Implementing

NATIONAL CURRICULUM

the da **ASSESSMENT** in the primary school

b
te
fr

42281

Implementing

NATIONAL CURRICULUM ASSESSMENT

in the primary school

Diane Shorrocks

with
Len Frobisher,
Nick Nelson,
Lynn Turner *and*
Andrew Waterson

Hodder & Stoughton
LONDON SYDNEY AUCKLAND

British Library Cataloguing in Publication Data

Shorrocks, Diane
  Implementing National Curriculum
  Assessment in the Primary School
  I. Title
  371.12

  ISBN 0 340 58766 0

First published 1993
Copyright © 1993 Diane Shorrocks, Len Frobisher, Nick Nelson,
Lynn Turner and Andrew Waterson

Printed and bound in Great Britain for the educational publishing division of Hodder &
Stoughton Ltd, Mill Road, Dunton Green, Sevenoaks, Kent, by Athenaeum Press,
Newcastle upon Tyne. Photoset by Rowland Phototypesetting Ltd, Bury St Edmunds, Suffolk.

Contents

Introduction   ix

1   Children, Teachers and Classrooms   1
Diane Shorrocks

2   Assessing Children: Theory, Practice and Implications   20
Diane Shorrocks

3   National Curriculum Assessment in England and Wales   36
Diane Shorrocks

4   Assessing English   50
Diane Shorrocks

5   Assessing Mathematics   79
Nick Nelson and Len Frobisher

6   Assessing Science   114
Andrew Waterson

7   Special Educational Needs   137
Lynn Turner

8   Assessing Bilingual Children   158
Lynn Turner

9   Conclusions, Issues and Prospects   174
Diane Shorrocks

References   187

Index   193

The Authors

The authors were all members of the research team at the School of Education, University of Leeds, that carried out the first national evaluation of the Key Stage 1 National Curriculum assessments in summer 1991 – the ENCA 1 project (Shorrocks et al., 1992). Dr Shorrocks was also involved in a smaller-scale national evaluation, carried out in conjunction with the National Union of Teachers, in 1992. All of them had gained experience in primary education before moving into the research field.

Diane Shorrocks, who directed the ENCA 1 project, worked in primary schools before moving into higher education and training primary teachers. Her special interests lie in children's language and literacy development.

Len Frobisher also worked in primary school before moving into teacher training, with special emphasis on mathematics education.

Nick Nelson was a primary teacher who moved into research with the ENCA 1 project, mostly focusing on mathematics assessment.

Lynn Turner is an educational psychologist with extensive experience of working with primary children. She has also taught in school and is currently gaining experience of educational psychology in Canada.

Andrew Waterson's interests are in science education in the primary school. He trained in science, moving on to teach in primary schools and becoming a primary head before joining the research team. He currently works in teacher training in Bradford College.

Diane Shorrocks, Len Frobisher and Nick Nelson are currently members of the MAK2 project at the University of Leeds, developing National Curriculum standard assessment materials for Key Stage 2 mathematics.

Acknowledgements

This book owes much to the thinking and discussion that took place in the ENCA 1 research team, both during and after the official term of the project. Members of that team who should be mentioned in particular are Robin Alexander, John Willcocks and the statisticians Sandra Daniels and John Bell. Grateful thanks also go to Anne Parkinson, project secretary, who has worked long and hard, over and above the call of duty, on typing the manuscript and deciphering our hieroglyphics.

We wish also to acknowledge the generous contributions made by John Joyce and Mike Haworth to the preparation of the chapters on special educational needs and bilingual issues. Their insights and comments greatly enriched those chapters.

The authors and publishers are grateful to the following for permission to reproduce copyright material:

Open University Press for Figure 4.2, adapted from figure 1.7 'Tree structure for a simple story' in *Language Understanding* by Judith Green (Open University Press, 1986).

The Controller of Her Majesty's Stationery Office for Figure 6.2, from *Science at Age 11: Review of APU Survey Findings 1980–84* (HMSO, 1988).

Multilingual Matters Ltd, of Frankfurt Lodge, Clevedon Hall, Victoria Road, Clevedon, Avon BS21 7SJ, for Figure 8.1, from *Bilingualism or Not: The Education of Minorities* by Tove Skutnabb-Kangas (Multilingual Matters, 1981); and Figure 8.3, from *Bilingualism and Special Education: Issues in Assessment and Pedagogy* by Jim Cummins (Multilingual Matters, 1984).

Longman Group UK Ltd for Figure 8.2, from *Bilingualism in Education* by J. Cummins and M. Swain (Longman, 1986).

Introduction

Assessment is all about making judgements based on valid and appropriate evidence. These judgements should then enable us to make well-informed decisions: decisions about what a child needs to learn next; decisions about the success of a programme of learning; decisions about the selection and placement of children for particular purposes; decisions about resource allocation.

The aim of this book is to explore the issues and implications of assessing children in a classroom-based way, when they are in the early years of their schooling, working within Key Stages 1 and 2. This is of special significance in Britain at the moment because of the implementation of the National Curriculum and the requirement to assess the progress of children, both formally and informally, within the framework of this curriculum.

The book is the product of several years' immersion in the issues of assessing children in Key Stage 1. The authors were members of the research group set up to evaluate the first full experience of assessing seven-year-olds at the end of Key Stage 1. It is not, however, a straightforward reporting of that evaluation work. Instead, it is a distillation of ideas that have emerged from the evaluation, which are of direct interest and use to teachers. It seeks to pose questions about the basic purposes of assessment, the nature of the judgements being made and how assessment can best be carried out.

The fundamental question in assessment is: how do we find out what another individual knows, understands or can do? To begin to answer this question, in relation to assessing young children in classroom contexts, we need to:

- understand more about the young child as a learner, both in and out of school;
- understand more about ourselves as the adults making the judgements, and about the characteristics of classrooms and classroom interactions;
- understand more about the nature of assessment and its role in the teaching/learning process;
- understand more about the nature of the subject-matter within the curriculum, and the issues this raises for assessment.

These points provide the organising framework for the book. Chapter 1 addresses the first and second items, giving an outline of current views on the nature of children's thinking and learning and the characteristics of the schools and classrooms where some of this learning occurs. It goes on to present a brief account of some of the ways in which adults (as well as children) reach judgements and make decisions.

Chapter 2 explores in some depth the basic ideas about the nature of assessment, different kinds of assessment and different purposes which are then addressed and developed in the context of national curriculum assessment in Chapter 3. Together, these chapters provide background information for the detailed analysis of assessment in the three core subjects – English, mathematics and science – which then follows in Chapters 4, 5 and 6 respectively.

Chapters 7 and 8 have a particular focus which relates to all the chapters that precede them. Certain groups of children require particular consideration when carrying out classroom-based assessment. Children with special educational needs and bilingual children, using a language in school that is different to that used at home, present special circumstances and challenges for assessment. Some of these major issues are addressed in these chapters.

Overall, the book tries to move away from the traditional litany of ideas on assessment and present instead a wider framework of ideas and information that should helpfully inform assessment in the classroom. Although the main emphasis is on assessment at Key Stage 1, the central issues are equally applicable at Key Stage 2 and explicit reference is made to this throughout the coming chapters.

Finally, a note on terminology. The National Curriculum assessment materials – Standard Assessment Tasks – have hitherto been fairly consistently designated 'SATs' within the education world. This term is not to be confused with SATs – Scholastic Aptitude Tests – as used in the USA. Partly because of this potential for confusion, and partly reflecting the trend towards greater use of pencil-and-paper testing, particularly at Key Stages 2, 3 and 4, the term is being superseded by 'Standard Task' and 'Standard Test', as appropriate.

1

Children, Teachers and Classrooms

To repeat the central message of the Introduction, the basic question we are addressing is: *How do we find out what another person knows, understands or can do?* The answer could be deceptively simple: we ask them or get them to carry out some task or activity and then make our assessment judgement. However, the reality is much more complicated than this. The responses given by the person being assessed may be ambiguous or partial, they may not like or understand the activity, the room may be cold or distracting. The judgements made by the person assessing may be biased, they too may be affected by the environment around, and they may interpret the responses in a different way to those intended.

The technical aspects, to do with devising activities and providing relevant answers, will be dealt with in the next chapter. Here, the focus is on the people involved, their characteristics and the classroom situation where the assessments may take place. It is about background factors and processes.

For decades now, researchers have been trying to find effective ways of discovering more about how people think, learn, judge and solve problems. But even in what we might consider to be 'optimal' conditions of one-to-one discussion and activity with adults, the process has been shown to be fraught with difficulties. Each individual brings many things to the interaction:

- a view of the purpose of the encounter;
- particular personality characteristics and attitudes and expectations;
- particular kinds of motivation;
- experience of social roles and interaction and views of other people;
- previous experience of communication;
- views about the physical situation, the room and setting for the encounter.

Even in an ideal situation, all of these will influence the responses and judgements made. Perhaps the only safe starting point is to recognise that all we are ever doing under these circumstances is *inferring* what a person knows or understands. Some of these inferences may be more valid than others. What is more, their quality will be directly related to the extent to which we recognise the characteristics and limitations of the process.

If this is the situation when adults are involved, then dealing with young children highlights them even more, especially in classroom situations. This is why it is important to spend a little time considering some of the evidence about how young children think, learn, communicate and relate: it may radically affect our approach to assessment.

But outlining these ideas immediately poses a dilemma. On the whole, our understanding of children's learning and development has advanced by asking questions about what is *general* or *common* to all children and what is *unique*. Clearly, at one level it is possible to see general characteristics and processes, but if we are not careful, this can lead to a view that is too uniform, too restricting. On the other hand, recognising the great variation that exists among individual children potentially leads us to a situation of not seeing the wood for the trees. The only solution is to try to do both: to point out common patterns but, at the same time, to acknowledge individual variation, gaining insight from both.

Young children thinking and learning

It has become almost part of the folklore of teaching that children, especially young children, think in very different ways to adults and have a very different view of the world. This has provided the justification for particular approaches to their education. But how valid a view is it? Are young children's thinking processes very different to those of adults or are there similarities, with children just being less advanced along the same route? Put more technically, if there are differences, are these *qualitative* or *quantitative* differences?

The evidence from research over the last twenty years or so has led to a move away from the former (fundamental, qualitative differences) towards the latter (differences only in amount, quantitative differences). This is not the place to present great detail on this topic: suggestions for further reading are given later. However, key points need to be made, as preparation for later discussion of approaches to assessment.

The work of Piaget has both informed and clouded our understanding of children's development and learning. The bookshelves of writings and research produced by Piaget and his co-workers have provided a most important archive of information and stimulus to further questioning. His whole theoretical framework has also acted as an important antidote to the earlier view of children as either passive receivers of experience and knowledge, or pre-programmed beings who merely matured in line with a predetermined blueprint.

This information about children was mostly obtained through a particular technique, the 'clinical interview'. Working on a one-to-one basis, the child would be presented with a particular task or problem and would discuss it with the adult. The questions asked by the adult were carefully structured, with very particular aims in mind. The child's spoken and behaviour responses were noted and, as these accumulated, so Piaget's theory of the development of logical thinking was elaborated.

In this, he suggested that children's thinking passes through a sequence of stages, becoming progressively more logical and more powerful with time and experience. By definition, then, young children were not capable of logical thinking and their view of the world was therefore different and partial, an argument for qualitative differences between children and adults. He argued that all children moved through these stages, but perhaps at different rates. However, intervention by adults would seldom speed up the process: instead, it would lead only to superficial change, not fundamentally new insights or changes in basic thinking and understanding.

It is easy to see that such suggestions would have an impact on education, particularly as the findings were apparently supported by a great deal of evidence. The result of his work has been to present us with a new view of children: children as active creators of knowledge rather than passive receivers.

Piaget's view of the process of development was that basic biological dispositions and behaviours (for example, early reflex responses) were progressively developed and differentiated as the children experienced and acted upon the world. A key process in this, according to Piaget, was *adaptation*. The theory goes that we are all (children and adults) constantly adapting to our environment, indeed this is how he defines intelligence. From birth, the world outside impinges and as a result of these dealings with the environment, sets of ideas or concepts emerge, which allow the child to begin to classify and predict what is being experienced.

When a new object or experience is met, the child's existing concepts allow some recognition of it and some categorisation/relating to go on. This is the process of *assimilation*. At the same time, each new experience changes these existing ideas somewhat, so progression and development are brought about. This is the process of *accommodation*. The two kinds of process work in a complementary way to each other and so ensure that there is both a degree of coherence in the child's ongoing representation and understanding of the world, but also change and growth. The suggestion is that these processes are at work in all of us, young or old, allowing us to continue to adapt to and understand a changing environment. This is an issue that will be taken up again later in this chapter.

But Piaget's legacy has its negative aspects too. In particular, it seems to have left parents and teachers essentially in the role of bystanders, providing appropriate experiences, but with apparently little opportunity to affect the process of developing children's minds. Also, there is now a growing body of counter-evidence which suggests that the way the information was collected (the clinical interview) may have acted as a barrier to children demonstrating their full capabilities. This is most impressively outlined in Margaret Donaldson's 1978 book, *Children's Minds*. It is a criticism which has a direct bearing on the issue of assessment so it is worth considering in a little more detail.

Diagram A   Diagram B

Figure 1.1   *Conservation displays for the two conditions*

Much of the argument concerns the classic *conservation* experiments. The child is, for instance, shown two rows of counters, and asked if there are the same number of counters in each row (see Diagram A in Figure 1.1). The researcher then pushes one row of counters more closely together (Diagram B), watched by the child, and the child is asked the same question again. Those children who can 'conserve' number (i.e. recognise that the number is the same, whatever the physical arrangement) say yes, whilst others say no. Criticisms have included the following:

- the whole situation is meaningless for the child, with no common-sense purpose to the task;
- the form of the question is structured in a particular way and rather odd;
- repeating the same question twice may give the child the wrong signals about their first answer.

It is suggested that these factors, and others, may have given rise to an underestimation of children's capacities. In fact, when various aspects of the activity were changed, more children gave correct answers in some subsequent experiments. Whether there has therefore been consistent under-estimation of children's abilities is not a topic to be pursued in detail here. The important message is that the **means** chosen to access children's understanding seem, in themselves, to have been acting as a barrier in this particular 'assessment' situation.

Piaget does not seem to have regarded interpersonal interaction and communication as problem areas in their own right. For him, language and conversation seem to be *'transparent'*, a straightforward means of access, not an *'opaque'* dimension which needs considering and resolving in its own right.

For an alternative view about children's learning and thinking (and for that matter adults too), we may turn to the computer. The growth of this technology over the past years has provided a suggestive model about how the human mind might work. The computer takes in information, processes and manipulates it, and retrieves it when necessary. There could be some parallels here that may help us to think about human mental functioning: after all, we too take in information, transform it, retrieve it and utilise it. This *information processing* approach has provided many useful insights and a possible model for comparing child and adult thinking and learning.

However, the process of taking in information is more complex than might appear. There is now a large amount of evidence to show that none of us, children or adults, ever just 'sees' and 'hears' information. We constantly try to give meaning to the vast array of incoming information and what we choose to attend to is a very *selective* process. This is why the term *perception* is preferable to 'seeing' or 'hearing'. Ambiguous information will be interpreted and filled out: from a mass of incoming information, only certain parts will be attended to and focused on. In other words, what we observe and hear will be heavily influenced by current preoccupations and needs. In unfamiliar situations or when anxious, the way we deal with information will be different.

However, once information has been attended to and perceived, it can be *worked on*; perhaps trying to make more sense of it; linking it to other information, seeing relationships, trying to remember it. The more these kinds of processes happen, the more likely are we genuinely to come to terms with new information, incorporating it into our framework of existing knowledge.

This long-term store of knowledge that each of us has, contains all a person knows about the world. It seems to be almost unlimited in capacity, although everyday experience tells us that relevant information is sometimes difficult to retrieve. The content of the store must be of many kinds:

- factual information (e.g. the names of our friends);
- procedural knowledge (e.g. how to ride a bike);
- memory of past events (e.g. the football match last week);
- recognition of bodily sensations and responses (e.g. pain);

- knowledge about what is in our memory (e.g. knowing we don't understand the rules of chess);
- knowing that some things are difficult or easy to learn.

Without this complex knowledge system we could not function in the world: we would have no way of recognising objects, anticipating events or linking past to present and future. When we converse, read or carry out a simple task such as recognising a cup as a cup, we are using this complex information processing system. It follows that, the more organised the information is, the more likely we are to be able to retrieve items efficiently when we need them. A large library of books would be virtually useless without an organising system.

This approach can be used to present an alternative view of children's developing skills and thinking in relation to that of adults. The idea of *novice* and *expert* is the starting point. As we try to grapple with a new skill or body of information, our approach seems fairly random and fragmented. Think about learning to ride a bicycle: at first there is too much to concentrate upon all at once. However, once we have a little more experience, everything seems to fit, and we can perform or understand easily and smoothly. As skills become more smooth and automatic, more of our attention and concentration becomes free to focus on new aspects or issues. The move is from being a novice to being an expert and dealing with information in more efficient and fluent ways.

In many ways, children are novices who have to become expert in a very wide range of skills and understandings: they have to learn to walk, talk, ride bikes, read, remember and solve problems. There is now a great deal of evidence (see Wood, 1989) about the ways in which children develop these skills, moving from clumsy and random attempts to fluent and skilled performance, able to consider situations and apply the correct strategies. This even applies to high-level thinking skills, which can be taught.

This presents us with a rather different view of children and their capabilities. Their thinking does not seem to be radically and un-changeably different to that of adults, as Piaget suggested. It seems to be just less far down a similar road and, in fact, under some circumstances children's thinking and strategies may be more advanced than adults.

An example of this is the game of chess. Chess is a highly complex game, requiring high levels of planning and problem solving. When adult chess players are compared to non-players, clear differences emerge. For instance, if they are all presented with particular and realistic groupings of pieces on a chess board, skilled players remember more of them than do the non-players. However, when pieces are arranged randomly, not in predictable chess patterns, then all subjects remember equally. Experts do not have superior memories in general, but what they do have is particular expertise, a large *vocabulary* of possible patterns stored away in memory. This enables them to see groups of pieces as meaningful *chunks* and therefore remember them more efficiently.

Chi (1978) set a similar chess-remembering problem to two groups of people and again found that the experts outperformed the novices. In this case, however, the experts were children and the novices adults, all of which seems to confirm the fact that children do not have radically different capabilities to adults. Under some circumstances they can be superior.

When we approach the question in this more *particularistic* way, taking specific areas of knowledge or specific skills, somehow more positive outcomes seem possible. The kinds of in-built constraints on children's learning that Piaget suggested may not exist. In fact there is ample evidence (see Carey, 1985) that adult thinking in science is often very partial and misguided. Perhaps children can learn and we can teach a great deal more than previously imagined. In broad terms, adults may be more expert in a wider range of skills than children, but viewing knowledge and skills in this much more differentiated and specific way opens up many more possibilities.

It is also not in conflict with the idea of the child as an active learner and constructor of knowledge. Children may indeed construct impressive amounts of knowledge and acquire impressive skills in particular domains. Other work by Chi tells of a four-year-old with enormous expertise about dinosaurs. He could recognise and name 46 kinds and, for a subset of these, give detail about their eating habits and diet, and categorise them according to the type of locomotion they used. Here was a four-year-old who was no novice, in one domain at least: he had also acquired the knowledge under his own volition.

Another criticism of Piaget's ideas is that he underplayed the role of other people in the child's learning and development. However, the **social** context is viewed as of much more significance by Vygotsky, a Russian psychologist writing earlier this century and only in the last two decades known about in the West. For Vygotsky, learning has an important social dimension: children learn much from other people and gradually grow into the mental life of those around them. He writes of the *zone of proximal development*, which focuses on ways in which children's learning and thinking can be advanced and helped along. This 'zone' is the distance between what the child can do alone and the level that can be achieved under the guidance of an adult or more capable peer. The adult *structures and scaffolds* the activity until the child can *internalise* the approach or thought processes and then accomplish the activity alone.

This is an important idea. It stresses finding out what the child already knows or can do, then building on this, being careful not to go beyond the 'zone' where the child is still capable of comprehending and following. It is in fact the essence of the learning-teaching process, based on sensitive diagnosis and guidance by the adult.

The conclusions that arise from this outline so far are as follows:

- Children are active in their learning and knowledge-constructing, as are adults. We are not just passive receivers of information, empty vessels as it were, into which knowledge and skills are poured.
- There is a complicated relationship between the information and experiences as present in the outside world and what any person takes in, digests and incorporates into their framework of knowledge. A simple input-output view of the way the human mind works is inappropriate.
- Taking in information is a highly selective process that is heavily influenced by existing knowledge. We are more likely to attend to and take in information and experiences which relate to what we already know and understand.
- Each individual will therefore have their own unique kinds of stored knowledge, with different aspects of knowledge and experience developed to different extents. Concepts will vary, as will characteristic ways of approaching information and tasks. Preferred problem-solving strategies are likely to vary, as are levels of motivation in any particular domain of knowledge or skills.
- Children's and adults' thinking and learning seem to have more in common than earlier theories would suggest.
- Ways of tapping into the knowledge and understanding of children, or for that matter adults, need careful consideration. The activities and approaches used can effectively allow knowledge to be demonstrated – or they can act as a barrier.

Teaching and teachers

The activity of teaching is all about promoting learning. This requires consideration of the nature of children's learning and approaches to intervening in the process. A possible model for this intervention is provided by Vygotsky's ideas. It seems to be the case that children are especially sensitive to information and concepts that are just a little ahead of their present level of skill or understanding. This is easily explained by referring to the ideas of selective attention and perception described above.

The zone of proximal development exploits this predisposition, and adds to it by indicating a way of leading children forward into new and relatively unknown territory. An adult or informed peer can act as a guide, the child's consciousness as it were, supporting the venture. The new information or skill thus becomes accessible, the product of two minds, as the first step towards *independent* performance or understanding.

The skill of the teacher (or parent) lies in diagnosing the existing level that the child has mastered, then implementing the programme of guidance. Given the wide individual variability that exists, this is not necessarily an easy task. For the teacher, Figure 1.2 outlines the process.

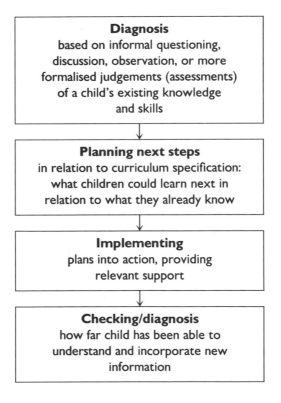

Diagnosis
based on informal questioning,
discussion, observation, or more
formalised judgements (assessments)
of a child's existing knowledge
and skills

↓

Planning next steps
in relation to curriculum specification:
what children could learn next in
relation to what they already know

↓

Implementing
plans into action, providing
relevant support

↓

Checking/diagnosis
how far child has been able to
understand and incorporate new
information

Figure 1.2   Diagnosis, planning and teaching

The process is ongoing. As a model, it may seem over-optimistic for the busy teacher with large classes. The counter-argument to this is, however, that teaching skills too become automatised and more efficient as they are put into practice, and it is important to be automatising an appropriate model rather than an inappropriate one. Observation and questioning skills, for instance, become more focused and efficient with practice.

What the model emphasises are *differentiation* – the fact that different children have different learning needs – and *match* – the appropriateness of tasks to the learners' needs. We need look no further than the work of Bennett and his co-workers (1984) to discover that these two aims frequently are not met in primary classrooms. In particular, they found that in classes of six- and seven-year-olds:

- more than half the tasks allocated to children were mismatched to their capabilities;
- the capabilities of high attainers were frequently underestimated and those of low attainers overestimated;
- significant proportions of language tasks (20%) and number tasks (30%) did not in reality exhibit the kinds of demands teachers expected;
- the majority of tasks, especially in number work, were practice tasks, rather than tasks which required children to restructure and understand, or enrich and extend.

According to this analysis, it is doubtful whether many of the aims of either differentiation or match were being met. The ratio of practice tasks to restructuring or enrichment tasks may or may not be appropriate. Clearly, children need to practise certain skills, but the key factor in effective teaching, as the points made earlier emphasise, must be the careful balance between novelty, challenge and consolidation in learning. There are no easy answers to this, but the question has to be kept in mind.

Stereotypes and halo effects

Just as it is important to understand more about children, so it is important to understand more about teachers and the judgements they make in class.

Much of what has been said already informs our view about likely teacher responses and judgements. Children and adults alike selectively perceive aspects of their environment, and take in information in ways that relate to their own existing knowledge and to characteristics of personality. The particular motivations, attitudes and values held will also affect what is attended to, perceived and acted upon. Teachers are, after all, human.

However, the perceptions teachers have and the judgements they make are of special significance, since they are likely to affect their relationships with children (individuals, groups and whole classes) and the ways in which they perceive pupils' learning needs. As a necessary part of our functioning we classify and label our environment, all in relation to our own particular experience, attitudes and values, but it is important that these do not have negative influences in dealing with children.

Three particular issues are worth examining a little further, since they have special significance in education contexts. The first of these is *stereotyping*. We inevitably need some broad categorisations about people and situations that enable us to respond quickly to any new object, person or experience. When relating to other people, these stereotypes or broad concepts imply making generalisations from a limited set of characteristics, and responding to the person as a type, rather than an individual. A grain of truth is set about with a whole range of other assumptions. Under many circumstances, we go on to find out more about a person and so are able to deal with them in more complex ways. However, the effects of stereotyping may continue, with negative outcomes. Stereotypes which may intervene in relationships with children in the classroom could be 'working-class child', 'low ability child', as well as the more usual gender and racial ones.

This leads on to the second important issue. In some cases, the result of not getting beyond the stereotyped judgement may be negative in educational terms. However, opposite outcomes can occur, often referred to as '*halo effects*'. Under some circumstances, a positive stereotype may be applied ('clever child') which may lead to a range of other positive qualities being attributed to the child (e.g. they are helpful, hardworking). This 'halo' may, of course, be as inaccurate as negative stereotyping and just as illusory.

Teacher expectations

The third issue is that of teacher expectations and their effects on the performance and behaviour of children. Once again, beginning with the obvious points, we all need to be able to predict and anticipate events and behaviour in our environment, and we can only do this by building up expectancies about people, objects and situations. It is also clear that we take in information differently, depending on these expectations. If we expect dogs to be aggressive and bark, then we are likely only to focus on and remember such examples.

There is now a large body of research in education that has explored teacher expectancy effects in schools and classrooms. In the late 1960s Rosenthal and Jacobson (1968) presented evidence of *self-fulfilling prophecies* at work among teachers and children. When teachers were informed that certain pupils were going to be high attainers, this was indeed the outcome, despite the fact that the initial information had been false. The research evoked much criticism but also a great many follow-up studies, some of which confirmed expectancy effects and some of which did not. The studies which did demonstrate that teacher expectations could act in a self-fulfilling way, were mostly those involving younger children and those where the teachers were not fed obviously false information (Rogers, 1982).

If expectancy effects occur, it is important to understand the process through which they manifest themselves. Several writers have tried to summarise the sequence of events, beginning with the kinds of factors that may influence teacher expectations. Figure 1.3 depicts a basic view of the factors and sequence.

There is evidence to suggest that all the factors arrayed around the top of the diagram – the 'input' factors to the teacher – influence teacher perceptions of children. This is even the case for children's names! For any of these expectations to have an effect, however, they must be shown to influence the teacher behaviour. Once again, there is evidence that teachers do behave rather differently towards some children in class, in the kinds of ways shown as teacher 'outputs' in the Figure.

The next phase of the process involves the pupil. The child must interpret the teacher's behaviour, filtered through their own set of attitudes, perceptions and previous experience, which in turn affects the child's performance and behaviour. So teacher expectations are not automatically self-fulfilling, but under certain circumstances, where all these conditions are present, they may be.

It is clearly a complex process, very subtle in its workings. Stereotyped judgements, or halo-effects, may not be very overt, but may nevertheless exert important influences. In all of these cases, the suggestion is not that teachers are in some way wicked or misinformed, deliberately trying to promote or do down particular children. Many of the processes will be subconscious: hopefully, being aware of the possibility of their influence will be the first step towards doing something about them. By way of final comment on this topic, however, if a teacher makes a deliberate effort to change behaviour towards a particular child, the outcome may not be as expected, nor even positive. The child's own perceptions of the teacher's behaviour may negate the best of intentions.

By considering something of the psychology of both children and teachers, therefore, it becomes possible to see new and problematic dimensions of the assessment process. Before drawing all the issues

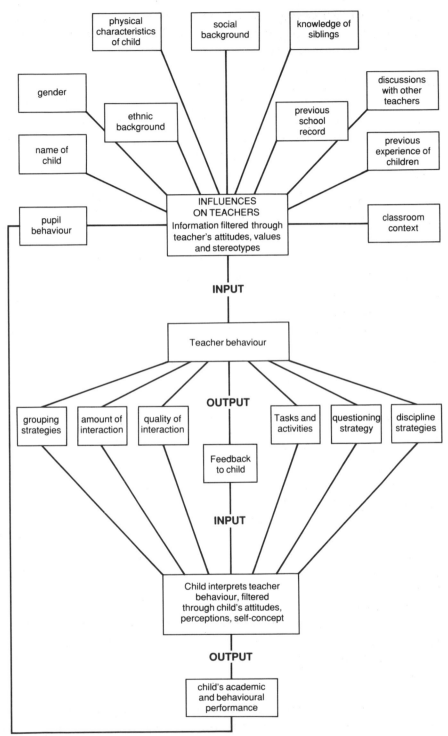

Figure 1.3 Factors and sequence in the expectancy process

together, however, some outline of classroom environments and influences is needed.

Classrooms

Back in 1968, Jackson described certain key aspects of classroom life.
These bear repetition since they still provide an insightful summary. He
suggested that classrooms are in the main about *crowds, praise and
power*. They are places where children and adults are brought together,
in a confined space, and required to interact with each other – the crowd
dimension. This sometimes poses problems both for teachers and
children. They are places where work and behaviour are publicly
evaluated and praised or otherwise, and they are places where significant
kinds of power relationships prevail. The child must come to terms with
an asymmetric power relationship with the teacher and a range of other
power and friendship relations with others. Classrooms may indeed
appear daunting places to young children.

Many studies have also attested to another characteristic of British
classrooms: their variety. There are enormous differences of size,
layout, organisation and management. They also vary in the extent to
which children are granted a degree of autonomy and freedom of
movement, and they are arenas for a wide range of teaching strategies.

Having stressed variety, however, certain common patterns can be
found. Early years classrooms, in particular, in line with a particular
educational philosophy, are frequently set out in an almost 'workshop'
way, with groups of tables and activity areas. Along with other studies,
the Key Stage 1 National Curriculum Assessment evaluation (the
ENCA project) found that in a national sample of classrooms with
seven-year-old children in them, roughly 80% were organised into
groups, usually four or five groups per class. On average each group was
made up of six children, although numbers varied greatly. The teaching
strategies also varied. About a third of the time was spent on whole-class
teaching, a third in groupwork and a third on individual activities.
Other adults were also present in the classrooms, helping the teacher in
some way, in about half the classes.

The time spent on various aspects of the curriculum is of interest too.
A 1988 study of 33 inner-city infant schools, by Tizard and her co-
workers, revealed that, overall, children spent only 46% of the time in
school engaged in learning activities in the classroom. The rest of the
time was spent on non-work activities such as register, lining up, lunch,
etc. Of the 'work time', 64% was spent on what might be termed the
basic subjects: reading, writing and mathematics. Children spent 17%

of classroom activity time on mathematics, 27% on such things as reading, discussion and storytime, and 20% on writing.

The way in which the curriculum is delivered also shows variation, both within and between the core subjects of English, mathematics and science. The ENCA evaluation project found that:

- reading activities were planned and delivered either in only a partly cross-curricular way or as a separate subject;
- other English activities were less likely to be delivered as a separate subject and more frequently in a partly or fully cross-curricular way;
- mathematics work showed a heavy emphasis on delivery either as a separate subject or in only a partly cross-curricular way;
- science activities were much more frequently planned and delivered in a fully or partly cross-curricular way.

Putting all this together, and from the point of view of children, any one day involves relating to the teacher on a one-to-whole-group basis (definitely being one of a crowd), relating on a one-to-one basis for short periods of time, working individually and working in close proximity to a small group of peers. In the course of these experiences, they are expected to interpret a range of instructions, comments, explanations, discussions, gestures and materials, and to work in different ways in different subject areas.

Children's academic performance is constantly being evaluated, often in very public ways: questions are openly asked, to which the child has to reply; reading aloud, to the teacher or peers, is a frequent occurrence; work is displayed, or not, around the classroom. There is fairly constant evaluation by the teacher and by peers. Children's characteristics are defined and redefined by those around, as evidenced by the many studies which have charted the course of a child's behaviour being progressively defined as 'troublesome'. Living down to labels, as well as living up to them, seems to be an important part of life in classrooms. Children have to negotiate relationships with other children, in relation to this well-understood status hierarchy, the pecking order of skills and power. These are complex social demands to which children must adjust: they must become socialised into the subtle and complex rules and roles of classroom life.

Teachers and children in conversation

With these characteristics and against this background, teachers and children engage in discussion, at least for some of the time. The reason for this last comment is the recurrent finding from many studies that the amount of constructive conversational interaction between teachers and individual children, even in early years classrooms, is not large. The content of such discussion may also be limited and fairly superficial, as the work of Edwards and Mercer (1987) suggests. Teachers talk a great deal, often posing many questions, but not necessarily on topics and in ways that enable children fully to participate and learn.

Yet a great many of the teacher's assessment judgements – ongoing and as end-of-year records – must be based on the outcomes of such conversations. Direct observation and discussion are two of the most important ways open to us to discover what young children know and can do. Both will be considered more fully in the next chapter, but both bear some analysis in the context of this chapter too.

As with most aspects of human behaviour, when we come to analyse particular kinds of issues or performance, it becomes instantly obvious that much of what is involved is so complex, we are left asking how do we manage to do it? So it is with conversation. Many complex, high-level mental skills are needed to participate as a conversational partner. Using language, topics have to be initiated, sustained and developed, and a whole range of purposes achieved through conversational exchanges. We have to build our own ongoing meanings and points of view in relation to the contributions and purposes of a partner. We have to be able to work out what our partner already knows and expects, and what kinds of conversational strategies will best enable us to reach our goals. Complex, problem-solving skills are needed, in order to devise and deliver this concerted set of interrelated messages.

In addition, however, we embellish the basic messages in a rich variety of ways – through tone of voice and intonation; through facial expression and gesture; through our eyes and eye contact; and through the way we position ourselves. In some cases, these extras add to the message (e.g. through gesture or eye-contact) whilst in others, they contradict it (e.g. when we are being sarcastic). Therefore, learning to participate in conversations requires considerable skill in message construction, topic building, ways of delivering messages and 'reading' the overt and hidden intentions of others.

Children seem to learn some of these skills from an early age. Studies of quite young babies show that they can begin to take their *turns* in conversation-like exchanges with their carers and to *initiate* conversation and interaction, albeit in fairly rudimentary ways such as looking, pointing, tugging or shouting out. As their knowledge and experience increases, this becomes reflected in the increasingly subtle and precise ways they gain attention and begin conversational exchanges. Children also rapidly learn to *respond to and ask questions*, both quite complex conversational skills, and, interestingly, to *repair* certain breakdowns in conversation, by requesting repetition or by clarifying points. All of this has been documented in detail by McTear (1985).

Creating coherent dialogue means not only thinking of appropriate *content*, but also learning some special conversational language devices, such as using pronouns to refer to something already mentioned or using connectors of various kinds ('in fact', 'mind you') which link various contributions together in a conversation.

However, not all conversational skills come easily, and for many children their previous experience has not necessarily enabled them to develop. The work of Elizabeth Robinson (e.g.1986) has shown that it may be well into the first years at school before children become competent, understanding precisely the kind of information that the listener needs, and why communication fails sometimes. Young children (around five years) seem to judge that all speakers' messages are adequate even when they are not, but older ones (around seven years) can detect that sometimes the information given by the other person is faulty or incomplete. Work in all these areas suggests that even young children can master some of the *mechanics* of conversation and basic conversational procedures, but find it more difficult to present and interpret some conversational *content* at a more sophisticated level.

The implications of all this for classroom conversation, particularly in assessment contexts, are considerable. It is likely that all children experience more difficulty than we imagine in fully interpreting the questions and intentions of adults in conversation, and that *some* have very great difficulty indeed. As we have seen, children may go to great lengths to try to work out what is expected of them and what the teacher wants them to say, and much classroom dialogue may have little significance for them. As we shall see in Chapter 3, speaking and listening skills may need to be very actively developed in young children, and if this is the case, it seems inappropriate to place too much reliance on a channel of information which they may only partially have mastered.

Teachers observing children in classrooms

Observing children in an objective way, then, in class or anywhere else in school, is no straightforward task, not least because it requires us to step back from the situation instead of fully engaging with it, as we are accustomed to do in normal teaching. Yet it is important not only in assessing academic progress, but in monitoring behaviour and behaviour problems and in providing evidence. If this evidence is to be helpful, it must provide an objective description, as free of *value judgements* as possible. *Explaining* and *interpreting* these behaviours is a different activity for the teacher. The two must always be kept distinct.

A given behaviour – for instance one child offering another a sweet – could be *described* or explained in many ways, which may be heavily prejudiced by the particular attitudes of the observer. In this case, the behaviour could be seen as an act of generosity, as an act designed to buy a favour, as an act designed to be seen in order to gain teacher approval. Interpretation is very much in the eyes of the beholder, and eyes differ. Only by making a concerted effort to keep these two elements separate are we ever likely to derive helpful observational information. If they come mixed up, the results of the observation will tell us more about the person observing than about the child being observed. Some of the different kinds of approach to observation for assessment purposes are outlined in the next chapter.

Assessment implications

This chapter has focused on some of the likely characteristics of the teachers and children involved in the making of assessment judgements, set against a context of classroom organisation and processes. This gives rise to major questions and issues that have to be addressed first, in order to provide the necessary background framework for considering assessment in more detail.

Above all, the teaching-learning process must be recognised as the complex thing it is: a simple input-output model will not do, as any experienced and sensitive teacher will attest. What we think we are teaching may not be what children are learning, and by the same token they may be learning a great deal that has not been formally taught. What is clear is that effective teaching is only likely to occur when children's progress is accurately monitored and built on.

Until now, this may have happened, but in an unexamined way: certainly (in Britain, at least) this must now be made much more explicit. In some senses, it no doubt exploits the existing teaching skills of many teachers: children's written work is marked and monitored, as are other 'products'; questions are asked; replies are developed and acted upon; problems are posed in order to see how children tackle them. However, all these skills may now need more honing, so that more detailed, productive and efficient judgements can be made. The only way to achieve this is to build *assessment thinking* into all planning and delivery of the curriculum, and progressively to make these skills more automatic. In the case of observation, the existing whole-class scanning skills used by teachers may need to be sharpened and to include much greater focus on individual children.

Another conclusion from this chapter is that the existing kinds of teacher-child classroom interaction and conversation may not be sufficient to meet these demands. Classroom language may well be of a fairly ritualised kind, sometimes rather superficial. The work of Tizard and Hughes (1984), studying children in nursery classes, hinted that many of the conversations between adults and children (girls) in this supposedly educational context were less rich and varied than children experienced in even fairly deprived homes. Conversation needs to be more focused and purposeful, bearing in mind also the enormous possibility of mutual misunderstanding, bias and incompleteness.

Assessment, as we shall see, comes in many guises, and one of the issues raised here is the question of matching the approach to assessment with the kind of classroom organisation and functioning which is most familiar for the children and most appropriate for the teacher. As we have already seen, most infant classrooms provide a range of organisational experience for the children. This in itself opens up the possibility of making valid decisions about what kinds of organisation permit what kinds of assessment strategy.

Certain kinds of assessment clearly take place on a *whole-class* basis, usually where an uncomplicated 'product' is required. However, if this form of organisation is unfamiliar to the child, then the assessment is likely to be less valid and dependable. In classrooms where *small groups* are the organisational norm, then assessment strategies clearly have to accommodate this. A central question, of course, is whether the groups actually function in a genuinely cooperative way, or whether they are just convenient seating arrangements for the provision of what is essentially varied but individual work. Again, this has major implications for assessment strategies.

Assessing children in a group context is fraught with difficulties, since the focus in assessment is mostly to find out what each individual knows or can do. There is a basic tension here between making valid assessments of individuals and a working context with which the children are familiar.

2

Assessing Children: Theory, Practice and Implications

Assessment is about making judgements based on sound evidence. It is about finding out in appropriate and detailed ways what another person knows, understands or can do. At best, the results should be valid and dependable, so that the inferences we draw from them are well grounded, and recognised as being made in relation to particular tasks. At worst, the results may be global, subjective opinions, leading to faulty and inappropriate decision-making. As we have seen, the process of assessing young children, in relation to a specified curriculum, in the context of the classroom, is potentially fraught with problems.

Information on which to make appropriate assessment judgements can come from three major sources (based on Salvia and Hughes, 1990):

- from general impressions of a child's performance or behaviour, based on unstructured observations and recollections, often very *unspecific* in character;
- from more structured observations, listening to a child or watching them with specific points in mind;
- from activities and tasks, which deliver more systematic information in a structured situation, provided that the tasks enable the child to demonstrate the necessary capabilities.

All three kinds of information are of use in reaching assessment judgements and should form part of the teacher's repertoire of assessment strategies, fully recognising the fact that the three sources of information vary in the inferences that can be made from them. A judicious combination of them may form the basis for ongoing *record keeping*, a vital source of continuing evidence in assessment. The role of more *impressionistic information* should not be discounted: teachers' intuitions and impressions may be an important source of insight, provided that these insights are then linked to more systematic information-gathering, to back them up.

Observation

Observation is about *noting or recording the overt motor and verbal behaviour of others*. It can take place in naturalistic settings (e.g. classrooms) or special settings (e.g. special 'experimental' rooms), or a sequence of behaviour can be recorded on videotape and then analysed. It is important to remember that using video recording has its strengths and weaknesses. Its strengths as a technique reside in having a permanent record, which can be analysed and re-analysed. Its weaknesses are that the record will perforce be a limited one and the presence of a camera may have a direct influence on the behaviour of the children. Neither of these is an insuperable problem since, for instance, children will gradually become used to a camera and begin to behave more naturally. These limitations should, however, be recognised (as should the fact that it may be appropriate to seek permission before making such a record of a child's behaviour).

Observation techniques may be of special usefulness with young children or children with particular learning difficulties, where the usual ways of obtaining information (e.g. by verbal or action response) may be inappropriate. Bearing in mind the points made in the last chapter concerning value-judgements and bias on the part of the observer, it is worth pointing out that *the more precise the observational focus, the less likely are biasing effects to occur*, unless, of course, the observational focus is itself biased. The more *global* the judgement, the greater the possibility of bias. Structured observation therefore requires careful identification of the kinds of behaviour that are to be the focus and the best ways of structuring the observations for the particular purposes in mind.

There are several kinds of structured observation that could be used, depending upon purpose. Observational evidence can be collected for monitoring a wide range of behaviours that children may display. The major approaches are:

- **Sequential observation.** In this approach, a child is intensively observed for a fixed and usually short period of time, say 10–15 minutes. Every behaviour is noted down, often using various forms of shorthand notes. Such an approach is useful for getting a sample of a child's typical behaviour in certain circumstances and for helping the teacher hone observational skills.
- **Time-sampled observation.** This technique is useful when some estimate of the frequency of a particular behaviour is required. This could be how frequently a child leaves their seat, or as a measure of time-on-task. For a specified time interval, every occurrence of the

particular behaviour is noted down, giving a frequency record. It can only be used, though, when a particular behaviour has already been identified.
- **Event-sampled observation.** Again, this is a technique for investigating particular behaviours or events in some detail, such as a behaviour problem (say, temper tantrums). The aim is to code in detail one particular episode from beginning to end, in order better to understand the causes and outcomes.

The kinds of observation used in the assessment of children's academic progress and learning are likely to involve elements of all of these approaches: the key point is always to match observation to purpose and to be as clear as possible about exactly what needs to be observed. Description and interpretation need to be kept separate in whatever technique is used.

More formal assessment activities and tests

The other source of information for assessment judgements may be from more formally arranged assessment activities or tests, whether teacher-made or already published. At a basic level, the process of devising all of these is the same: the concepts, knowledge or skill must be identified, then activities or items must be devised which allow the child to demonstrate the knowledge or skill they have. Finally, definitions must be established about what will constitute success. The approach is in principle the same whether the assessments are constructed by teachers for their own diagnostic and curricular purposes or whether more formalised, published tests are involved.

Different kinds of tests

Having so far used two terms – tests and assessments – we shall define them and consider what we mean by them. The term *assessment* is usually taken to have broader connotations than *testing*, implying that judgements are based not only on the results of more closely defined and focused measures, 'tests', but also on systematic observation and analysis of a wider range of factors in a child's performance. However, tests themselves come in a variety of forms – from informal, teacher-devised versions to published tests which are standardised. In this latter group, there are also some important distinctions which need to be clearly understood. Two broad categories are:

- **tests of ability**, which seek to use past and present performance to predict future performance and to determine potential;
- **tests of attainment or achievement**, which seek to measure what a person has learned to do and know.

Each of these will be examined in some detail, since the distinction is an important one, not only in terms of assessment but in terms of the way we view children and their competencies.

Tests of ability

It is an idea deeply ingrained in our education system, and to some extent in our wider culture, that it is possible to distinguish between people in terms of the possession or non-possession of the quality we have chosen to call 'ability'. The selective education system that prevailed in Britain for most of this century was grounded in this notion. As such, it implicitly informs much of our thinking – even the thinking of experienced teachers – but it is an idea that needs a great deal of clarification.

To understand the issues, we have to go back to the development of tests of intelligence as they were initially conceived and elaborated earlier this century. These represent ability testing in its most direct and obvious form. The pioneering work carried out by Binet was motivated by practical and social aims. Certain children in French schools were not functioning in school as well as might be hoped, so measures were needed which would enable 'retarded' children to be screened and provided with special education. Without any theoretical underpinning, any definition of what 'intelligence' was or how it might develop, Binet listed what he thought were the most important mental attributes – memory, comprehension, reasoning, speed of judgement – and developed a wide range of items and tasks that would test these.

The strategy he employed was to trial each test item with a large sample of children aged between 3 and 15 years. Some of the items proved more difficult than others, being passed by a small proportion of children. By trialling a range of items in this way, key ones could be chosen according to the percentage of each age group that passed them. In this way, an age-graded set of items was developed which provided the basis for many subsequent measures of 'intelligence' and IQ. It is, however, an approach that is fraught with problems, the most significant of which concern the meaning and nature of 'intelligence' and the implications it has for our view of the process of child and adult development.

This fairly *ad hoc* approach to the measurement of ability was not informed by any rigorous theoretical view of the nature of intelligence. It was presumed that the test items were in some way indicators of this central quality, and that a valid measure was being gained, in much the same way that we use a thermometer to measure temperature. In fact, IQ scores are *not* very good predictors of educational achievement and subsequent occupation.

Such theorising that *has* happened, has largely consisted of statistical manipulations of scores, once measured, in order to try to find common mental qualities that might underlie and account for the pattern of outcomes. This led to the major controversy as to whether 'intelligence' was a *general ability* that entered into our performance on all test items, or whether it was better thought of as a *range of abilities*, which together accounted for individual differences in levels of performance. More recently, much research energy has been deployed in trying to analyse the basic cognitive processes that may be involved: in other words, an information-processing approach. The findings and outcomes of this work are still not fully worked through, but the indications are that it is in many ways as atheoretical as earlier attempts. Individuals differ in the speed with which they react to stimuli and in the time they take to make certain judgements, but it is still not clear how such factors relate either to each other or to wider mental performance (Richardson, 1991).

The second major problem concerns the view of development implied in this form of ability testing. If we consider the traditional intelligence test, the test scores for children of different ages show a smooth line of progress as children get older. They should do, of course: it is what the tests were designed to produce. This is not a valid description of the development of mental ability, but it is an artefact of the way the tests are constructed.

Moreover, what such an approach also tends to create, is a view of this 'ability' that is more or less fixed at birth, is predictable at an early age, and merely 'grows' from then on to different extents in different children. The *psychometric* view that has been outlined here almost seems to presuppose this. *Development* equals *maturation* and is a relatively pre-determined, smooth and predictable process.

However, much of what was said in the last chapter would give the lie to such views. The current view of children's development emphasises the fact that it is a complex process of gradually differentiating knowledge structures and skills, which are constantly being restructured, and characterised by many spurts and plateaux. With this view of children and their development in mind, a major question mark is raised about how we measure a *constantly changing* set of qualities and compare them at different points in time on the same scale.

It is likely that we would be measuring different qualities at different stages, which would necessitate careful description of those qualities and the devising of appropriate ways to measure and relate them to each other. But this is not at all what traditional intelligence tests have done, as we have seen.

A score derived from a traditional intelligence test is meant to represent and encapsulate the relevant range of a person's capabilities into a single (or sometimes double: verbal and non-verbal) value. However, it is important to recognise that this number (or numbers) is not really a *measure*, it is a *ranking*: in other words, it is expressing the performance of one particular person *in relation to* the typical, age-related performance of others. Essentially, if a child performs at a level above that of their chronological age, they will be awarded an above-average score. Similarly, performance less than that expected by chronological age will produce a below-average score.

This is an important point. It emphasises the fact that, as it stands, any score or number is meaningless. It can only be given meaning by relating it in some way either to the scores and performance of other people (*norm-referenced*) or to performance in a particular domain of knowledge or skill (technically *domain-referenced* but more often designated *criterion-referenced*). These are significant distinctions that will be taken up again later.

It is clear that the kinds of tests that have attempted to measure ability have not proved entirely successful. This does not imply that they have no value: it is sometimes helpful to know that an individual possesses the kinds of qualities measured, for instance, in traditional intelligence tests. Such information can give new insight and expectations to teachers and parents, and in this way enable further progress. However, the kinds of assumptions involved – that a few factors influence all cognitive behaviour; that 'ability' is easily measured by a few test items; and that a score can be used as a predictor of future performance and achievement – are open to considerable question.

In the 1950s and 1960s, dissident voices were beginning to be heard, suggesting that the psychometric approach was of little relevance in educational settings. The scores contained too little information to be of much direct use to teachers in their classroom teaching. Glaser (1963) made the distinction between the kinds of *psychometric* approach implied by some of the previous work, and *educational measurement* that would be much more directly useful in educational decision-making and planning. His answer was to suggest a move away from notions of *ability* and focus instead on *attainment*.

Tests of attainment and achievement

Earlier in this chapter, tests of attainment or achievement were defined as assessments that seek to measure what a person has learned – what they know, understand or can do. Adopting this approach immediately opens up a wider prospect in teaching contexts, of much more direct usefulness, for it allows us to define the knowledge, skills or characteristics deemed important and then to assess whether they have been acquired or demonstrated. The two terms are set alongside each other here, since there is some difference in use and meaning on both sides of the Atlantic.

So far, the distinction between tests of ability and those focusing on attainment or achievement has been presented in a clear-cut way. A traditional analysis of the two approaches might focus on the following distinguishing factors, in a very general way:

- **the use made of the information** – ability tests focusing on prediction, achievement tests on what has been learned;
- **the nature of qualities being measured** – ability tests focusing on more general, high-level cognitive processes, and achievement tests on knowledge skills and more specific elements;
- **the relationship to heredity** – ability tests supposedly measuring innate capacity, and achievement tests, learned accomplishments.

In reality, however, the distinctions are more blurred than such a listing would suggest. Specific learning, knowledge and skills interact in complicated ways with more general cognitive processes, and hence any response that a child makes to an assessment item is likely to be the product of both, in unknown ratio. In fact, one of the criticisms of traditional intelligence tests is that they frequently assess attainment rather than ability in the 'pure' form. Such outcomes are, no doubt, partly the result of learning and of particular kinds of educational, social and cultural experiences. The holy grail of pure 'ability' is very elusive. This throws question marks over the notion of testing *ability*, and at the same time strengthens the argument for a focus on *attainment*.

Tests that focus on attainment and achievement come in many forms: they vary from fairly formally constructed, standardised published tests in specific areas of the curriculum (for example, certain tests in reading or mathematics), to informal, teacher-constructed tests related to specific work in the classroom. In their most useful form they are closely related to a specific curriculum and to the teaching-learning process: the content of teaching determines what is to be assessed and at what point in time. They pursue goals that are specifically educational in nature, rather than abstract, psychological constructs. Because they are more specific, they are perhaps more in line with what is known about children and their developing skills.

Norm-referenced tests and criterion-referenced tests

Both these terms have already been encountered in this chapter. The central message is that once an assessment activity or test has been completed by a child (or adult, of course) the score that is yielded means nothing until some sort of referencing scheme is applied. This enables the score and the performance to be interpreted. In *norm-referenced* assessment, the referencing is to other children in the wider population – a comparison of performance, as it were. In *criterion-referenced* assessment, the reference is to a particular area of knowledge or skill. The child's performance is judged by how much of this *domain* (of knowledge or skills) has been mastered.

An example may make this clearer. I want to assess how well a child knows the basic sight vocabulary of the fifty most commonly used words in English. Having presented these words in an appropriate way, I discover that a particular child could rapidly read 32 of them but could not read the rest. I could interpret this score in two ways. The norm-referenced interpretation would be that this score of 64% (consulting a list of typical scores for the population) meant that this child did better than most children of that age and in fact could be located in the top 25% of the population. This is essentially information about *ranking*, which may be of use to me for some purposes.

The criterion-referenced interpretation would be different. The domain of knowledge in this case was the fifty most used words and this particular child had only read 64% of them. On this basis, can we say that the child has *mastered* this domain? The only answer to this would be to decide upon a *criterion* for success and then categorise the child as either a *master* or *non-master* of the relevant content of the domain. This criterion may be arrived at in many ways, perhaps by judging how many of the words occur in the class reading books and therefore judging how many would need to be recognised for progress to continue. In this case, if the criterion were set at 80%, then the child would be assessed as not having mastered the domain criterion. However, I would have detailed information about which words caused difficulty and therefore where further teaching/learning was needed. On this basis, the child, after a period of time, may go on to demonstrate mastery, and reach the necessary criterion level.

The idea of norm-referencing or criterion-referencing relates to the previous distinction between ability and attainment/achievement tests. Almost by definition, ability tests are norm-referenced, since they invariably require population comparisons. This also applies to such measures as tests of personality traits. Attainment/achievement tests can be norm-referenced in nature (as in some standardised, published tests of reading, for instance) or criterion-referenced, when they are used in the ways just exemplified. Teacher-made, informal tests would usually fall into this last category.

Historically, there has been a gradual move away from norm-referencing and towards criterion-referencing in much educational measurement, although both have a place. In the 1950s, the work of Bloom (1956) acted as a considerable stimulus. By specifying many different kinds of knowledge and skills in many facets of human thinking and behaviour, he provided a foundation for this much more specific kind of approach to assessment. Particularly in the USA, a society more besotted with testing and assessing in schools than our own, much dissatisfaction had arisen with norm-referenced approaches and the way in which they seemed to highlight comparative ignorance rather than positive achievement. As Glaser argued in 1963, what was needed in education was helpful measurement not abstract preoccupation with test theory and prediction.

Criterion-referencing emphasises differences *within* an individual's performance (some things known and understood, others not) rather than differences *between* individuals. According to Wood (1986), it is a form of assessment that *opens* doors, not *closes* them. It is an approach that is more responsive to and reflective of learning, teaching and school experiences. In an ideal form, it embodies a *constructive* outlook, looks for *competence* and for *best performance* from the child. It deals with individual achievement in relation to self not to others. The acid test for any assessment must be: *does it lead to greater understanding and to more constructive action on the part of the teacher?* It seems to be increasingly accepted that approaches that stress achievement and criterion-referencing are more likely to deliver these.

Some further ideas in testing and assessment

So far, we have considered tests and assessment in terms of the qualities they seek to measure, the generality or specificity of their focus, the interpretation or 'referencing' of the scores and their usefulness to the teacher. To some extent, it has also been made clear that tests and assessments vary in terms of their formality and informality. Tests may range from highly formalised, standardised measures, through to highly informal measures constructed by the teacher with particular curriculum aims in mind. However, there exists another distinction frequently made with regard to assessment, and that is the *formative* versus *summative* one. The distinction refers to the function or purpose of assessment, and to some extent its timing.

Formative assessment emphasises judgements and recording made as an integral part of the teaching-learning process. In order to fulfil this role, formative approaches need to be detailed and cover all relevant elements of an area of knowledge or skill. Only in this way can useful information be gained about a pupil's progress and gaps or errors in their understanding. On the basis of such insights, the teacher and pupil can locate difficulties and plan a course of action. Formative assessment is closely linked to a *diagnostic* approach. The aim is not necessarily to assign grades or marks, but to provide feedback for the teacher and learner, which can confirm present understanding and remedy problems. Because of the requirement for detailed analysis, the scope of formative assessment may be limited to particular areas of knowledge or skill within the wider curriculum.

Summative assessment, on the other hand, essentially fulfils a summarising and reporting function. As such, it involves judging overall mastery or competence, and assigning grades or levels. To do this, it should necessarily encompass a broad sweep of the total curriculum that has been addressed within a project, term or year. It therefore has a very different character and purpose to formative approaches. The important distinction between the two is not just in terms of timing: *continuous assessment*, a term commonly used, can be continuously *summative* in nature and function. It should also be pointed out that the terms summative and formative actually apply more properly to the *uses* of the assessment information.

However, in principle and in practice, some crossover of function occurs between the two. For instance, an assessment developed to provide summative information can also be used formatively, if the responses to particular items are analysed individually and used as a basis for further planning. The opposite process is also, in theory, possible, since a detailed, formative assessment could be summarised in some way in order to present a 'snapshot-in-time', and give a summative view. The words to stress here are *in theory*; very careful thought would be needed as to *how* to summarise, particularly if the level of detail involved wide coverage of a total area of curriculum knowledge or skill.

The issue that has not yet been addressed concerns the **quality** of the outcomes as true measures of the characteristics they seek to probe. Here, it is important to emphasise the point made at the beginning of this chapter. Assessment is about making judgements that are as accurate and well-evidenced as possible. These judgements are, however, basically *inferences* about what a person knows and can do, based on their responses and behaviour. As such, all assessment judgements are likely to contain a degree of *error*. This error may be the result of the kinds of measures we are using, the attitudes and motivation of the person being assessed and the assessor, together with problems inherent in the communication process itself.

Because of this, much time and energy has been spent trying to ensure that, in standardised assessment, at least, this error is reduced to a minimum, particularly the kinds of *random error* just outlined. It is worth remarking that measuring complex human qualities is not at all the same kind of enterprise as measuring qualities in the physical world. When I step on the weighing scales in the morning, I recognise that the reading I get may contain a slight element of error (the scales may be on a bump in the carpet) but that it basically delivers a reliable value. Educational measurement is very different, since these random errors could be quite large.

The technical **reliability** of such measurement is usually estimated using various statistical techniques, either by test-retest methods or by using parallel and equivalent versions of the same test. The principle common to both these is that a similar score should be obtained by the same individual on two occasions, provided conditions have been broadly the same. The closer they are under these circumstances, the more reliable the assessment.

It is important, however, also to ask a further question about a test or assessment activity: *Does it measure what it is supposed to measure?* Are the inferences we are making useful for the purposes we have in mind? This is the question of the **validity** of assessment. The questions conventionally asked relate to the *content* of an assessment (do the items sample appropriate characteristics or knowledge?), to the relationship with other *concurrent* measures (do the results bear some relationship to other relevant results?), and to the *predictive* value of the outcome.

All this theory has been developed in relation to norm-referenced assessment: the different nature of criterion-referenced assessment implies somewhat different interpretation of these ideas. When the assessment is criterion-referenced, the issue of reliability becomes one of estimating the *dependability* of the categorisation into masters or non-masters of a particular area of knowledge or skill. The validity of criterion-referenced assessment is a question of the definition of a domain of knowledge or skill and the way in which this is translated into assessable objectives, items or activities.

Which knowledge and skills should be assessed?

The distinction has already been made between tests and assessments, with one having potentially wider focus and basis than the other. Bearing this in mind, it is important to recognise that a common criticism made against formalised testing of children is that tests focus on a limited area of knowledge or skills, and seldom on other more important qualities, which are difficult to measure. As Gipps and her colleagues (1983) point out, they may lead to the dangerous misapprehension that qualities that cannot be clearly delineated and measured are not important. Qualities such as generosity or perseverance are difficult to define and measure, yet they are no doubt qualities we wish to encourage in children. Such considerations have been the prime motive force behind the movement for the use of Records of Achievement, which not only stress positive factors but also address wider issues than academic attainment.

In the school situation, the curriculum documentation provides the usual source of detailing of academic and social aims. Such documentation may vary from highly formalised, written statements to informal agreed procedures. Barrow (1984) defines the curriculum as 'the programme of activities (by teachers and pupils) designed so that pupils will attain, so far as possible, certain educational and other schooling ends and objectives'. Without going too deeply into more philosophical issues, it seems clear that curricular statements may take on a broader or more narrow brief, but at some point should address the issues of what is to be taught, in what sequence, and how learning outcomes are to be evaluated, for individual children and for the school as a whole.

In primary schools, particularly during the early years, a central issue concerns the designation of the areas of knowledge or skills. Should the knowledge and skills be designated or delivered along traditional subject lines, or should they be conceived and delivered in more cross-disciplinary ways? It is a topic outside the direct remit of this book, so it can be sidestepped at this point. However, it does give rise to further questions. If the designation is into traditional subject areas, how can the dictates and demands of the logic and sequence of the *subject* be reconciled with the learning/developmental needs of the *child*? In an ideal world, the curriculum should embody and reconcile both, so that there is a developmental coherence in the subject matter and also an approach and sequence which reflect the capacities of children to deal with increasingly complicated and difficult ideas.

Whichever approach is adopted, whether subject-based or based on some other broad designation of areas of skills or knowledge, in assessment terms the question is the same: *How can we best translate broad curriculum aims or statements into smaller, more assessable areas or items?* In the case of published, standardised tests, of course, this stage of the process has already been carried out: items have been devised, trialled and selected so that the final product is as reliable an instrument as possible for its purpose. The problem with such formalised tests is the nature of the match or mismatch with the particular curriculum in a class or school. Clearly, some existing assessment instrument may well accord with the precise needs and content of the curriculum: in such cases they may prove useful comparative tools in the teacher's repertoire.

However, for the evaluation of learning against a specific curriculum, the process must begin with decisions about the domains of knowledge and skills which are to be assessed. There is a fundamental tension between defining domains in as 'closed' and specific a way as possible, and relying on more open definitions with less precisely specified items within them. The first may result in lengthy, detailed and ultimately questionable lists of objectives, highly assessable but fairly meaningless: the second may result in very wide and loose descriptions which may prove difficult to assess. Nitko (1983), one of the foremost writers in this field, makes an important set of distinctions which may help us think in a more focused way about defining domains. He distinguishes between:

- **Well defined and ordered domains**, where the domain contains elements within it that can be arranged along some kind of scale of difficulty or performance. Examples might be 'addition of single digit numbers' or a scale that reflects different qualities of handwriting.
- **Well defined but unordered domains**, which represent the most common circumstance, since they are likely to be varied in content and in need of very careful description of this content or specification of the properties. An example might be 'uses capital letters and full stops when writing'.

Both of these contrast with domains of knowledge or skills that are very general and poorly defined.

Having decided and defined the domains in useful ways, the content has to be sampled, which in itself is no simple task. In ordered domains, the selection may be more obvious: in unordered ones, it is a matter of some judgement *which* properties or content should be chosen and *how* these elements will relate to and in some way 'represent' the rest. The maxim usually followed is that, for criterion-referenced assessments, items should be selected which represent the range of difficulty within the domain.

How should the knowledge and skills be assessed?

Once domains have been defined and described, giving rise to statements or objectives that are in principle open to assessment in its broadest terms, then a fairly clear-cut process of developing assessment materials occurs. This is shown in Figure 2.1.

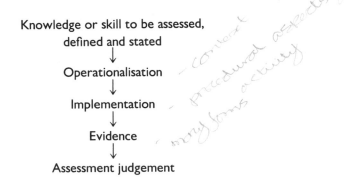

Knowledge or skill to be assessed,
defined and stated
↓
Operationalisation
↓
Implementation
↓
Evidence
↓
Assessment judgement

Figure 2.1 *The process of developing assessment materials*

Tasks, activities or test items have to be devised which will allow children to demonstrate the relevant knowledge or skill: the statement must be *operationalised*. In particular, the *context* in which activities are set may exercise an important influence on outcomes. For instance, a child's ability to add particular digits may be heavily influenced by whether an activity is about adding counters, or about adding up numbers of animals in a zoo, or adding numbers of pencils. This is very much in line with the view of the development of children's thinking outlined in the last chapter. Knowledge gained in one particular context may not be triggered or perceived as relevant in another. Children may give very different responses to what, on the face of it, seem very similar tasks. Given the unpredictability of this, the more contexts that are offered the child, the less likely it is that a biased response will be the outcome.

Procedural aspects of the assessment activity or item must then be considered – the *implementation* aspect of the process. The crucial concern here is that the way the task is presented, the actions involved, or the kinds of responses required should not inhibit the possibility of children demonstrating their competence. Presenting tasks orally (by tape recorder) or in picture or written form will each engage children in different ways. Written responses may be inappropriate for some children, as may oral ones for others. A variety of response modes would overcome this problem. There is little point in trying to assess, say, children's knowledge of multiplication facts, if the requirement to write down answers becomes, in effect, what is being assessed.

The matter of **evidence** is an important one. It may take many forms: a piece of written work or drawing; a model; an audio tape recording or videotape; a record of what a child said or did in particular circumstances; a photograph. However, there clearly are practical limits to the amount of evidence that can be collected or stored for any child or any activity, especially if this evidence forms part of an ongoing portfolio of a child's performance and achievements. Perhaps the best criteria to apply are those of *recency* and *high quality*. Best performance is always important in assessment contexts.

Assessments and testing are about coming to valid and informed judgements, sometimes based on test scores alone, sometimes on wider evidence, including observations. Having devised and implemented relevant tasks or items as appropriate, a judgement must be made as to whether the outcome represents success or failure for a given activity, or mastery or non-mastery in a given domain. The criteria for reaching such a decision should be as explicit and valid as possible.

Conclusions

The central message of this chapter has been that assessments come in different forms, but that all of them should be as valid, helpful and well-evidenced as possible. The outcomes should inform the teaching-learning process and educational decision-making. The kinds of processes teachers have deployed previously, often implicitly, must now be made explicit and must be justified. Under ideal circumstances this should lead to more effective teaching, more integrated learning and to better educational decision-making.

In making assessments more explicit and open to scrutiny, key problems and issues are also brought to the fore. Given a comprehensive, classroom-based approach to assessment, then questions relating to the characteristics of young children, their development, thinking and social relationships gain significance. They clearly impinge on our approach to assessment, as do the characteristics of teachers and classrooms.

This chapter has outlined some key concepts in assessment and testing: different kinds of tests; different purposes; different kinds of interpretation of outcomes; and questions about the quality of the assessments being made. All these ideas should inform the approach to assessment as part of ongoing teaching.

However, in making any decision, it is the wisdom of the decision-maker that is important. Given what we know about the limitations and weaknesses of certain kinds of assessment, it becomes obvious that an arid adherence to test scores will not necessarily make for productive decision-making. The aim of providing the technical information in this chapter is not to suggest a straitjacket for teachers, but to broaden and enhance the judgement repertoire.

3

National Curriculum Assessment in England and Wales

The National Curriculum specifies, for each of the prescribed subjects, the skills, concepts and content to be taught progressively through the years of compulsory schooling. Children's learning within these curriculum specifications is monitored through the assessment system introduced almost alongside the curriculum itself. Simultaneously, both the content and the criteria by which such content is to be assessed, are provided.

The assessment system, as first formulated by the Task Group on Assessment and Testing (DES, 1988), was to have the following characteristics:

- **it should be criterion-referenced**: the results were to give information about pupil achievement in relation to objectives.
- **it should be formative in nature**: the results were to provide the basis for decisions about a pupil's further learning needs.
- **it should demonstrate progression**: the scales and levels used should give continuity to a pupil's assessments at different ages.
- **it should be moderated**: the outcomes should be capable of comparison across classes or schools.

These principles, elaborated in the TGAT Report, were to inform the development of the curriculum specification in the designated subjects. From the beginning, the curriculum was specified in a subject-based way, although no requirement was made that this should necessarily be its mode of delivery in the classroom. The principle established was that children should be assessed summatively at the end of each of four **Key Stages** (at ages 7, 11, 14 and 16), these summative assessments being based on the formative assessments made throughout.

The Group's deliberations and the subsequent decisions made in the ensuing months, gave rise to an hierarchical breakdown of knowledge and skills in each subject. The first broad sub-categories, the **Profile Components** (PCs), were to be the major areas of knowledge and skills within the subject. These Profile Components were in turn delineated into **Attainment Targets** (ATs), smaller but definable areas of knowledge and skills, each of which was to contain ten specified **levels** within it. Each level was to achieve this specification through **Statements of Attainment** (SoAs) at each of the ten levels. This scheme of ten levels within each Attainment Target would provide the framework for progression between the ages of 5 and 16. The number was arrived at by examining other systems that sought to scale pupil achievement (usually 5 or 6 scale points for single age groups) and then rationalising this over the eleven-year age-span of the National Curriculum.

The precise nature and specification of knowledge and skills in each subject was left to the relevant curriculum working groups. Guidance was, however, offered on the matter of breadth versus specificity with the outlining of the curricula. Paragraph 5 of the First Supplementary Report of the Group states:

> *'On the one hand, a small number of targets, each couched in fairly general terms gives maximum room for flexibility in teaching and learning, but lacks clarity and precision for assessment purposes. On the other hand, many and highly specific targets may increase clarity and precision, but leave little room for flexibility and may indeed become unmanageably complex.'*

On the matter of progression through the ten levels, the following points were made:

> *'It is not necessary to assume that the progression defined indicates some inescapable order in the way in which children learn or some sequence of difficulty inherent in the material to be learnt. Both of these factors may apply, but the sequence of learning may be the result of choices, for whatever reason, which those formulating and operating the curriculum may recommend in the light of teaching experience.'* (TGAT Report, para 93)

The assessments were to be made by teachers in a classroom context, within this curriculum-based framework. Such assessments would be *formative*, yet capable of becoming *summative* assessments at the ends of the Key Stages. Alongside these assessments made by the teacher, **Standard Assessment Tasks** (SATs) would be introduced, covering a small proportion of the total curriculum, which would allow for a degree of 'external' assessment, in the interests of wider accountability.

These 'SATs' were to be as varied as possible in approach, using a range of activities, presentation and response modes. Among these methods, there should be scope for more formalised testing. The tasks should *'be designed to elicit a particular type of response in a stan-dardised manner, and to rate this, using standard methods, so that the pupil assessed would be assigned a score, grade or category'* (TGAT Report, para 44).

It is also worth drawing attention to a particular point in relation to the assessment of seven-year-olds at Key Stage 1. At this stage, where fewer Attainment Targets may apply, the aim of the asssessments, with such young children, should be to *'identify children in need of help which is exceptional for a child of that age, whether because he or she is making so little or so much progress in a Profile Component'* (TGAT Report, para 147). Such a comment is entirely in line with a formative approach to assessment, linking it directly to a subsequent programme of teaching provision.

With this background information in mind, we can now look in more detail at the characteristics of the system, and some of the issues it raises. So far, the major experience of assessment has been in the three core subjects: English, mathematics and science. These will therefore be the focus of analysis, but with the principles applying more widely to the other subjects too.

The four major characteristics of the system envisaged by the TGAT group were listed above. Each of these characteristics will now be considered in turn, pointing out theoretical and practical issues that arise. The focus here is initially on Key Stage 1, but with the points and principles applying equally to Key Stage 2. The points also apply, whether it is Teacher Assessment that is the focus, or assessment through the Standard Tasks.

The approach should be criterion-referenced

The content of the curriculum in each subject is set out and extended within the Statutory Orders and the related Programmes of Study. The former provides a fairly precise kind of specification, the latter more general principles and advice. For assessment purposes, however, the main focus is likely to be on the Statements of Attainment at each level, informed by the more general approach of the Programmes of Study. The statements potentially provide the objectives in the criterion-referenced system.

The processes by which these statements were arrived at are not clear. No doubt the principles outlined earlier provided the basis: the way in which children learn; the logical sequence of some of the subject-matter; the experience of teaching certain ideas to children. What is clear, however, is that some of them may need even more rethinking as experience of curriculum delivery and assessment increases, this notwithstanding the fact that the specifications in mathematics and science have already been modified. A further point rapidly becomes obvious too. Even a cursory glance at the statements at the first three levels, even within the three core subjects, reveals that at some levels a great deal is specified and at others, very little. This clearly, of itself, has enormous implications for the ease or difficulty of attaining that level. Having to satisfy the requirements of five or six statements is a very different proposition to satisfying only one or two.

In the three core subjects, even considering only the first few levels in each Attainment Target, the statements vary tremendously in their specificity or generality and the clarity with which they outline a particular aspect of content. Using the terminology established earlier (see page 32):

- Some of them represent fairly closed and *ordered* domains, for instance under the early specifications:
Mathematics, Ma3/2a
'know and use addition and subtraction facts up to ten.'

- Some represent more usual *unordered* kinds of domain:
Science, Sc3/1a
'be able to name or label the external parts of the human body/plants.'

- Some represent very vague and poorly defined domains:
English, En1/4d
'participate in a presentation.'

- Some have an enormous number of elements within them:
English, En2/4d
'find books or magazines in the class or school library by using the classification system, catalogue or database and use appropriate methods of finding information, when pursuing a line of inquiry.'

Added to this, a wide range of *performance verbs* are used, among which are:

understand	*listen*	*predict*	*select*
explain	*find*	*construct*	*demonstrate*
identify	*sort*	*sequence*	*use*
design	*apply*	*convey*	*interpret*

Certain of these verbs cause considerable difficulty in assessment. What does it mean to '*understand*'? How does understanding show itself in order to be assessed? In a similar way, what does it mean to '*know*'? Does it mean being able instantly to provide an answer or can 'thinking' be involved? A rather different kind of problem arises with the verb '*listen*'. How do children demonstrate that they are listening? Many teachers have had the experience of a child who fidgets constantly and appears to be paying little attention, during a story perhaps, but who can then go on to recount every detail. There are apparently no clear-cut behaviours which would reliably indicate 'listening'. The only proof seems to lie in the outcomes, children demonstrating listening by their subsequent responses. Of a different order completely are terms such as '*appreciate*' or '*explore*', which seem almost impossible to assess.

These comments are not designed to put teachers off the idea of systematic assessment: they are discussed here with the aim of encouraging further consideration of some of these crucial first steps in approaching assessment. There may be no easy solution to such variety and difficulty contained within the statements of attainment: it was pointed out earlier that the process of specifying a curriculum must involve reconciling a degree of generality and flexibility with some specificity. Some consistency of interpretation is, however, vital. Without this, there will be a great deal of variability and hence undependability built into the system.

In the Key Stage 1 national assessments in 1991, it was obvious that teachers interpreted these statements in very different ways. There was little agreement about the meaning of words such as '*sight vocabulary*' (the '*reading*' AT) or '*understanding*'.

It was also clear that some teachers required children to demonstrate competence on only *one* occasion, whereas others required evidence from children on more than two occasions, in order to credit them with attainment of a particular statement. Continuing this theme of mastery levels, many teachers seemed to apply a criterion of about 70–80% correct for a child to be credited with attainment, but this was by no means universal. As far as *evidence* was concerned, teachers seemed to show some consistency in taking into account the full range of quality in a child's work. 'Best' and 'worst' examples were mostly considered alongside 'usual' work. Very few indicated that they relied only on the child's most *recent* products.

Earlier, the distinction was made between *norm-referenced* assessment and the approach of the National Curriculum assessment system, *criterion-referenced*. The two basic approaches are different, but in criterion-referenced assessment, an element of norm-referencing may creep in, since, to some extent, all criteria are interpreted in relation to certain norms. The 'criterion' level for deciding mastery or non-mastery must be set, preferably according to rational means rather than arbitrarily deciding on a cut-off point. In the absence of other information, 'expected' performance for an age group may be the only starting point.

Some of the statements of attainment are very general in their content specification, although located at a particular level. Under these circumstances, it is almost impossible not to introduce an element of norm-referencing in deciding upon mastery levels. For example, given a statement such as *'talk in simple terms about the content of stories'* (En2/1d) the 'simple terms' can really only be defined in terms of what might reasonably be expected of a child of the appropriate age. This is likely to be based on the standards set by a group of children on whom the activity was tried.

The assessments should be formative

We saw earlier (page 29) that *formative* approaches to assessment stress detailed analysis of the kinds of knowledge and understandings possessed by a child in order to plan further learning experiences. This contrasts with *summative* approaches where overall judgements are made. In principle, the distinction between the two can be blurred, and it seems to be the case that formative assessments, kept as a detailed and accurate record, could indeed provide the basis for summative judgements. In the context of the National Curriculum, detailed teacher assessments can be summarised and used summatively for reporting purposes.

However, a further dimension is added to this process, in the form of the Standard Assessment Task. In order to begin to clarify their nature and purpose, reference needs to be made to the original suggestions of the TGAT group. SATs were envisaged as an important means of securing comparability of judgement across teachers and schools throughout England and Wales. In theory, they should help produce results on a common scale, with no doubt a 'backwash' effect into teacher assessments. From the beginning, the implication was that they should cover only a *part* of the curriculum on any occasion, particularly at Key Stage 1. The TGAT group advocated a wide variety of assessment strategies within these standard tasks, together with 'flexibility of use' (para 50).

All of this suggests that the Standard Assessment Task should have three major purposes: they should act as *calibrating* devices within the assessment system, ensuring common standards and judgements; linked to this they should act as a vehicle for the further *professional development* of teaching and assessment skills; and they should have the potential for providing measures that would encourage *accountability* within the system.

Against this background it is useful to examine the actual workings and outcomes of the system, at least for Key Stage 1. Experience thus far suggests three major issues that bear further examination.

The first concerns the meaning of the word **'Standard'**. The original definition (TGAT Report, paras 44–50) stated that they should elicit a particular type of response in a standardised manner, using standard methods. The word *'standardised'*, in assessment parlance, refers to the degree to which the procedures, equipment and materials of an assessment are *fixed* (Nitko, 1983). However, it is also used in a slightly different way, to refer to the fact that some formal assessments and tests have been tried out on large representative samples of subjects, and norms developed for scoring. These are then known as 'standardised tests'. The meaning of 'standard' in the National Curriculum is clearly in line with the first definition and not with the second. 'Standard' when used in this way can improve the objectivity and comparability of the assessment. The reality of the 'standard' quality of the Key Stage 1 assessment tasks, as so far developed, will be discussed in subsequent chapters, when the core subjects are considered individually.

The second issue continues the theme of **comparability**. The Standard Tasks were, in part, a vehicle for ensuring some comparability within the system, and to some extent they functioned in this way. In the standard assessment materials, teachers are presented with (mostly) clear interpretations of the statements of attainment and clear indications of what to look for as evidence of attainment. As time goes on, this developing body of information and experience will no doubt give rise to more common standards and greater comparability of judgement, which in the short term is lacking.

But this in turn begs the question of the nature of the relationship between the assessment judgements made by teachers, and the assessment outcomes produced by the SATs. Since the Standard Assessment can inevitably only occur for a small part of the curriculum (certain Attainment Targets), how should these relate to teacher assessments made in the same Attainment Targets? Furthermore, what are the implications of the two scores in the same Attainment Target being different? Certainly there are arguments to suggest that the two scores might be different. The assessments recorded by teachers are likely to be based on full and detailed work by the children over a period of time. The Standard Assessments, on the other hand, mostly represent a one-off summative judgement, made under particular circumstances and frequently addressing only limited aspects of an Attainment Target.

In practice, under present arrangements within National Curriculum assessment, the SAT score, if it is different to the score arrived at by teacher assessment, overrides the teacher assessment and in effect replaces the teacher's score for that particular Attainment Target. Mechanisms exist, however, for appeal, negotiation and moderation, should this not be satisfactory to the teacher or school. Indirectly, these points raise further questions about whether and in what ways the two kinds of scores should be combined. Experience so far, however, shows SAT scores are frequently *higher* than teacher assessment scores, making the appeals and moderation procedure less likely. In a situation where this did not prove to be the case, or as the two sets of scores converge, more urgent consideration may need to be given to the nature and implications of combining scores with these particular priorities.

In the 1991 assessments, the combined effect of SAT scores often being higher than teacher assessment scores, together with the particular rules of the aggregation system, meant that the SAT scores had a disproportionate effect in some Profile Components (for example, Science 1) yet played a minimal role in the outcomes in others (Science 2). The changes in the number of Attainment Targets in mathematics and science may go some way to even out this problem.

The third issue concerns **aggregation**. Summative information can be derived from more extensive and detailed assessment information by some process of selection and aggregation. In the case of the present system, rules exist for aggregating scores from Attainment Target to Profile Component level, and for aggregating scores from Attainment Targets direct to subject level.

This highly summarised information can therefore be obtained, but at a price. The price is the loss of important information along the way and a more gross, less detailed characterisation of a child's attainments. Clearly, summarised information *is* needed within the system, but the crucial point is deciding at what level this should happen. The more the stages of aggregation to a single value, the more likely the move towards precisely the global and unhelpful judgements that the system seems to have been designed to avoid. The paradox is that the guiding principle behind the National Curriculum seems to have been one of *differentiation*, enabling a fuller and more helpful appraisal of children's progress and discouraging *labelling* and wider *expectancy effects*.

The present system may well be a level of summarising and aggregation that is appropriate for parents (though they may request more), but as teachers it is important to maintain a clear distinction between these global assessments and the more detailed assessments that not only inform teaching but also encourage a more constructive view of children. Teachers themselves must be clear about the purposes the different kinds of assessment are serving.

The assessments should demonstrate progression

The ten levels of attainment within each Attainment Target provide the framework for monitoring progress, on the same scale, throughout the school years, from age 5 to 16. The specification of the curriculum throughout these levels is intended to represent the likely progress a child will make, and was no doubt arrived at through the kinds of considerations outlined earlier. Whether, in reality, the levels outline the changes accurately will only become obvious with time, as the curriculum is further implemented and the more formal assessments evaluated.

The hierarchy does, however, have considerable implications in terms of the **accuracy** of summarising a child's progress at the early Key Stages. Inaccuracy, particularly over-estimation, would have knock-on effects for subsequent Key Stages. With so few levels against which to represent progress, the scores of some children may remain fairly constant, as they move through their schooling – particularly the summarised, aggregated scores at Profile Component or subject level. These aggregations may conceal particular areas of progress within them. It may also be the case that more detailed specification *below* Level 1 will be needed in order to do justice to the achievements of some low-attaining children.

Marking children's progress in terms of these levels may also have implications for teaching. The range of attainment in a class, even within particular areas of the curriculum, and including classes that supposedly contain children of similar 'ability', may be very great. This may well have the effect of highlighting for the teacher what perhaps might have remained previously implicit. By the same token, it ought to facilitate greater insight into any child's attainments and further learning needs, and potentially improve the 'match' between the child's needs and the tasks provided.

The assessments should be moderated

Given a situation of formative assessment against objectives/statements that are highly varied in character, then moderation takes on enormous significance, if comparability of standards is to be ensured. There are in principle three sources for national consistency of interpretation and judgement; the national training for LEA staff; the SAT information and materials; and the central advice on interpretation and standards provided by SEAC in their additional documentation.

Based on the information with which they are provided, it is the responsibility of the local education authorities to create mechanisms for moderation and to monitor the quality of the assessments made. The response of most, so far, has been to group schools and appoint staff as moderators for these groups. Their role is to support teachers in schools and to try to ensure common assessment standards.

Agreement trials are a popular mechanism for beginning to achieve these. Teachers from within a school or group of schools consider children's work and agree judgements. In the process of so doing, interpretation of the statements is being discussed and agreed, as well as mastery levels of all kinds. As we saw earlier, issues such as how *much* does a child have to demonstrate a particular knowledge or skill and *how often* are of major importance.

However, under these circumstances, the tendency is often to focus on direct and measurable products (children's writing, number work, books) rather than to address the difficult matter of agreeing standards for more **intangible** aspects, such as *process* science, or speaking and listening skills. Until ways are found of agreeing these also, then the assessment judgements will always contain a degree of variability and non-comparability. Possible mechanisms for this might be to audio-tape, video-tape or visit other classes to agree judgements in a 'there-and-then' way.

The national evaluation project (ENCA 1) found agreement trials to be highly valued by teachers as a direct and practical help in facing the difficult situation of the new assessments. They seem to have proved a major force for effective professional development, as predicted by the TGAT Report. The National Curriculum introduced a framework and vocabulary for the discussion of curriculum content and delivery issues. The assessment system has the potential to do the same, and in so doing, to enhance insight and teaching skills.

Responses to the initial proposals

Responses to the proposed new assessment system were mixed, but most commentators seemed reassured that the kind of approach being suggested might not be as disastrous as many had anticipated. However, many also pointed out some of the basic problems associated with any assessment, even one with these characteristics. These can be sum-marised as follows:

- Even with a wide range of subjects within the National Curriculum, and a reasonably broad specification within each subject, any assessment or set of tests would be likely to have a narrowing effect on teaching and the classroom experiences of children, especially young children.

- Introducing the assessment system at such an early point in time, almost alongside the implementation of the curriculum itself, raised the question of assessment-led curriculum change. This has not always been seen as the most productive approach to change, although many would argue that it has sometimes proved successful, as with the GCSE, for instance.
- Criterion-referenced assessment demands the setting of mastery levels – cut-off scores – which determine success or failure. These risk being almost arbitrary decisions, lines drawn at random as it were, unless care and sound judgement are exercised. Yet such mastery definitions are necessary for measuring change and progress over time.
- The role and status of the statements of attainment may become rather confused. Should they be seen as *educational objectives*, the *curriculum specification* or *performance criteria*? Are they only the means of defining the boundaries between each level?
- Theoretical problems exist in the matter of aggregating scores. It is not clear on what basis scoring outcomes from one aspect of the curriculum can legitimately be combined with the outcomes from other, potentially very different dimensions. The paradox is that valid assessment of a broad specification of knowledge and skills requires a range and variety of assessment, but it is then not clear that all the disparate dimensions can be reasonably combined or aggregated.

Putting the proposals into practice at Key Stage 1

A long process of development and trialling went into the production of the Key Stage 1 Standard Assessment Tasks used in the pilot run of 1990 and the first full national deployment in 1991. Many approaches were tried out by three development agencies, one of which was finally adopted. The early attempts were detailed and in line with what was deemed good practice in infant classrooms – that is, thematically-based, small-group activities, mostly practical in nature, and frequently administered orally rather than in a pencil-and-paper way. They required detailed observation and recording on the part of the teachers. The end-result was major protest that they were time-consuming and almost unmanageable in classrooms

Since then the SATs have undergone a considerable streamlining, becoming shorter, more self-contained and addressing only a small part of the curriculum in each of the core subjects. The hope has been that they are thus more manageable in classrooms and more acceptable to teachers.

The central issue is one of balancing the often conflicting demands of producing genuinely standard and dependable assessments, with classroom manageability and acceptability to teachers. As assessments take on the characteristics that render them reliable, they are likely to generate the disapproval of teachers commited to what they see as appropriate methods and activities for young children. There clearly has to be a compromise between the two, particularly at Key Stage 1. But, unless this is a sound and principled compromise, which produces outcomes which are dependable and comparable, then the idea of using these as the basis for comparing attainments in different LEAs, schools or classrooms is open to question.

Implications for Key Stage 2 assessments

The knowledge and skills of eleven-year-olds are obviously different from those of seven-year-olds. They have been in school longer, have a wider understanding and experience, and hence are more likely to respond to more traditional and familiar approaches to assessment and testing. For many years, eleven-year-olds up and down the land experienced formalised testing, the 'eleven plus' exams, for purposes of selection. These tests were mostly intelligence-type tests, focusing on such dimensions of performance as verbal reasoning. They were not curriculum-based tests, although general knowledge clearly entered into them. The outcomes were, however, of considerable significance in children's lives. It is not the intention here to go into the pros and cons of this debate, but only to point out that formalised assessment at age 11 was and is still a common experience.

It seems likely that standard assessment at Key Stage 2 will have this more formalised character, so eliminating some of the problems encountered at Key Stage 1 – for example classroom manageability issues. However, there will no doubt still be significant matters to address, not least those of the nature of the curriculum specification and appropriate interpretations of the statements at the higher levels, in relation to interpretations and standards established at Key Stages 1 and 3. The possible range of attainments within a class of eleven-year-olds is likely to be greater than at Key Stage 1, with attendant problems for the organisation of the assessments. The ongoing problem of not insulting or boring the high-attaining child nor daunting the lower-attaining, within appropriate packages of materials, must be confronted. An assessment context must be created that allows each child to demonstrate their maximum performance through sets of items and activities that are dependable and easily organised in the classroom. To some extent, these are also problems that confront teachers in their own assessments and record-keeping.

Assessment and record-keeping

The National Curriculum spells out, in each subject, what should be taught, whilst the parallel assessment system provides the basis for deciding how well children have gained the knowledge or skills. This is an important change of focus required of teachers. Information that may previously have remained implicit, in teachers' heads as it were, must now be formalised and made explicit.

As Merttens and Vass (1991) suggest, in the past, teacher records in the primary school have often noted what has been *taught* rather than precisely what the children have *learned*. Any focus on learning was likely to be in relation to learning difficulties or problems, for particular children. The demand is now for detailed evaluation of what has been learned and careful record-keeping. The records should encourage ongoing, formative assessment that can give rise to summative assessment at certain points. It is not possible to keep separate any longer what the child has done and the level of their performance and understanding. Effective planning of activities cannot take place without a clear idea of the learning needs and levels of performance of individual children and groups of children.

It is also the case that reporting to parents now needs to be done in a more detailed and structured way. This is a time-consuming activity when done properly and should be acknowledged as such. The evaluation of the 1991 assessments as analysed in the ENCA 1 Report (Shorrocks et al., 1992) showed that reporting to parents took many hours of teacher time, often in the evenings and at weekends. The reports were, however, well received by parents, who said they found the information comprehensible and useful. Of the parents surveyed, 37% were in favour of teacher assessments but not the SATs, and 57% said they were in favour of both.

Conclusions

This chapter has set out the major characteristics of the National Curriculum assessment system, relating particularly to the three core subjects (English, mathematics and science) since these are the ones where most information is available. It represents an attempt not only to specify a curriculum, but also to set alongside this an integrated assessment system, which is classroom-based.

When the ideas were first mooted, many eyebrows were raised, especially among educators of young children in infant and first schools. The idea of exposing young children to this kind of assessment raised negative responses in many quarters. Only time will tell whether such responses proved well-founded or not.

However, it would be naive to assume that children of seven, and even younger, were exposed to no kind of assessment previously. In first and infant schools up and down the land, many children were exposed to spelling tests, reading aloud, 'review' pages in mathematics workbooks, etc. Also, on a one-to-one basis, a number of children are formally assessed by educational psychologists and teachers if there appear to be problems.

As long ago as 1983, Gipps and her associates discovered that 79% of LEAs had some kind of formal testing programme, often directed at primary-age children. A total of 38% were formally testing reading by age 7, and a few mathematics and IQ. By the age of 8, these figures had risen to 50% for reading and 17% for mathematics and IQ. The increase up to age 11 was then considerable, so much so, they reported, that testing was at its heaviest in primary schools. The reason given for this widespread testing of every child in some age cohorts was *account-ability*, following very public airing of the issue during the 1970s. For children beginning to cause concern, the reason has always been one of screening and offering help at as early a stage as possible.

More recent studies have shown that, in the case of reading, around 62% of LEAs have administered formal reading tests, most commonly Young's *Group Reading Test* (NFER, 1992).

It would be wrong to suggest, therefore, that formal assessment is unknown for this age-group. What is new is the systematic and overt way in which it must now be carried out, at least in the core subjects.

The National Curriculum itself is still rather new in its implementation and the assessment system even more so. This chapter has pointed up some of the problems and issues to do with both principles and practice. Some of these are clearly the product of the newness of the requirements and the inexperience of some teachers. The speed of the whole enterprise has also played a part. Some aspects, however, perhaps need further consideration. Only constructive feedback will allow for its improvement and development.

4

Assessing English

The National Curriculum specifications for English essentially represent the end product of a decade or more of debate about the nature of competence in language and how this competence should be taught. The Bullock Report (1975), the Kingman Report (1988), HMI documents (the 'Primary Survey', 1978) and 'Curriculum Matters' (DES, 1984), all raised important issues which the Cox Report (1989) sought to reconcile within the English curriculum. The National Curriculum embodies an approach to English teaching that, even at Key Stage 1, is broad in scope and requires children to begin to reflect on language use as well as to develop particular competencies. As in the other core subjects, the Programmes of Study provide the wider teaching framework, and the Statements of Attainment within the levels the criteria for judging children's performance.

There are three broad areas outlined, the three Profile Components, concerned with *speaking and listening, reading* and *writing*. At Key Stages 1 and 2, the writing Profile Component is, in turn, divided into three Attainment Targets: writing, handwriting and spelling. This subdivision is important, since it encourages a more differentiated approach to children's writing: it is too easy to merge all three in practice and thereby to lose the learning and developmental insights that are potentially available.

Although there are five Attainment Targets, nevertheless certain themes cross most of them at Levels 1 to 5: children's growing familiarity with and understanding of narrative, a focus on meaning and an emphasis on effective communication in all modes.

Speaking and Listening (En1)

The aim of the curriculum in Speaking and Listening is:

> 'The development of pupils' understanding of the spoken word and the capacity to express themselves effectively in a variety of speaking and listening activities, matching style and response to audience and purpose.'
> (*English in the National Curriculum*, DES, 1989)

At Levels 1–3, certain themes are evident:

- communicating effectively with peers in one-to-one and group situations;

- communicating effectively with adults;
- responding to and giving instructions;
- listening and responding to stories, poems and other reading materials.

Some background considerations

This apparently simple listing belies a very wide range of skills and knowledge to be encouraged in children, all of whom will arrive at school with a varied experience of language use. As we saw in Chapter 2, using and interpreting spoken language is a highly complex problem-solving activity, for adults and for children.

The study of children's language development that has taken place over the last two decades has clearly established the fact that children do not learn to talk by processes of parrot-like repetition: it is a much more constructive and personal process. The framework of children's development presented in Chapter 2 applies to language process too. Children actively engage in the process of working out what language is and what it can do, a fact evident from the beginning when mothers and infants are interacting together.

What seems to be happening between them is that *meaning* is being *negotiated* during the course of conversational exchanges. The messages from the child are initially quite rudimentary, but as experience and skill increase these messages become more extensive and precise. In the most productive interactions, the adult provides the structure – the framework of the conversation – with the child feeding in their 'turns' when they are able. To use Bruner's terminology (1987), the adult *'scaffolds'* the conversation and the child gradually learns to join in and develop the idea or topic. Children learn spoken language *through* conversation and, at the same time, learn *about* conversation.

What they have to learn about conversation, as we saw in Chapter 2, is a complicated set of skills, insights and understandings. In order effectively to communicate with adults or with peers, they have to be able to:

- gain the attention of the other partner, using language or some other means;
- initiate a topic;
- judge how best to do this by deciding what the person already knows or has in mind and therefore what the best strategy might be for an 'opening';
- interpret the responses their partner makes;
- work out the meaning of non-verbal behaviour – the gestures, facial expression, tone of voice and intonation of what is said;

- make judgements whether what is actually said is meant: messages are often conveyed in very indirect ways;
- sustain a theme or topic of conversation and clarify meaning along the way;
- repair conversations if they break down, by repetition, requests, etc.;
- change topics or themes in a conversation;
- end conversations.

If the conversation is taking place in a group, then a further layer of skills is required in order to establish a role, present messages and information in ways that are accepted by the group, and interpret the messages and intentions of several people at once.

As in all learning, children's experiences of and with language will vary during the pre-school years. Some of the best evidence we have on this matter comes from the work of Gordon Wells and the Bristol Language Development Study (Wells, 1987). The detailed analysis of children's language learning before and during the first years at school not only endorses the views outlined here, but also draws attention to the issues of children from supposedly 'impoverished' home language backgrounds.

It is a pervasive idea in the minds of many teachers that children from 'working-class' homes experience language in very limited ways, a notion outlined by Bernstein back in the 1960s. The sample of children in the Bristol study came from a representative range of home backgrounds, allowing for realistic analysis of the *'language deficit'* debate. What the findings show is that, at the extremes of social background, there are indeed differences in the language experience of the children, but that for the vast majority, the differences are nowhere near clear-cut. The experiences of many 'middle-class' and 'working-class' children were similar in home contexts. All the children experienced a wide range of language and the differences between them were not sufficient to justify the ideas perpetrated in the earlier studies. Indeed, the work of Tizard and Hughes (1984) showed that, for their sample of children, the language experiences at home – whatever the social background – were richer than many of their language experiences at school or nursery.

All of which leads to important questions about the kinds of talk and language experience provided in classrooms for young children. With twenty to thirty children in a class, it is clearly an immense task of imagination and stamina for the teacher to ensure appropriate conversations are held with each child, according to their needs and for educative purposes. However, the requirements of the curriculum dictate that high-quality spoken language development should take place.

One step on the way to achieving this is to be very clear about what is involved and how children learn: these insights should enable a much more focused and relevant set of experiences to be provided. The Programme of Study for speaking and listening is a source of further help.

It is also important to consider the *nature* of teacher talk in the classroom. Many studies bear witness to the fact that much of what is said by teachers consists of questions, and often very *'closed'* questions to boot. Such questions, by their very nature, constrain the conversational possibilities and contributions that can be made by children in response. Even more *open-ended questions* can place constraints on the kinds of ways in which children can elaborate their thoughts. Perhaps the golden rule for teachers should be to rely less on questions as a means of initiating conversations, or even eliciting information from children. A well-chosen *comment* or *statement* may prove more provocative in gaining involvement, since it is an opening gambit that is in many ways more natural and familiar among children themselves. It also helps minimise the pervasive classroom litany of teacher question, child response then teacher comment and evaluation.

Assessing children's spoken language

The Programmes of Study for speaking and listening provide a range of ideas for activities and experiences which help children to develop these skills and understandings. The same activities should also provide the context for making judgements about children's progress, using the statements of attainment as focus points.

Apart from the TGAT recommendations (DES, 1988), specific advice for assessing the various strands of English was offered in the proposals from the National Curriculum Working Group (DES, 1989). Their comments provide a useful starting point, giving five criteria for assessment in this Attainment Target:

- the nature of skills requires that they be assessed in a *continuous* way and as *informally* as possible;
- the assessments should be in the context of activities and experiences *familiar* to the child;
- the speaking and listening dimensions are *closely related* to each other and this should be reflected in any assessment;
- the assessments should both reflect and promote a *wide range of classroom activities;*
- the assessments should be as free as possible from the influence of *social and cultural bias.*

The third and fifth criteria on this list bear further comment here, since the rest have to some extent been addressed either in this chapter or elsewhere. Listening and speaking are two sides of the same coin: in order effectively to shape and deliver our messages and information we need to listen to the contributions of others, gaining as much meaning as possible. We also need to listen to ourselves. A few activities do *not* involve both – listening to a radio programme or tape, watching television, listening to a story, for instance. Apart from these kinds of situation, separating out speaking and listening for assessment purposes may distort the outcomes.

In assessing speaking and listening, social and cultural bias may readily enter into the judgement. Focus on *how* a child speaks (accent, 'sloppiness', slang) may easily divert attention from *what* is said and the kinds of structures and vocabulary being used. Teacher expectancy effects may also intervene in the case of children from different social or cultural backgrounds. Part of the solution lies in being as *specific* as possible in our observations and our own listening, focusing only on the relevant aspects of what the child says.

If the assessments are to be continuous and informal, then considerable observational skills and listening skills are required of the teacher.

What are we watching and listening for?

The statements of attainment are not specific about the kinds of 'conversation' and 'participating' behaviour that is appropriate. Other work outlined above, however, provides a more detailed framework. For *formative* purposes that will help us to plan for further learning, we can look for the kinds of behaviours listed on page 16:

- How does the child open conversations and initiate topics?
- How do they respond to the responses of others?
- Can they ask for clarification of meaning?
- Do they contribute at appropriate points in a conversation?
- Are they confident, dominant, or more reserved in groups, pairs or with adults?
- Do they understand and use gesture when they communicate?
- Can they ask as well as respond to a range of questions?
- How long are their contributions?

As well as these 'conversation management' aspects, what about the content of what children say?

- Can they use a range of vocabulary?
- Do they use a variety of types of sentences?
- Is intonation and expression used appropriately?

- How imaginative is their speech, in role play, for instance?
- Do they talk about feelings and motives?
- Can they hold the attention of another child, adult or group by what they say?

Observing and assessing a child's speaking and listening with an adult presents special problems. This communication situation may present difficulties for children overawed by a teacher or not so familiar with this 'asymmetric' power situation.

On the other hand, observing two children communicating, a more 'symmetrical' communication situation may give rise to certain kinds of exchanges, because more may be taken for granted when communicating with a peer: less may need to be made explicit. Only careful devising of activities can help counteract this. In a *dyad* of this kind, observation may need to focus on one child then on the other, for sustained periods.

Observing children interacting in a group context is one of the most difficult of all assessment activities. Tape recording is often no solution either, since voices are not easy to recognise in a situation of such complex interactions. One solution would be video, an activity that would necessarily have to be infrequent because of the costs and time involved. More practically, one of the few solutions would be to focus for a time on each of the members of the group, noting their contributions, gestures, etc., and at the end compiling not only these individual records but also a view of the sequence of interactions for the whole group.

Assessing whether a child is listening – either to another child, adult, or to a story or TV programme – is not easy. As we saw in earlier chapters, there are few ways that can unequivocally judge 'listening' behaviours. Only by requiring children to *demonstrate* that they have listened, and by implication understood what has been said, can an indirect assessment be made. They have to act upon an instruction, talk about a TV programme, draw a picture, or make something to demonstrate that they have indeed listened.

These may appear to make overwhelming demands on the teacher in a busy classroom. They require the development of new skills, new elements in a professional repertoire. As with any skill learning, at first the process will be slow, partial and time-consuming. The advice given in the booklet produced by SEAC (*A Guide to Teacher Assessment: Pack A*) is helpful. What we do know is that, with time, as it becomes second nature to observe in particular ways under particular circumstances, the process becomes enormously speeded up. As with any skill, it becomes automatised.

Reading (En2)

Even a cursory glance at the Programme of Study or statements of attainment in Reading at Key Stage 1 reveals the very broad conception of the nature and purposes of reading embodied there. The aim is:

> *'The development of the ability to read, understand and respond to all types of writing, as well as the development of information-retrieval strategies for the purposes of study.'* (DES, 1989)

The Programme of Study at Key Stage 1 specifies experience with a wide range of books and other reading materials, pupils' written work as reading material, drama, book-making, discussion of reading experiences and familiarity with information books and dictionaries. So far as judging performance is concerned, the statements of attainment at Levels 1 to 3 include the following dimensions:

- Developing reading skills:
  - letter and word recognition
  - the use of picture, phonic and context cues in reading
  - developing fluency, accuracy and expression in reading aloud
  - developing independence in reading
  - the ability to read silently
- Understanding of what has been read and that print serves important functions in the environment.
- Familiarity with and response to narrative forms, with developing insight into narrative structure.
- Familiarity with and response to poetry.
- Familiarity with other kinds of text and a range of reading materials.
- Appreciation of the pleasure and value of reading.
- Expression of opinion about what has been read.

This is a tall order, both for teaching and for assessment, even if the latter is undertaken in an ongoing way in the classroom. Again, a little background information may set the scene for the discussion of assessment issues and strategies in reading.

Some background on the reading process and children learning to read

At no point in the section on speaking and listening was the word *sentence* used. This was deliberate. Listening to conversations around us or on the radio rapidly makes it clear that we certainly speak in 'units' or 'utterances', but very few of these could be termed sentences. In fact, much of our speech is laden with what could be termed 'grammatical' errors: we half-finish our 'sentences'; plurals or singulars don't agree; tenses of verbs frequently do not 'match'. Spoken language is essentially intended for here-and-now communication, where much is shared in the situation and can be taken for granted. It therefore has special characteristics such as shorter 'units' of language within it, more general kinds of vocabulary and the heavy use of referring terms such as 'this/ that', 'here/there'.

Written language is not speech written down. As soon as we commit language to paper, we change it: the 'units' of language we write become longer and more complex and we tend to use more unusual vocabulary. The reasons for this are obvious. When we speak, we have to create messages there and then, on our feet, as it were. Writing allows for more thought and deliberation to go into construction of messages. The communication has to stand alone, with no intonation or gestures to moderate meaning. It is for this reason that only for written language does the word 'sentence' have any real meaning. Much of the grammatical and linguistic analysis that has developed for language is based on written language, on permanent forms of text.

Interpreting written text therefore requires more and often different kinds of mental processing than spoken messages. This is probably why *literacy* appears to have higher status than merely being able to cope with spoken text. In introducing children to literacy, these are important considerations to bear in mind. Further reading on this topic can be found in Halliday (1989) and O'Rourke (1990).

There exists a very large body of research on the reading process, mostly from cognitive psychology. This can be summarised briefly as a starting point. It is important to understand more of the adult skill before we can effectively help children to attain these competencies and to monitor their progress.

Effective and skilled reading is about *creating a meaning* in the mind of the reader, *guided* by the information presented in written form by the text. This contrasts sharply with the idea that reading is simply a matter of decoding a printed symbol to a sound. Reading a piece of text without understanding its meaning, at some level, is not reading. In line with the ideas given in Chapter 2, reading is an *active* and *constructive* mental process, which involves high levels of thinking and problem-solving. It is also clear that skilled readers use *many sources of information* when engaging with text, and bring different kinds of previous *knowledge* and *experience* to the activity.

The kinds of meanings created and their richness will be influenced by many factors. Some of these will be to do with the *reader* themselves.

The most important of these will be the reader's purpose and motivation in reading, their existing knowledge, and their ability to go beyond literal meanings and to question the text. On the other hand, some of the outcomes will be influenced by qualities in the text itself: its format and structure; the kind of language used; the effective sequencing of ideas; the inclusion and placing of illustrations or diagrams. There will be complex interactions between all these factors that will influence the outcomes of the reading for any child or adult.

Because of this, skilled reading involves many processes, all of which must go on at once. Words and groups of words have to be recognised, their meanings have to be retrieved from memory and on this basis the *propositions* or 'meaning units' have to be created in an ongoing way. There have to be back-up procedures for when the system fails (knowing when to go back and re-read, or check). At some stage, the *integrated meaning* of a sentence or paragraph has to be generated. The whole of this process is shown in Figure 4.1, in a very summarised way.

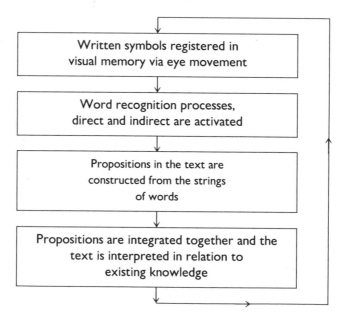

Figure 4.1   Processes that go on during skilled reading

When the skilled reader reads, most of these processes happen so quickly they are not easy to disentangle. What is clear, however, is that being a skilled and effective reader, who can create valid meanings as efficiently as possible, means being able *flexibly* to deploy a wide range of strategies appropriate to the materials being read.

If this is the developed competence, how do children learn how to read, and what is the role of teaching in this? It is commonly suggested that children just learn to *talk* but have to be taught to *read*. Both of these propositions are open to question. As we have seen, parents and adults play an active part in children's developing spoken language and it is also the case that some children learn to read without apparently any overt teaching, often before they arrive at school. This should give us pause for thought.

However, it is no doubt the case that the majority of children arrive at school with little experience of literacy and it is the role of the teacher to aid learning. As recent debate indicates, there is no accepted view about how this should be done: historically, many approaches have been suggested, none of which has come to hold sway. *Mixed approaches* seem to be the order of the day, as recent findings from many studies have shown (HMI Report, 1990). The schools involved in the ENCA project (a national sample) reflected previous findings, in that 75% of the teachers indicated that they used *mixed methods* in the teaching of reading, 13% used terms such as a *'developmental'* or *'apprenticeship'* approach, and a total of 7% wrote comments indicating that they used a primarily *phonic* approach. This should be set alongside the additional information that *all* said they carried out phonic work with the children as part of the approach they were using. A total of 67% said they used reading schemes in their class, and the schemes they mostly indicated embodied a 'mixed' approach to teaching. What is also interesting is that almost all the schools/classes in the sample said they encouraged children to take books home to read with their parents. Of these, 79% said it was a weekly occurrence and 23% said it happened on a daily basis. The parents had been given advice and encouragement to read with their children in 91% of these sample classes.

Assessing reading

Reading is probably the area of the language curriculum, perhaps the curriculum as a whole, where most assessment has gone on in school. During Key Stages 1 and 2, this is likely to have taken the form of:

- diagnostic assessment for those children with potential problems in their reading development;
- published standardised tests, mostly at ages 7 and 11;
- informal methods of analysis/assessment (e.g. miscue analysis).

The standardised reading tests most likely to be used, according to a recent NFER survey (1992), are Young's *Group Reading Test*, *Edinburgh Reading Test* (Stage 1), and the *Primary Reading Test*. In the ENCA project, 64% of the sample schools said they used formal reading tests, with Schonell being most frequently mentioned alongside Young's *Group Reading Test*, the *Neale Analysis of Reading Ability* and the *Salford Sentence Reading Test*.

Although much assessment of reading seems to occur, these measures used are *norm-referenced* tests, often covering only limited aspects of the range of reading competence. For instance, Young's test is basically a word recognition and sentence completion test, while Schonell focuses only on individual word recognition.

They are not necessarily appropriate in the context of the curriculum-based, criterion-referenced assessments required in the National Curriculum. The range of requirements for reading in this context are so wide that they could not be covered by any existing measure, or even battery of existing measures.

The challenge for the teacher in making assessment judgements against the statements of attainment at Levels 1 to 3 is to decide on the meaning of such terms as *'read accurately'*, *'fluently'* or *'independently'*. Words such as *'inference'* and *'deduction'* (Level 3, 3d) also need careful consideration. Having established and agreed some interpretations, issues of mastery level must be addressed (see Chapter 3) and suitable activities found that enable children to, for instance, show that they can use 'picture and context cues', 'phonic cues' or have an appropriate 'sight vocabulary'. Given the wide range of activities available in most infant classrooms, imaginative task planning does not seem to be a problem for teachers. What is less easy is the devising of activities which allow for the more precise kinds of focus dictated by the curriculum.

The problem for the developers of the Standard Assessment Tasks for reading was even more difficult. Tasks had to be devised that not only covered the majority of the skills and knowledge listed in the statements of attainment, but could be carried out in a reasonably economic time-frame. The outcome, as far as the 1991 materials were concerned, was to focus only on the reading of narrative and to assess most of the *reading process* aspects through one or two reading-aloud tasks. The choice was made, for reasons of familiarity to the child (and hence the *validity* of the task), to select these passages from 'real' books, potentially available in many infant classrooms already. However, the problem with such an approach lies in the comparability of the passages, since a wide range of choice was available. Unless the passages can be shown to be comparable in their demands, the dependability of the outcomes is brought into question. This is also an issue for teachers to consider when making their own assessments.

The development agency (NFER/BGC Consortium) went to considerable lengths to ensure comparability. Five possible aspects of the texts were examined: the *readability score* of the passage (using the Spache formula); the number of *words per line*; the supporting *illustrations*; the degree of *repetition*; and the *location point* of the passage within the total story/book. Using calculations based on these criteria, the selection of books was made. It is open to question whether choosing books already available in the classroom increased or decreased the dependability of the scoring. The issue of familiarity to the children has to be set against the possibility of practice and coaching. All assessment has to deal with this very basic question, and reach a compromise.

As the children read aloud, a version of *miscue analysis* was carried out by the teacher. A little more information about this technique will inform the subsequent points to be made. The theory behind miscue analysis stresses that all readers, including skilled readers, miscue when they read aloud, particularly if the text is a little difficult. They change words, miss words out, insert words, hesitate and pause. Miscues are *not errors*: they are better seen as 'windows' into the kinds of processes and strategies being used by the reader. Because of this, analysis of the number and kinds of miscues made provides very important information about whether the reader is developing and using positive and productive *reading strategies*. It is a technique widely advocated in education circles, but not yet widely used by teachers.

It is a technique that certainly can indicate whether or not a child is using some of the reading strategies outlined in this Attainment Target, but as important, it is a technique that the teacher can take further in order to make fuller, formative assessments in reading. Details are given in Arnold (1982, 1992) of ways to analyse the words the child *substitutes* in the text as they read aloud, for example:

1. ' Where are you going ? ' ~~said~~ *says* Cat

2. ' I ~~want~~ *will* to ~~go~~ *you* for a ~~run~~ *rabbit* ' ~~said~~ *says* Dog

The aim of looking at these substitutions is to see whether the words they substitute are *phonically, semantically* (word meaning) or *syntactically* (understanding of the way sentences flow and are constructed) appropriate. In example 1, the substitution is similar and appropriate on all three aspects, so it is a *positive* example, showing that the child can use all three kinds of cue, even though a word has been misread. The four substitutions in the second example show other characteristics. The substituted *'will'* and *'rabbit'* bear some phonic resemblance to the text, but neither makes sense in the context of the sentence (semantic dimension) or is grammatically appropriate (syntactic dimension). As such they represent somewhat negative reading strategies. The substitution of *'you'* for *'go'*, however, does not even bear a phonic resemblance to the text word, so it is negative on all counts. The substitution '*says*' is positive as before. This information provides a starting point for more focused work on the relevant aspects of reading, in order to develop more positive strategies and therefore more effective reading.

Once again, however, the issue of familiarity for the child crops up. The ENCA study asked teachers whether they carried out any such monitoring as children read to them in normal classroom circumstances. Having the teacher make notes as they read aloud may be a very unfamiliar and disconcerting activity for some children. The responses indicated that only 29% of this sample of teachers made any kinds of notes as the child read and only 10% ever used full miscue analysis techniques. It was also significant that a large proportion of these assessment activities were carried out by someone other than the class teacher. Again, with young children, this may compromise the quality of the outcomes.

At Level 3, the words '*inference*' and '*deduction*' appear in the statements of attainment, ideas which perhaps need further explanation. Earlier, it was pointed out that reading is all about creating meaning in the mind of the reader, guided by the words on the page. Almost by definition, this requires the reader to go beyond what is actually written, by bringing a wider knowledge and experience to bear, in the interpretation process. An example may help to illustrate this, as in the following passage:

> '*Mary went to a restaurant. The waiter gave her a menu and she ordered a salad. She was served quickly. She left a large tip.*'

This is an experience (restaurants) common to many people. If the question was posed 'Who paid the bill?', you would be able to provide the answer, even though it is not stated in the passage itself. The author has required and expected the reader to make the *bridging inferences* needed, fully to interpret the meaning. Texts would be rather boring if every detail always had to be stated explicitly.

Young children's ability to make such inferences and deductions about what they read is likely to be less than that of more experienced and skilled readers. But they can make them, and in the interests of developing a more reflexive attitude to what they read, these insights should be encouraged and monitored. Careful questioning is needed, as well as a clear understanding of the nature of the inferences required in the story or other piece of text, on the part of the teacher. The SAT assessments in 1991 tackled this through the provision of questions for each of the selected passages. These may well provide a useful guide for the teacher in their own assessments, but it should also be pointed out that the work carried out by the ENCA study found that many children were capable of even more subtle kinds of inference-making. It is important not to underestimate their capabilities.

At Level 3 also, mention is made of children's developing understanding of story structure. This again is a topic where much research has been carried out, in a psychological frame. The basic idea is that through experience of hearing a variety of stories, we come to develop a sense of the *underlying structure* of narrative, even though the *surface form* of any story may have its own particular characteristics. The central aspects seem to include the setting, theme, plot and resolution of the story, with added dimensions of characters, locations, goals and outcomes. It is possible to *map* stories, almost in the form of tree diagrams as in the following example of the classic princess being rescued by the handsome prince who wishes to marry her (Figure 4.2). They naturally live happily ever after!

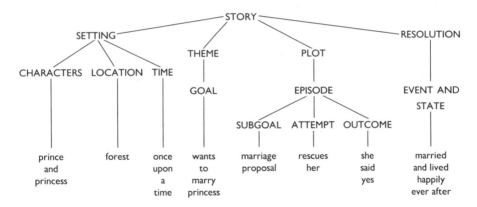

Figure 4.2   *The structure of a simple story (based on Greene, 1986)*

It may be useful for children to be helped to map out stories in this simplified way as part of encouraging further reflection and insight. Such mapping also helps the teacher to recognise the salient points in any text, which in turn may be an important focusing device in the assessment process. Similar processes can be carried out with other kinds of text, for example information text. The information and line of argument can be plotted. Further reading on these processes (including inferences) can be found in Greene (1986) and in Lunzer and Gardner (1984). Neither of these has a specific focus on young children, but both provide important background theory and principles which may inform the practice of teachers of young children. It is especially important because of the emphasis on narrative forms across most of the English Attainment Targets.

Other assessment issues in this Attainment Target (Reading)

In the course of evaluating the 1991 Key Stage 1 assessments, other issues emerged in relation to particular aspects of the curriculum specification or statements of attainment at Levels 1 to 3 which it may be helpful to summarise.

Alphabetic knowledge   At Level 2, one the statements refers to *'knowledge of the alphabet'* using word books and simple dictionaries. In trying to assess this, the first issue that had to be settled was what is to constitute such 'knowledge': should success be defined in terms of the *product* (finding a word eventually) or the *process* (how the word was found). Many children in the sample could find words, but often by a random process of flicking through a wordbook or dictionary. Only about two-thirds of those who succeeded found the words by a systematic search strategy, beginning at roughly the right place initially, then homing in on the word. Important questions of what 'knowledge' is in this context, need to be settled.

Using a range of cues in reading   In a sense, this issue has already been addressed in the earlier discussion of miscue analysis. However, it is important to point out that the cues listed in this statement are distinct from the qualities listed in statement En2/2f, at the same level, which stresses reading with *'fluency, accuracy and understanding'*. Some quite detailed listening and observation is needed, with the children over a period of time, to monitor whether they indeed can use context cues, picture cues and phonic cues in their reading, as well as demonstrating that they are developing an appropriate sight vocabulary. This could be made up of:
– high frequency words (*and, the*)
– general social vocabulary (*street, bus-stop*)
– classroom terms (*library, pencils*)
– personal vocabulary (*names*)
– curriculum-specific vocabulary (*word, letter*).
    These aspects can be assessed, even though children may not yet have the ability to read an appropriate passage out loud, as in En2/2f.

Reading with independence, fluency and accuracy   At Level 2, this is perceived to be a very important statement, one that was a major focus in the SAT assessments. It is important to note that the phrase *'read a range of material'* is also added to this requirement. In the ENCA assessments, children read not only from a story, but also from an information text and from poetry. Approximately 300 children attempted to read all three kinds of text, and children who could read narrative text with fluency and accuracy could also cope with information text and poetry in a similar way. However, over the whole of this sample, only 58% of the children could read all three kinds of text to an appropriate standard. The children needed more help in reading poetry aloud.

The issues to be addressed by teachers for their own assessment purposes are somewhat different to the issues of more formalised assessment through the SATs. Given the wider range of possibilities open to the teacher, in the course of normal classroom activities, then clearly all aspects of the curriculum can be monitored, in both formative and summative ways. The problems in more formalised SAT assessment revolve around time and content constraints. In the 1991 assessments, this was the only Attainment Target where, in the SAT, *all* statements had to be achieved at a level in order to be awarded that level. In this sense it may have been more in line with teachers' own assessments. However, bearing in mind the points made in Chapter 3, the fact that there are so many statements at each of these Levels, makes this a very difficult AT. It may also lead to a situation where, as presently conceived, children apparently remain at one level for a prolonged period of time.

Writing (PC3)

The separation of the three aspects of writing as distinct Attainment Targets within this Profile Component (writing, spelling and handwriting) is important. It enables different focus points to be addressed, all of which should allow for more detailed formative assessment and clear indications for the kinds of experiences the child needs in order to progress. They are separate, but integrated together in the act of writing.

In this section, each Attainment Target will be discussed separately in the first instance.

Writing (En3)

Reading and writing, taken together, are the two sides of the literacy coin which clearly feed into each other, as do all language skills and experiences. As we saw earlier, spoken and written language have rather different characteristics, with which children have to come to terms, particularly in the context of their writing development. '*Literate language*', the kind embodied in written text, has structure of a particular kind and also permanence. It requires writers to step back a little, reflect on the messages they wish to convey, and reflect upon the nature of writing itself. Because of this, many researchers (e.g. Donaldson, 1978) have suggested that it encourages a different, more complex kind of thinking, moving away from the here-and-now quality of face-to-face communication, towards more abstract and reflective thinking.

As with many of the activities we have been considering, writing is an activity which involves high-level thinking and problem-solving. It is important not to underestimate the scale of the task facing young children. One influential outline of the nature of the thinking process has been provided by Hayes and Flower (1980).

In essence, their suggestion is that writing involves three processes: *planning, translating* and *reviewing*.

- **Planning** – this involves generating ideas for what is to be written, setting goals for the writing (who is the audience, for example) and organising the ideas in some rudimentary ways. It involves thinking, either mentally or on paper.
- **Translating** – this is the process of turning these ideas and plans into a product on paper, choosing words and sentences and generally formulating the ideas in an appropriate language.
- **Reviewing** – once the writing has been produced, this is the stepping-back phase, when it is reviewed, edited and changed if necessary.

In order to carry out these processes, memory must be searched and appropriate ideas and content retrieved, and complex decisions must be made about the kinds of language and style that must be employed to make the writing appropriate for the particular audience in mind. Some quite sophisticated skills are needed in order to make final judgements about quality and how changes should be made.

Children arrive at school with varied experiences of literacy. They must gradually be introduced to the purposes and nature of written language in both its receptive mode (reading) and its productive mode (writing). Hall (1989) provides a useful anthology of ways of doing this. One of the major hurdles is the recognition of the special characteristics of written language, a threshold often marked in young children as they begin to 'talk like a book'. But much confusion reigns, a fact that is evident from children's writing when it is clear that they are writing down speech, rather than using more 'book' forms of language.

When children have progressed beyond these early stages and can produce more sustained and coherent messages in writing, other characteristics become clear. Much writing at this stage is dominated by straightforward recounting of ideas or sequences of ideas. This has been referred to as *'knowledge-telling'* by Bereiter and Scardamalia (1985): it is as though children call up from memory all they know about a particular topic, and just 'tell' it. They contrast this with writing that is *'knowledge-transforming'*, where the process of devising and producing effective writing actually develops thinking and understanding in itself.

The National Curriculum specification for writing mentions *chronological* and *non-chronological* writing, a way of classifying writing according to whether or not a time-sequence is involved. In the main, young children seem to be most exposed to and to produce *chronological* writing, usually in the form of stories and accounts of activities, in a sequenced way. Non-chronological writing includes such things as descriptions or listings, which are not time-ordered. Along with this kind of distinction, it is appropriate that children also have experience of creating writing for a range of different *purposes* and *audiences*.

The 'review' stage and the Level 3 requirement to *'begin to revise and redraft'* frequently seems to prove difficult for younger children. Once writing has been committed to paper, children seem to experience major problems in considering, evaluating and changing it. Again, the work of Bereiter and Scardamalia (1982, 1985) is interesting in this context, since they report the results of trying to encourage children to review their writing, using specific techniques. The kinds of *facilitation* they used included providing children with certain kinds of questions, written on pieces of card, which they had to use as they composed their writing. Examples might be *'Will the person understand?'*, or *'Is this a good sentence?'*. These are ideas which could clearly be adapted to the needs of young writers in order to help them in their evaluation and redrafting. Even so, it has to be admitted that, even after sensitive discussion with the teacher about a piece of writing, it is not easy to encourage redrafting and reviewing beyond simple changes in vocabulary or phrases.

En3 clearly focuses on the process of writing, on the content of what is written, how it is composed and the amount of structure and appropriateness it exhibits. We will now turn to consider issues of assessing these developing capacities.

Assessing writing

The first, fairly obvious point to be made is that whereas the Programme of Study in this Attainment Target focuses on activities and the *process* of writing, the statements of attainment focus very much on evaluating the written *product*. Since they are criteria for judging performance, this may seem inevitable.

The merit of separating out the three dimensions of writing within this Profile Component becomes clear in the context of assessment. The detailed encouragement to consider the products in a differentiated way means that elements in the judgement are not, or should not be, blurred. In this AT, the emphasis is on what is written, the kinds of language used and the structuring of the work.

It is also important to make another fairly obvious point. For assessment purposes, especially summative teacher assessments, the *quality* of work produced is significant: such an approach to assessment requires that *best performance* be assessed, which in this case means ensuring high levels of motivation and involvement in the task, on the part of the child. Since much writing that is required in classrooms is of a very routine, even desultory kind, some imagination needs to be exercised in order to engage and sustain the interest of the children. Given the focus of En3, it is also important that children are absolutely clear about the nature of the writing that is being asked for, its purpose and its audience. It would be unfair to judge writing against criteria which were not necessarily required of, nor made clear to, the child. This may involve talking through, for instance, the qualities that make a good story, or the importance of using interesting words and thinking hard about what would be the best way of telling the sequence of events. The work on the structure of stories (story grammars) referred to earlier in the context of reading (En2) also has applicability here.

Most of the content of the statements at Levels 1 to 3 is fairly clear, especially in relation to the kinds of information just presented here. However, some aspects merit attention:

'Producing sentences with capital letters and fullstops.'
Defining a *'sentence'* in the wording of young children is not a straight-forward matter. As we have seen, it is very much a product of experience with written text and, as a concept, it takes some time to develop. Much early writing, especially narrative writing, is dominated by the 'contin-uous stream' strategy, clause upon clause, joined together by 'and' or 'then', and often extending for pages. It is not uncommon to find two pages of writing that formally might be designated a single sentence.

A second problem concerns the use of capital letters. At this stage, letter formation may be so varied as to render it difficult to decide whether a letter at the beginning of a sentence is upper or lower case.

Neither of these matters is trivial. Deciding where the sentence boundaries are and how they are demarcated is central to the judgement that has to be made. It is also important in going on to judge what kinds of *sentence connectives* have been used.

Common sense seems to be the answer. A sentence is essentially a unit of thought and as such relatively easy to note. Judgements about upper and lower case letters must also rest upon comparison with other renderings of a particular letter in the writing. All of these are matters for discussion, moderation and agreement, if consistent standards are to be applied nationally.

In the 1991 SAT assessments, the mastery level required using '*at least two capital letters and at least two full stops*' for Level 2 and '*more than half, and at least five sentences correctly punctuated*' for Level 3 attainment. However, an important message emerged from the ENCA analysis of children's writing. Only 38% of the sample children met the Level 2 criterion of two full stops and two capital letters, and only 18% the Level 3 criterion. But, by only marginally changing these mastery requirements, the percentage failing or succeeding could be radically changed. For instance, if the requirement at Level 2 was just one full stop and capital letter, then 54% of the children succeeded: if the Level 3 requirement were changed to three quarters of all sentences produced being properly punctuated, the proportion succeeding dropped to only about 6%. Just one or two changes in mastery criteria can make an enormous difference to outcomes.

Also at Levels 2 and 3, judgements must be made about the **structuring** of stories and other chronological accounts. As we have seen, this requires careful thought on the part of the teacher to decide what the elements and structure of any particular story are, and to judge accordingly. The major guidance in 1991 again came from the SAT performance criteria, which at Level 2 required '*more than one character, at least one event and an opening*' and at Level 3, in addition to these, '*some description of setting, or feeling or motives of characters, and a defined ending*'. In terms of the information presented earlier, these may or may not be appropriate: again they are matters for discussion and moderation. However, applying them to the writing samples collected on the ENCA project, 71% of children succeeded at the mastery criterion of Level 2, and approximately 15% at Level 3. Discussion of feelings and motives seemed especially difficult for them. It is a moot point, exactly what is meant by '*complexity*' in these circumstances.

On the whole, children in infant classes have less experience of producing **non-chronological** writing: much writing is of stories and other accounts. As such the specifications of the National Curriculum are an encouragement to give children a wider range of writing experiences. The SAT assessment did not include non-chronological writing, but the ENCA evaluation did. When assessment of non-chronological writing (a poster and a listing) was included in overall scoring, the effect was to *lower* the overall scores.

At Level 3, the issue of **redrafting** written work is introduced. The background information on this showed that, on the basis of other studies, it seems that children find this difficult to do, at least beyond simple editing for punctuation and changing the odd word. This trend was confirmed in the ENCA data when children were encouraged to redraft their stories. The criterion employed in the 1991 SAT was that the work should show *'at least one example of improved clarity, order, style or consistency'* with spelling corrections alone not counting. On this basis, applying similar mastery requirements, only 13% of the ENCA sample succeeded. Taking this further, only 4% of the children indulged in any redrafting that could be said to be a fundamental change to the ordering or structuring of the story.

So far as this Attainment Target (writing) is concerned, several key assessment issues emerge. These concern the clarity of meaning of the requirements of the statements, the clear separation of focus of the En3 in relation to those of spelling and handwriting, and the importance of addressing all aspects of the curriculum in providing classroom experiences for children. Particularly in the case of *non-chronological* writing and *redrafting*, perhaps the assessments reveal that more time should be devoted to extending children's experience in these areas.

Spelling (En4)

The aim of this Attainment Target is that, by the end of compulsory schooling, pupils should be able to spell confidently most of the words they are likely to use in their writing (DES, 1989). The aim is not *perfect* spelling, since this is a virtual impossibility for even the best writer. The specifications for the Attainment Target at Levels 1 to 3 cover early distinctions between drawing and writing, spelling common words with increasing accuracy and the beginnings of the recognition of pattern in the way many words are constructed.

English is notorious for its irregularities in spelling. There are many words in English whose written form bears no relationship to the way they are pronounced. Historically, English words were spelled as they sounded, and spelling would vary from region to region and from person to person. The *conventional forms* that are now set down in dictionaries are the result of the fossilisation of various versions created at different times in the past. For example *'yacht'* is a product of Dutch printers' imposing their own spelling in the fifteenth century and *'debt'* is the result of the insistence, in the sixteenth and seventeenth centuries, on continuing to mark the Latin origin of the word. However, now a conventionalised system has been created, it is these – irregularities and all – that children must somehow learn.

Quite a lot of research has been devoted to how children learn how to spell, with the finding that two kinds of processes could be involved. The first and obvious one explains spelling by suggesting that we *assemble* spellings for words as we write, working from sounds within the word and presenting these on the page. This seems plausible, until we recognise that many words we use have the same sounds but are spelled differently. These are *homophones* such as 'their' and 'there', or 'great' and 'grate'. So this cannot be the complete explanation. The alternative is to suggest that, after some experience with written forms of words, we gradually build up complete word-units in memory, which we retrieve as whole units. The spellings are not assembled, they are *addressed* as whole units. Skilled spellers seem to use a combination of these processes, as circumstances dictate. Known words could be *addressed* and unknown ones *assembled*, perhaps using information from similar words, by *analogy*.

However, research with *poor spellers* suggests that some people may have difficulty with one or other of these processes, which gives rise to particular patterns of mistakes. People who have problems working out sounds in words can often spell quite *irregular* words accurately but cannot so easily work out regular sound-symbol relationships. On the other hand, those who have difficulty with the whole patterns of words, misspell irregular words, but can spell regular words quite well.

What is also clear is that very little of our memory for spelling comes from memorising the *hand movements* that make up a word. We write words in many ways (print, upper case, lower case) and we also use different modes altogether (for example typing), yet we still spell correctly.

It has been suggested that children's spelling passes through certain general phases, even though some children may show preference for one or other of the two strategies just outlined. Beginning with the phase of representing words by squiggles and marks of various kinds, they then seem to move towards a phase of focusing on sound-letter rules – in other words, a *phonological* phase. During this period the words they write may be phonologically correct but incorrect in terms of standard spelling. After this, comes a phase when the focus changes to whole words and to the patterns of conventional spelling, an *orthographic* phase. During this phase, quite difficult, irregular words may now be spelled correctly.

The subject of how to teach spelling is not easy, particularly in the context of the information just presented. However, one useful source is still Todd (1982), who does not exactly present her model in the way outlined above, but who does provide some useful background information as well as classroom teaching ideas. The only further point to be made, is that the present emphasis on allowing children some scope to develop their spelling abilities in more natural ways, potentially provides the teacher with important insights into the child's understanding and development. Useful reading here is Read (1986) on children's invented spellings and what they reveal.

The Attainment Target in spelling covers some of this ground. At Level 1, insights into the nature of writing and its distinction from drawing, alongside an increasing ability to represent letters in print, are mentioned. Level 2 focuses on the growing ability to spell common and *monosyllabic* words with some accuracy and upon an increasing recognition of the patterning of words. At Level 3, this understanding of patterning is increasingly demanded, along with the capacity to spell correctly *polysyllabic* words and to be able to *check* accuracy. As in many of the statements, these specifications are very open-ended.

The SAT, however, had to pin down the requirements more precisely for assessment purposes. The development agency chose to indicate Level 2 attainment by specifying that three letters/sounds had to be represented and evidence had to be present of children spontaneously using letters in their 'written' products. It should be pointed out, however, that at Level 1 in the *writing* Attainment Target, children can attain, in principle, by drawing as well as writing.

At Level 2, the SAT developers chose to set the criteria of children being able to spell at least four common words in a recognisable (though not necessarily correct) way, and to attain five correct spellings of one-syllable words. Evidence was also needed of patterning in words, in the form of examples such as '*ck*' or '*tt*'. At this point, it is useful to mention that no indication is given whether any of these selected examples should be *regular* or *irregular* in terms of their spelling. Yet as we have seen, this is an important distinction. Being able to spell '*cat*' is rather different from being able to spell '*comb*', yet they are both monosyllabic and relatively 'common'. There is also no indication how the patterning within words might vary in level of difficulty. Analyses that indicate children's development in phonic awareness and representation, might provide more detailed help in this context, help that is developmentally based (see Read, 1986).

At Level 3, '*longer*' words were indicated, five examples of which had to be spelled correctly. However, these were not to be '*irregular, technical or adventurous*'. Visual patterns in words were also to be assessed, with again little guidance about what these might be for Level 3 attainment. Once again, these are interesting criteria, not only in terms of their vagueness, but also the theory that informs them. By this level, it would not be inappropriate to consider the child's growing insight into irregular spelling: it is, after all, the phase into which their understanding must move. Yet *length* of word seems to be what is stressed – *polysyllabic* words. It is not beyond the bounds of possibility that a child could spell correctly *'paramedic'* yet not be able to spell *'smudge'* or *'known'*, both of which are monosyllabic but embody certain kinds of irregularity. Once again, it is a question of the kind of theory that informed curriculum development in the first instance. Certainly teachers would find it helpful to possess more knowledge about the characteristics of English spelling and the development of these skills in young children. Only in this way can valid examples be chosen for teaching and assessment purposes.

Another general issue that arises with reference to En4 concerns what phrases such as *'common words'* mean. The term could be used in several ways. It could mean the words most commonly used in written English; it could mean the words most commonly used in text for children; it could mean the words most commonly used by children in their own writing. Drawing up word-lists under each of these headings would probably result in very different outcomes. Once again, clarification seems to be needed about exactly what we should be expecting of children at different points of their development.

The overriding picture that emerges in trying to give guidance on assessment in this Attainment Target, is that the specification itself is of little help in reaching assessment judgements. One solution would be to continue with the present criteria and develop more informative *guidance* alongside it. Another would be to contemplate changing the criteria to reflect a more detailed and appropriate pathway of progress.

Handwriting (En5)

This 'secretarial' aspect of writing is included within the writing Profile Component, as Attainment Target 5. It is termed 'handwriting' from Levels 1 to 4 and (with spelling) 'presentation' at Levels 5 to 7. It is clearly concerned, at least in the early stages, with the development of the *motor skill* of writing, shaping letters in a controlled way, producing properly aligned letters and words and, at Levels 3 and 4, producing 'joined-up' writing.

The Bullock Report (1975) devoted little attention to handwriting, except to suggest that legible and fast-flowing handwriting was unlikely to develop without some kind of instruction. Some focus on handwriting was also provided in two other documents, *English from 5 to 16* (DES, 1984) and *English from 5 to 16: the response to Curriculum Matters 1* (DES, 1986).

The HMI survey of 1978 suggested that handwriting was practised in at least 80% of the schools surveyed, although other, more recent studies have indicated that the teaching is seldom consistent. In fact, in 1982, Rubin and Henderson reported that 12% of nine- to ten-year-olds had some difficulties with handwriting. This should be taken alongside the APU finding that 3% of children at ages 11 and 15 had great difficulty with writing.

The course of children's development of *graphic* skills has been extensively charted, from the first stages of tool holding, through scribble of various kinds, to the development of formal writing skills in a particular language. For instance, Kellogg (1969) analysed the drawings and scribbles of young children (over one million examples) and has shown how these change and progress. However, scribbling has its own character, and does not require the considerable *hand-eye control* needed for writing letters and words.

As with many of the language capacities considered in this chapter, once analysed, it becomes clear that highly complex activities are involved. These include:

- the integration of *visual, auditory* and *tactile skills*;
- the development of *fine* motor skills in order to execute the various letter shapes, with often only small differences and distinguishing features;
- the development of *directionality* – left-right movement in the case of English;
- the development of *sequencing* skills;
- the development of *memory*, remembering the appearance of letters and digits and the movements that make them;
- the development of *visual matching* skills in order that a product can be judged by the pupil against a 'model' of some kind, and standards required by the teacher.

Once again, this is not to suggest that this is how the skill should be taught: it merely indicates the complexity of the overall activity and the kinds of skills that must be integrated in order to carry it out.

To help the teacher, checklists are available which set out schemes for evaluating children's writing and for the kinds of planning experiences that should therefore follow. Best-known among these are the Alston Checklist (Alston and Taylor, 1981) and the diagnostic scheme developed by Stott, Moyes and Henderson (1985). In the main, these scales focus upon similar dimensions of the *writing product* and *writing process*:

– writing posture and pencil grip;
– letter formation;
– letter size, slant and spacing;

– word spacing.

However, in a recent study, Mojet (1991) provides a most detailed analysis based on a large sample of children aged 6 to 12 years. In addition to this conventional focus on the *quality* of the product (spacing, shaping, uniformity), he emphasises *speed* of writing also, a factor seldom considered or emphasised by teachers. His overall findings show that:

– speed of writing increases with age/grade;
– size of writing decreases with age/grade;
– the regularity of up/down strokes improves with age/grade;
– the regularity of shaping increases with age/grade;
– the pencil pressure decreases with age/grade.

In other words, both the *product* and the *process* change with age and experience.

Assessing handwriting

The specifications in the Attainment Target emphasise increasing control over the *'size, shape and orientation of letters and lines of writing'*, moving on to legible and clearly defined writing, in one style. By Level 3, reference is made to producing *'clear and legible joined-up writing'*.

Again, these very general performance indicators had to be firmed up in the more formalised SAT assessments. For letters, this was achieved by specifying the dimensions to be considered: formation; letter heights; clear ascenders and descenders; letter spacing and consistent size. At Level 3, the writing had to be *'joined up'*, and show these qualities too.

In many ways, the same issues arise with reference to En5 as with spelling. The specifications of the curriculum and of the evidence of performance are minimal, which in many ways is useful for the teacher in the latitude it gives, but which in other ways is less helpful. Given that so much information exists about how children's handwriting abilities develop, it seems unfortunate not to be able to recognise this in making formal assessment judgements. Informally, of course, such information *can* be utilised, provided that it is agreed and in line with the specifications.

Conclusions

In broad terms, the content of the curriculum in English is full, innovative and in line with the most informed views of the nature of the subject and the development of the necessary competences in children.

Only time and experience of implementing this curriculum, and assessing it, will establish areas where changes to the specifications are required. It will be revealing to see the nature and scale of any revisions that do occur, such as those that seem to be at present planned.

The three designated Profile Components seem a viable division into the broad areas within the subject, and the subsequent division of the writing Component into three Attainment Targets is potentially a useful focusing device. However, having said this, specific issues for teaching and assessment arise within each Profile Component/Attainment Target.

Speaking and listening is an area of the language curriculum often highlighted in schools and classrooms, but seldom addressed in the detailed ways now required. The guidance and specifications given for this area are helpful in outlining not only the curriculum but also the performances required. They encourage teachers to *listen* to and *observe* children's communicative behaviour with great care, and perhaps also to monitor their own language use and communicative style in the classroom. Taken to their logical conclusion, they have considerable implications for overall classroom organisation and teaching methodology.

The curriculum for **reading** is very wide-ranging indeed and is likely, when implemented properly, to extend children's experience in the classroom. It is a field where teachers are more likely to be familiar with the assessment dimension of teaching, though not necessarily in this curriculum-based way. The approach to assessment adopted in the 1991 SAT assessment was novel to many teachers, but gave a useful measure in the context of both the curriculum and teaching methods. The major issue in the Attainment Target is the enormous amount specified at many of the levels. It is important to reach agreed judgements about whether *all* criteria must be met or only the majority of them, for achievement to be credited.

In the Key Stage 1 Standard Assessments of 1992, two innovations were introduced into the reading assessment which warrant some comment. The children read aloud as before from selected passages, with the teacher noting their performance. Certain key words had been chosen from each passage, and a measure of reading accuracy was gained through counting up the number of these key words that each child had read without error. The passages and words in each book were clearly different, and therefore, the ways of converting these scores into a standard 5-point scale (grades A to E) had to encompass this. Depending on the difficulty of each passage, it was sometimes the case that misreading only one word could make the difference between grades. In many ways, such apparent arbitrariness is inevitable in focused assessment of this kind, but when the passages themselves were so short, questions must be raised about the reliability of such scores. Lengthening the passages would be one option, but this would have time and resource implications, a difficult balance to achieve in this context.

The other innovation of 1992, was the optional use of a reading comprehension test with children attaining at Level 2. This took the form of a booklet, with coloured illustrations, roughly 15 pages long. The presentation of this was lively and attractive and it covered many of the dimensions of reading specified in En2: using picture cues; use of context; information interpretation and comprehension of key ideas. It was untimed but the guidance suggested that it should take 30 to 40 minutes. The general response of teachers seemed to be that it was an activity unfamiliar to the children (a comment not entirely borne out by the evidence on the extent of the use of reading tests by local education authorities) and that it required concentration by the children for a very long period of time. The last point is a significant point of criticism, given the age of the children. If the move in the future is towards this more formalised kind of assessment at Key Stages 1 and 2, then such aspects need further consideration.

In **writing**, the separation into three Attainment Targets provides a useful set of focus points, both for teaching and assessment. The focus on the *composing* aspects in En3 draws attention both to grammatical skills of presentation and to the content and the way it is structured. In teaching and assessment terms, it is important to recognise the *breadth* of the curriculum, with its wide range of purposes and types of writing.

The **spelling** and **handwriting** Attainment Targets raise similar kinds of issues for both teaching and assessment. In both of them, there is only a small amount of advice and specification given for the curriculum, yet in both areas there exists an enormous amount of theoretical and developmental information, potentially useful, but not embodied there. Given the very general nature of the specification, an appropriate response is to turn to this information for further guidance and fleshing out of the items. Many would argue that this is vital in order properly to monitor children's progress in these important aspects of communicating in written language.

In 1992, an optional spelling test was introduced into the Key Stage 1 assessments, for children attaining at Levels 3 and 4. This was in the form of a continuous piece of prose in a coloured booklet, with gaps for the children to fill in as the appropriate words were told to them. These words varied in difficulty from short, monosyllabic words ('*sun*') to long, polysyllabic and irregular words ('*building*'). It was interesting to note that the words selected did not bear much relationship to those qualities and criteria specified in the curriculum.

Overall, then, the English curriculum provides many useful and innovative suggestions for teaching at Key Stages 1 and 2, with the aim of developing a wide range of language competences. In terms of assessment, however, this very richness poses some problems, particularly in the context of the Standard Tasks, where time is at a premium and where the need is for focused and dependable summative scoring outcomes. It is to be hoped that any revisions to the curriculum in the future are not constrained or even dominated by such considerations.

5

Assessing Mathematics

Two years after its introduction, a major revision of the National Curriculum in mathematics took place. The need for revision arose partly as a result of difficulties encountered by teachers in assessment, particularly at the end of Key Stage 1. Pressure from other sources – the exam boards, for instance – was also implicated.

In mathematics the number of Attainment Targets was reduced from fourteen to five, with the overall curriculum content remaining essentially the same. The reduction in number was achieved by broadening the scope of the new Attainment Targets.

The restructuring of the National Curriculum resulted in a change in the *relationship* between Statements of Attainment and the Programme of Study. The original curriculum content has been maintained in the Programme of Study, in the form of elements, but the number of statements of attainment has been reduced, with a consequent move to greater generality. Where there used to be an almost perfect one-to-one correspondence between Programme of Study and statements of attainment, there are now some elements in the Programme of Study which are not represented in the statements of attainment. This seems to mean that there are parts of the mathematics curriculum which are to be taught at a particular level, but which need not be assessed at that level: assessment of some elements of the Programme of Study is deferred to a later level, while other elements are not assessed at all.

Educationally, this approach has much to commend it. Teachers will be encouraged to introduce children to new terminology, techniques and ideas at an early stage. Thus children will have time to develop their understanding and practise their skills more thoroughly, through a variety of experiences, before formal assessment is required. In assessment terms, however, this approach leads to an additional complication.

In order that appropriate assessments tasks can be devised and informal observations made about a child's attainment, the rather general nature of many of the new statements of attainment may need to be refined by teachers into more precise objectives. The National Curriculum Council, in its *Non-Statutory Guidance* (1991), suggests '*teachers will need to refer to the appropriate PoS (Programme of Study), the statements at adjacent levels and the examples provided*'. So the elements in the Programme of Study become important for assessment purposes. The *Non-Statutory Guidance* also outlines the following procedure for teachers who find difficulty working out how to assess their pupils on a statement of attainment:

> *First look to any appropriate Programme of Study for*
> *amplification.*
> *For more guidance read the examples which illustrate the*
> *Statement of Attainment.*
> *Study SEAC's anthologies of assessed pupils' work.*

The first step in this procedure may cause some difficulty for teachers, since it is not always obvious which elements in the Programme of Study are appropriate and which are not. Where there is some doubt whether a Programme of Study element is appropriate to a statement of attainment, it is worth looking at higher levels in the same Attainment Target to check if the material in the Programme of Study is assessed explicitly elsewhere. If this is the case, it is probably safe to conclude that the Programme of Study is not appropriate for assessment at the lower level. Some statements of attainment may relate to elements in the Programme of Study from *earlier* levels in the curriculum, in which case the Programme of Study for one or two levels below the level of the statement of attainment will need to be considered.

The yearly Standard Assessment materials are likely to become an increasingly important resource through which teachers, schools and LEAs gradually reach these common interpretations. Although materials for the first two years of implementation of the assessment system (Key Stage 1) were based upon the old Attainment Targets and statements of attainment, they seem to have made a significant contribution to teachers' understanding of the assessment process, and they may still be helpful in arriving at agreed interpretations of statements of attainment within the revised Attainment Targets.

In general, statements of attainment demand a particular *action* or *behaviour* (for example '*describe*'), which in turn is associated with particular mathematical content. Mathematical content can take two forms. The first is a mathematical *operation* (for example '*addition*'); the second is a description of the *content* on which the 'operation' has to be performed (for example, '*numbers no greater than 10*'). In the discussion of particular Attainment Targets that follows, the second of these will be referred to as the *content domain*. Some statements of attainment, however, also include a reference to the *context* in which the action or behaviour takes place (for example, the context 'money' is referred to in Ma2). The possibilities for inconsistency of interpretation in each of the areas – action, content domain and context – are numerous.

The National Curriculum Council, when issuing the revised Attainment Targets in mathematics, included a poster labelled 'Strands in Attainment Targets'. The intention of this large matrix of statements of attainment is clear. As already stated, many of the old statements of attainment were merged into single statements, making the new ones less specific. The NCC sensibly concluded that the curriculum would make greater sense and have more coherence if each Attainment Target was presented in the form of 'Strands'.

Each of the new Attainment Targets will now be discussed, bearing in mind their relationship to the old versions where appropriate. Each of the Attainment Targets has different characteristics and emphases, and some of the issues in mathematics assessment are more obvious in some than in others. For this reason, and to avoid unnecessary repetition, we have chosen to highlight important issues in those ATs where they are most pertinent. Teachers should bear in mind, however, that the issues raised are of general importance, not restricted to the particular attainment target in which they are discussed but relevant throughout the mathematics curriculum, and often in other subject areas as well.

Using and Applying Mathematics (Ma1)

Ma1 is unique among the five targets in the mathematics National Curriculum. It is the only one which does not contain any reference to what is normally considered to be mathematical content:

> *'Pupils should choose and make use of knowledge, skills and understanding outlined in the programmes of study in practical tasks, in real-life problems and to investigate within mathematics itself. Pupils would be expected to use with confidence the appropriate mathematical content specified in the programmes of study relating to other attainment targets.'* (*Mathematics in the National Curriculum*, DES, 1991)

Assessment of Ma1 aims to determine the ability of pupils to use and apply the content of the mathematics curriculum as described in Ma2 (Number), Ma3 (Algebra), Ma4 (Shape and Space) and Ma5 (Handling Data). These four Attainment Targets cover all possible areas in which mathematics can be utilised, whether in practical tasks, real-life problems or in mathematics itself.

A thorough assessment of Ma1 would require tasks set in all three contexts, and would involve the content (at appropriate levels) of all of the other four Attainment Targets. To do this formally on one occasion, or even over several occasions, in a Standard Task is obviously unrealistic, if not impossible. This is perhaps one reason why the 1992 Key Stage 3 assessment of Ma1 was not included as part of the Standard Tests.

Teachers were, however, provided with material for the assessment of Ma1, to be used to assist them with their own teacher assessment of pupils. Assessment at Key Stage 2 is likely to follow the same pattern.

The *Non-Statutory Guidance* (1991) classifies the 28 statements of attainment in Ma1 into three strands:

(i)   **Applications** – choosing the appropriate mathematics and approach for solving problems.
(ii) **Mathematical communication** – formulating, discussing, interpreting, recording and presenting findings in a variety of ways.
(iii) **Reasoning, logic and proof** – finding answers, giving explanations, reasons and justifications.

The statements of attainment for Levels 1 to 6 in the strands is given in Table 5.1.

The *progression* in each of the strands is clear; this is of considerable assistance to teachers when assessing Ma1. The nature of the statements at successive levels, together with the common terminology used in a strand, suggests that assessment by *outcome* is more appropriate here than assessment by *task*. In practical terms, this may mean that teachers observing children working at mathematical tasks should look for evidence of attainment at the *highest possible level* in a strand, rather than considering one level and deciding whether children have or have not attained at that level.

For example, a teacher may decide to study children's behaviour on a mathematics task so as to assess the 'applications' strand. If it is seen that a child is '*finding ways of overcoming difficulties when solving problems*', then they should be recorded as having attained Level 3 in that strand, for that specific task. Because of the progressive structure of the strands in Ma1, it is unnecessary, in this case, to consider the statements at Levels 1 and 2. It may be advisable to concentrate on observing and assessing only one strand at a time. Attempting to assess two or more strands in the same task demands that teachers hold in their memory too many criteria to make assessment manageable and the outcomes dependable. However, assessing one *strand* at a time in Ma1 has crucial advantages over assessing one *statement* at a time. Tasks which assess only one statement may not access a child's knowledge and skills appropriately, and may fail to provide pupils with the opportunity to show their ability to perform at the highest level of which they are capable.

A difficulty arises, however, with an approach to assessment which looks for children performing at their highest level. There is no guarantee that they will do so. Put rather crudely, the distinction is between

Level	Applications	Mathematical Communication	Reasoning, logic and proof
1	a) Use mathematics as an integral part of practical classroom tasks.	b) Talk about their own work and respond to questions.	c) Make predictions based on experience.
2	a) Select the materials and the mathematics to use for a practical task.	b) Talk about work or ask questions using appropriate mathematical language.	c) Respond appropriately to the question 'What would happen if. . . ?'.
3	a) Find ways of overcoming difficulties when solving problems.	b) Use or interpret appropriate mathematical terms and mathematical aspects of language in a precise way. c) Present results in a clear and organised way.	d) Investigate general statements by trying out some examples.
4	a) Identify and obtain information necessary to solve problems.	b) Interpret situations mathematically using appropriate symbols or diagrams.	c) Give some justification for their solutions to problems. d) Make generalisations.
5	a) Carry through a task by breaking it down into smaller more manageable tasks.	b) Interpret information presented in a variety of mathematical forms.	c) Make a generalisation and test it.
6	a) Pose their own questions or design a task in a given context.	b) Examine critically the mathematical presentation of information.	c) Make a generalisation giving some degree of justification.

Table 5.1   Statements of attainment in Ma1, classified in strands

saying 'Do your best', hoping that the child will do so, and saying 'Can you do this?'. At least in the latter case the child has a specific goal at which to aim.

It becomes increasingly obvious that assessment of Ma1 must take place over a long period of time and on many occasions, and that tasks should be set in a variety of contexts, involving different aspects of the mathematics curriculum. The decision of SEAC not to assess Ma1 during the formal period of national assessment using Standard Tasks or Tests seems eminently sensible. The consequence of this decision, however, is that it places considerable responsibility on teachers to respond in a professional manner to the challenge of assessing this wide-ranging dimension of the curriculum in a dependable way.

Because much of Ma1 is concerned with children's *communication* of their mathematical thinking, tasks which are appropriate for the assessment of Ma1 frequently involve two or more children working *cooperatively*, sharing their knowledge and skills, and talking about their work. This may be conducive to learning mathematics and to solving problems, but it hardly assists the assessment of *individuals*. In such circumstances, teachers may resort to requiring each child to record the findings of their group and also to write about what they did, offering explanations for any resulting conclusions. This may be appropriate for older children who are able to communicate their thoughts in writing, but can be quite inappropriate with younger children or for those who experience difficulty in language or written communication. The evidence which is provided using this approach may be valid and appropriate, but should not be used as the *only* evidence in determining a child's level of attainment.

The skill of assessing children when working in groups is one which teachers will need to develop further – a recurring theme in this book. Observation of the behaviour of one child when operating in a group requires a concentration of effort which many teachers have seldom experienced: observation alone may not be sufficient. If a child is reluctant to contribute to a group's efforts and decision-making, *intervention* from the teacher may be necessary to encourage the child to exhibit behaviour appropriate to the strand being assessed. The composition of groups becomes very important, too. The choice of which children should work together must be made in the knowledge of the pupil or pupils who are to be assessed and the likely ways in which they will contribute to the solving of the problem.

Ma1 permeates all the work children do in mathematics. Thus, there are very many opportunities to assess pupils in the normal course of classroom activities, particularly as 'Using and Applying' should not be assessed in isolation. The observing and collecting of evidence can be greatly assisted if thought and planning precedes any conscious effort to assess pupils. For example, a wide range of materials and apparatus can be made readily available for an activity and pupils' attention drawn to it before they commence. In this way they have the opportunity to make selections and demonstrate possible attainment in the 'applications' strand.

It can be argued that it is manifestly unfair to expect children to show evidence of attainment related to particular statements of attainment if they are unaware of what they are expected to show by their behaviour. If pupils understand the strands and are made conscious of what a teacher is expecting of them, then they are more likely to provide appropriate evidence in line with the assessment requirements.

As the three strands tap different aspects of 'Using and Applying', teachers should not expect pupils to attain at the same level in each of the strands. Indeed, the levels could be markedly different, as was discovered in the ENCA project, even though only Levels 1 to 4 were assessed. Thus at Key Stage 2 and higher, the *range* of levels of attainment over the three strands could increase as pupils move through the ten levels of the mathematics curriculum.

The ENCA project assessed 551 children on the original version of Ma1 and the results are worthy of mention even though the statements have been revised. There is, in any case, a very close match between the new and the old statements. Two tasks were used, so that the effect of context could be investigated.

The first task required children to construct a card container which would hold a small tin of beans. Each child was provided with a tin, a piece of card, a pair of scissors, a ruler, a pencil and adhesive tape. They were told that they could have anything else which they felt they needed to assist them in making the container. The second task presented children with a box of blue and red Multilink cubes with which they had to make as many different sets of 'railway carriages' as they could. Each set of carriages had to use three and only three cubes, using the colours in various ways. When the carriages had been made, pupils had to perform tasks on their set, such as sorting them according to the colour of the 'first' carriage. Both tasks were used to assess the three strands of the Attainment Target, covering Levels 1 to 4.

In general, children performed somewhat better on the 'containers' task than on the 'carriages' task. However, the agreement between the two tasks, in terms of pupils attaining the same level in both tasks, was poor. Given that both tasks had been very carefully developed and trialled, and that the assessors had been specially trained to use them, the lack of comparability was surprising. The most likely explanations were that the context in which the tasks were set influenced children's attainment, or that the mathematics content of the tasks demanded different knowledge and skills.

The ENCA experience only serves to reinforce the points made earlier. *Repeated* assessment, on a variety of tasks, is necessary to provide children with the opportunity to show the highest level of which they are capable in Ma1.

Number (Ma2)

The goal of this Attainment Target is stated as follows:

> '*Pupils should understand and use number, including estimation and approximation, interpreting results and checking for reasonableness.*'   (DES, 1991)

It subsumes more than three of the previous Attainment Target statements:

> '*Pupils should*
> (i)   *understand number and number notation* (old Ma2).
> (ii)   *number operations (addition, subtraction, multiplication and division) and make use of appropriate methods of calculation* (old Ma3).
> (iii) *estimate and approximate in number* (old Ma4).'

The revised Ma2 also includes aspects of the old Ma5 (Number/Algebra) and Ma8 (Measures).

As before, in order for teachers to assess attainment in 'Number', it is essential to begin with a careful and systematic study of the statements of attainment. Without a full understanding of the different mathematical themes within Ma2, it is not possible to develop an approach to assessment that will do justice to any child.

With the present emphasis on children learning the 'basic skills' in mathematics, it is essential that assessment of the statements of attainment in number are as detailed and accurate as is possible, within the constraints of everyday classroom work. 'Number' is perhaps the most hierarchical of the four 'content' Attainment Targets, so it is especially important that assessments should reflect the ability to perform the operations appropriate to a stated level of the curriculum.

Creating the new Attainment Target has not necessarily made its assessment any easier for the teacher. The old Attainment Targets 2, 3 and 4, which form the core of the new Ma2, contained, in total, 61 statements of attainment. These have been combined to produce 31 statements in the ten levels. This number does not include those statements which were previously in the old Ma8, which now have been incorporated into 'Number'. It is worth considering how this contraction has been achieved. Table 5.2 shows the relationship between the old and new statements of attainment at Level 1.

At Level 1, the new statement Ma2/1a has replaced three previous statements. However, the old ones have not been lost since, with slight changes in wording, they appear in the Programme of Study at this Level. This is useful, as reference to the appropriate Programme clarifies, to some degree, what is otherwise a very general statement of attainment.

The second revised statement at this Level, Ma2/1b, replaces only one old statement. The wording of the new and the old are very similar, but the differences are of significance. In the old statement, the phrase 'add or subtract' left teachers in some doubt as to whether a pupil could attain the statement by only attaining one or other of the operations, 'add' *or* 'subtract'. The amended statement of attainment has clarified this uncertainty. It is now clear that to attain the revised statement, a pupil must achieve in *both* operations.

The five statements at Level 4 in 'Number' replace fourteen previous statements, including two from the old Ma8 (Measures). The revised statement, Ma2/4a, is particularly interesting and worth close scrutiny:

Old Statements of Attainment	Old AT	Corresponding New Statement of Attainment	New AT
Count, read, write and order numbers to at least 10; know that the size of a set is given by the last number in the count.	Ma2/1a	Use number in the context of the classroom and school.	Ma2/1a
Understand the conservation of number.	Ma2/1b		
Give a sensible estimate of a small number of objects (up to 10).	Ma4/1a		
Add or subtract, using objects where the numbers involved are no greater than 10.	Ma3/1a	Add and subtract using a small number of objects.	Ma2/1b

Table 5.2   The old and new statements of attainment at Level 1

> *'Solve problems without the aid of a calculator, considering the reasonableness of the answer.'*

This replaces five previous statements of attainment, one of which, because of its complexity, now appears as *four* separate elements in the Programme of Study, so there are now eight elements which relate to the statement. These are mainly directed at pupils learning how to compute with numbers:

- reading, writing and ordering whole numbers;
- learning multiplication facts up to 10 × 10 and using them in multiplication and division problems;
- adding and subtracting mentally two two-digit numbers;
- adding mentally several single-digit numbers;
- adding and subtracting two three-digit numbers, without a calculator;
- multiplying and dividing two-digit numbers by a single-digit number, without a calculator;
- estimating and approximating to check the validity of addition and subtraction calculations;
- solving addition and subtraction problems using numbers with no more than two decimal places, and multiplication and division problems starting with whole numbers.

These eight elements draw attention to the enormity of the demands of this particular statement. They also emphasise the fact that the assessment of computational skills is important, as well as children's ability to apply them in problem-solving situations. However, given statements of attainment of this magnitude, individual assessment of the elements or attributes would be time-consuming and would in any case then require guidance on aggregating the individual items. Few children would attain the statement under these circumstances!

It is perhaps advisable to adopt a less atomistic approach, assessing pupils more subjectively and informally over a long period of time. The day-to-day classroom work of a child can make a valuable contribution to a less formal method of assessment. However, if more objective evidence is needed or thought to be advisable, then each test could be more global, containing items which cover in total as many of the Programme of Study elements as possible. Care should always be taken to ensure that such assessments never become overwhelming for children, particularly for those who work more slowly.

Each *strand* in Attainment Target 2 reflects some, but not necessarily all, of the old Attainment Targets which are now part of 'Number'. The strands, listed as part of the *Non-Statutory Guidance* (1991), are:

(i) **Knowledge and use of number,**
(ii) **Estimation and approximation,**
(iii) **Measures.**

Strand (i) includes statements of attainment which are modifications of those in the old Ma2 (Number Concepts) and Ma3 (Number Operations). Strand (ii) is basically the old Ma4 (Estimation and Approximation), and the third strand is part of the previous Ma8 (Measures). On the NCC poster some of the statements of attainment are shown as part of two or more of the three strands, in an attempt to indicate that relationships exist between them. Each strand can be further broken down to show *themes* from Level 1 through to Level 10, providing deeper insight into the progression which is inherent in the curriculum.

The breaking down of the strands into seven themes provides teachers with a greater understanding of the progression in the various aspects of 'Number'. This is particularly evident in the two themes associated with the operations of addition, subtraction, multiplication and division, popularly known as the 'four rules' of number. Even taking into account the additional information in the Programme of Study, however, most of the revised statements of attainment have not yet been sufficiently well defined. SEAC produced a helpful document, *Pupils' Work Assessed at Key Stage 1*, which attempted to clarify, amplify and exemplify selected pre-1992 statements. The Key Stage 1 Standard Assessment Tasks in 1991 and 1992 also contributed to further elucidation of the meaning of debatable statements.

It was pointed out earlier that, in general, a statement of attainment demands of a child a combination of *action* or *behaviour* and a mathematical '*operation*' on some mathematical content (*content domain*). These are then set within some *context*, or given some purpose. In the case of Ma2, not every statement contains all these, nor do they always appear in the same order described. For example, Ma2/2d states: '*Recognise the need for standard units of measurement.*' Here the *action* is 'recognition', applied to the *content domain* 'standard units of measurement' with 'need' as the *purpose*. There is no mathematical operation involved in this statement.

To give a different example, the statement Ma2/3c states: '*Solve problems involving multiplication or division.*' The *behaviour* which the teacher has to observe is children producing solutions. The mathematical *operation* is either multiplication or division. The *content domain* is 'problems', which is rather indefinite as no information is provided to indicate the context of the problems nor, indeed, their complexity.

In many statements, the action or behaviour required of a child is lacking in precision. The action '*use*' appears in a number of statements of attainment and its meaning differs, depending on the context. Occasionally (in Ma2/2a, for example) its meaning is not at all clear.

The content domain of statement Ma2/1a, which has already been highlighted, is stated to be '*a small number*'. The word 'small' is relative and undefined. Following the suggested procedure, clarification is sought from the Programme of Study element which corresponds to this statement. This states: '*using addition and subtraction, with numbers no greater than 10, in the context of real objects*'.

This seems to define the content domain. However, on closer examination, it is clear that it leaves open the question of whether the *answers* to an addition sum can be more than 10, or should all three numbers involved be no greater than 10? As the statement stands, both these interpretations are equally valid.

Does it really matter? Do we really need to arrive at a consistent and agreed meaning of every statement? To answer these questions let us take two scenarios, both involving only the *addition operation*. Teacher A decides to assess children using only additions where the answer does not exceed 10. This choice of content domain produces a possible *45 combinations*, ranging from 1 + 1 to 9 + 1. Teacher B chooses a different content domain by allowing answers to exceed 10. This interpretation produces a content domain of *100 items*, ranging from 1 + 1 to 10 + 10. Thus Teacher B is likely to include examples such as 7 + 8 which Teacher A would consider inappropriate. Can both teachers be right in their different interpretations of the content domain of the same statement of attainment?

It is well known, and confirmed during the ENCA assessments, that most children who are operating at Level 1 when presented with objects to 'add' will use a counting procedure to arrive at the total. The likelihood of a counting error occurring when a child is using larger numbers than when operating with smaller numbers is obvious. Teacher B is therefore making greater demands on the children than is Teacher A. The outcomes of any teacher assessment in relation to both sets of children on Ma2/1a could not be considered at all comparable. Until issues of this nature are satisfactorily resolved, teachers will inevitably differ in their assessment demands for the same statement of attainment.

A similar difficulty arises when the statement Ma2/2b is analysed. This states: '*solve whole-number problems involving addition and subtraction.*'

The *size* of the whole numbers in the content domain is not specified and reference to the Programme of Study is unhelpful in this case, except that mention is made of money being included in the problems. Clarification can be sought by looking at the two examples adjacent to Ma2/2b, both of which relate to money. The numbers used in the examples range from 5p to 34p, which suggests that numbers greater than 10 would be appropriate to this Level 2 statement. On occasions it may also be necessary to consider statements in different Attainment Targets at the same level, or different statements in the same Attainment Target at prior levels. The search for interpretation and meaning of statements is inescapable, if teachers wish to make assessments of children which are both accurate and comparable.

The *actions* or *behaviours* which pupils are required to show are sometimes open to a number of interpretations too. Ma2/2a is an example of this: *'demonstrate that they know and can use number facts, including addition and subtraction.'*

The old statement to which the revised one corresponds differs only slightly: *'know and use addition and subtraction facts up to 10.'*

Both demand the *behaviour* 'know' in relation to number facts, and different teacher interpretations of *'know'* can readily influence pupils' attainment.

SEAC recognised that it was necessary to define the word *'know'* before the administration of the SATs in 1991. The definition used there required that pupils should provide correct answers to addition and subtraction facts *'using recall (without any obvious counting or computation)'*. The SAT activity required numbers to be added and subtracted which had been produced by the throwing of two dice. Children were closely observed by the teacher, who had to decide if their responses satisfied this interpretation of 'know'.

In 1992 the SAT activity which assessed the same statement, Ma2/2a, took a different form as the tasks moved toward pencil-and-paper testing. On this occasion, pupils were presented orally with addition and subtraction sums. They were allowed *'no more than 5 seconds to answer each one'*. The implications of this are that if pupils need more than five seconds to answer then they are either counting or using some means of computation, or alternatively, that if children answer within the stipulated time they necessarily 'know' the fact.

The ENCA project recognised at an early stage that not only is it difficult to judge if a child is computing, but that many children who 'know' the answer to an addition will perform a calculation so that they are more certain of obtaining the correct answer. The task devised on the ENCA project to assess this statement took the form of a game which involved a quick response. Despite this, many children resorted to calculating answers. As the task was conducted on a one-to-one basis with children, the assessor was able to observe closely the mannerisms, facial expressions and use of fingers when children were providing answers. In this way the assessors decided whether children were using recall or were calculating. The results which are given in Table 5.3 show

Item	Percentage of pupils who responded correctly by		
	knowing	calculating	knowing or calculating
3 + 3 = 6	75	19	94
4 + 1 = 5	74	23	97
8 + 1 = 9	72	23	95
1 + 7 = 8	67	27	94
3 + 2 = 5	57	38	95
2 + 7 = 9	48	41	89
2 + 6 = 8	46	44	90
5 + 4 = 9	37	52	89
5 + 3 = 8	38	56	94
3 + 7 = 10	34	56	90

Table 5.3 *Percentage of pupils who responded correctly to various items*

the considerable difference in attainment if children are allowed to calculate quickly as well as recall facts.

This task was administered to 570 seven-year-olds, using ten addition facts for which the answers did not exceed 10. The facility value (the percentage of pupils who got the item right) varied dramatically, according to whether calculation was allowed or not. Every one of the ten items exceeded 89% when the criterion for assessment was that a correct answer was given irrespective of the method used. However, when the criterion was that of responding correctly by rapid recall only, the facility values were very much lower. These two approaches quite clearly give different assessment outcomes for the same children. Teachers should recognise that whatever their own thoughts and beliefs on the criterion for achievement of a task, they must base their own assessments on criteria which match those used in the Standard Assessment Tasks. Only by doing this will they be able to provide evidence to challenge a result if it differs from their own assessment of a pupil.

In 1991 and 1992, the SATs which assessed Ma2/2a differed in the *context* in which the items were set. There was also a difference in the *number of items* which each included from the total number of possible items in the content domain. The possible content domain of Ma2/2a is made up of 45 addition facts and 45 subtraction facts, assuming that none of the numbers involved is greater than 10. There are thus 90 possible items, number facts, from which to choose for assessment. In 1991, four addition facts and four subtraction facts were tested. Thus a total of eight items were randomly selected from the 90 possible ones. In 1992, teachers read out seven addition facts and then seven subtraction facts. The facts to be read out were specified and no randomness was therefore involved. On this occasion, 14 facts made up the assessment domain. As the number of items used to assess the same statement differed markedly in the two years, the outcomes from the tasks do not really allow valid comparisons.

In the same way, when teachers are assessing their pupils, it is essential that they use the same number of items with each child. It would be patently unfair to assess pupil A on only one fact and pupil B on all 90 facts. This consistency of assessment domain applies whether the tasks are formal, by written testing, or informal, by observing children working in the normal classroom setting.

A less obvious but more significant difference is apparent between the two SATs in the two years. In 1991 the facts were determined randomly by the throw of dice, so it was possible for one child to throw:

$1 + 1, 1 + 2, 2 + 1$, and $2 + 2$

while another child had to give answers to:

$2 + 6, 5 + 4, 5 + 3$, and $3 + 4$.

There is little doubt that the second child's task is more difficult than the first child's task. This injustice was rectified in 1992, as every child was asked the same facts. The implication for teacher assessment is obvious: never assess two children on a different set of items, unless it is known that the items are of comparable difficulty.

This last requirement is problematic, as many teachers lack the knowledge or information which would enable them to make such a choice. Teachers should begin to collect their own data on the relative difficulty of items within the same content domain, since it seems unlikely that such information will be provided by an outside agency. This is a weakness of our national testing. Valuable data about children's responses to tasks, and to individual items that comprise the tasks, remains in schools and is not collected on a national scale. It is, therefore, left to teachers and schools to do what SEAC should have already started. When such information becomes available it will be possible for teachers to select items for assessment which are represent-ative of the range of difficulty in the content domain, hence avoiding the problem of inadvertently choosing items for informal assessment pur-poses that are all easy or difficult. It would be manifestly unfair to compare results on this basis.

The *performance criterion* for attaining Ma2/2a in the 1991 Standard Task was three out of four correct additions and three out of four subtractions. In 1992 this changed to six out of seven, in both addition and subtraction. The mastery level for the two years was therefore so different – 75% in 1991 and 86% in 1992 – that comparison of the results in Ma2/2a for the two years would be misleading. If yearly outcomes are to be compared to decide if standards are improving or deteriorating, then changing the mastery level from year to year invalidates any conclusions which may be reached. The same reasoning applies to teachers making their own assessment of pupils. If teachers wish to ensure that the judgements they make of their pupils are comparable with the SAT results, they must adopt the same or very similar mastery levels. To make this point even more strongly, a comparison of the mastery levels used in selected statements of attainment in the first two years of Standard assessments are shown in Table 5.4.

Further information collected by the ENCA project in 1991 is of interest here too. A survey asked a small number of teachers about the mastery level they used in reaching their teacher assessments for Ma2/2a. The responses ranged from 60% to 100%. Although many teachers suggested a mastery level in the 70% to 80% range, a small minority had other opinions. Unfortunately, if consistency of assessment and dependability of outcomes is an objective of national assessment, then this variability is unacceptable. Unfortunately, teachers have been given little guidance on what levels of mastery to use for different statements of attainment. Until such guidance is forthcoming, it would appear that the appropriate level of mastery to adopt is that which is used in the Standard Assessment Tasks.

Although this discussion of the issues associated with the content and assessment domains and mastery levels has focussed on one particular statement of attainment at Level 2 of Ma2, the warnings are appropriate

Year	Old SoA	Number of assessment items	Number required for attainment	Mastery expressed as a %
1991	1a	4	3	75%
1992	1a	5	4	80%
1991	2a – add	4	3	75%
1992	2a – add	7	6	86%
1991	3a – subtract	6	5	84%
1992	3a – subtract	6	5	84%
1991	3c – know	6	5	84%
1992	3c – know	5	4	80%

Table 5.4   Mastery levels in various SAT tasks in 1991 and 1992

to statements at other levels. For example, Ma2/5b states: '*Find fractions or percentages of quantities.*' Here the content domain is limitless, making the choice of the assessment domain much more complicated. Selecting items to achieve comparability of assessment outcomes becomes nearly impossible. The whole of this Attainment Target is fraught with such problems, and teachers need to be aware of them if the problem is to be solved.

Algebra (Ma3)

This Attainment Target requires that children should '*recognise and use symbolic and graphical representations to express relationships*'.

This is a relatively new content area in the mathematics curriculum of primary schools, especially in the early years. Many teachers' own school experience of 'algebra' has left them with unhappy memories of the subject, and it may be the case that teachers need to increase their own knowledge and understanding of the content of Ma3 if they are to assess children effectively.

The mathematics *Non-Statutory Guidance* (1991) sets out the statements of attainment for 'Algebra' in three strands:

(i)   **Patterns and relationships,**
(ii) **Formulae, equations and inequalities,**
(iii) **Graphical representation.**

These strands are also apparent in the Programme of Study, to which it is necessary to refer to shed further light on the statements of attainment. There are few statements in the revised curriculum and the number of them which apply to each strand is very limited. However, a knowledge of how each strand progressively develops through the levels appropriate to Key Stages 1 and 2 is helpful in the assessment process, since the strands highlight the *hierarchical* relationship between statements at the progressive levels. Table 5.5 lists the thirteen statements of attainment in the three strands for Levels 1 to 6.

The statements at the six levels appropriate to the vast majority of primary school children place emphasis on the understanding and use of pattern. But, as with Ma2, they are very general and lacking in detail, providing little information about the *content domain* for assessment purposes. Two have been chosen to illustrate some of the difficulties which confront teachers in assessment.

The single statement of attainment at Level 1 requires children to be able to '*Devise repeating patterns*', but no information is given about *which* repeating patterns should be assessed. There are an infinity of

Level	Patterns and Relationships	Formulae, Equations and Inequalities	Graphical Representation
1	a) Devise repeating patterns.		
2	a) Explore number patterns.	b) Recognise the use of a symbol to stand for an unknown number.	
3	a) Use pattern in number when doing mental calculations.	b) Use inverse operations in a simple context.	
4	a) Make general statements about patterns.	b) Use simple formulae expressed in words.	c) Use coordinates in the first quadrant.
5	a) Follow instructions to generate sequences.	b) Express a simple function symbolically.	
6	a) Explore number patterns using computer facilities or otherwise.	b) Solve simple equations.	c) Use and plot Cartesian coordinates to represent mappings.

Table 5.5 *Statements of attainment in Ma3, classified in strands*

such patterns, from the relatively simple to the very complex, and it is vitally important that teachers know which repeating patterns are appropriate to Level 1 assessment. The statement also fails to describe the contextual setting in which the patterns should appear. For valid assessment, much more information is needed about both the *content domain* relevant to Level 1 and the *contexts* in which the content should be set. Both the examples which are given in the Statutory Order, and the elements in the corresponding Programme of Study, go some way toward this necessary amplification.

The Programme of Study refers to activities which involve '*objects/ apparatus or single-digit numbers*'. Much of the apparatus which is available in infant and junior classrooms – such as beads, Unifix and

Multilink cubes – could be used. There is, however, a major difference between a child using objects or apparatus and writing single-digit numbers. The former are moveable and a child is able to try out possibilities before deciding which is correct. In contrast, once a digit has been written on paper, it has taken on a permanence which inevitably influences a child's thinking and decision-making processes. Although little research has been conducted in this area, it is reasonable to suggest that as the two activities have different contexts, they necessarily make different cognitive and motor-skill demands on children. It would appear that, in order for a teacher to ensure that a child has satisfactorily attained this statement, success in devising repeating patterns with objects, apparatus and single-digit numbers should be established. For a child who has problems writing numbers, a set of cards could be produced on which are written single-digit numbers. In this way a child can move the numbers around as 'objects'. This would satisfy the statement, as there is no requirement that a pupil should write the digits in a repeating pattern.

The Programme of Study provides some help with the *context* in which repeating patterns can be devised, but to obtain assistance about the *content domain* it is necessary to consider the examples which are set out adjacent to the statements of attainment in the Statutory Orders. These suggest a variety of content which is applicable to this particular statement:

> '*a potato print pattern: red, red, blue, red, red, blue, . . . ;*
> *a number pattern: 2, 1, 2, 1, 2, 1, 2, 1, . . . ;*
> *a shape pattern:* △ ☐ ○ △ ☐ ○ △ ☐ ○ . . . '

It is important to recognise that these are only examples and merely illustrate the many possibilities. Children could also be assessed on this statement by providing them with four letter 'A's and four letter 'B's and asking them to devise a repeating pattern. The examples have no legal authority and it would be a mistake to assume that they completely describe the content domain of a statement.

There is, however, an interesting mathematical difference between the three suggested examples: the structure of the repeat is different for each. The number pattern uses only two digits, 1 and 2, with the repeat taking place after two digits; the shape pattern uses three shapes, with the repeat taking place after three shapes. The first example uses only two colours, red and blue, but since red is repeated, the cycle, 'red, red, blue', repeats itself after three elements. As these examples begin to indicate, there are no bounds to such possibilities as the number of elements used could be increased to 4, 5, 6 or more, and different elements in a cycle could be allowed to repeat.

Although Ma3 was not assessed by the SATs in 1992, evidence of some appropriate kinds of pattern is available from the 1991 assessments of the old statement of attainment: '*copy, continue and devise repeating patterns represented by objects/apparatus or one-digit numbers*'. The 'copying and continuing' aspects of the 1991 task can be ignored in any assessment as they do not appear in the new statement, but the 'devise' part of the task provides insight for teachers' assessment of Ma3/1a.

The 1991 assessment task instructed teachers to '*Ask the children to devise a pattern of their own and show it to you.*' This very open invitation provides the opportunity to produce patterns which may not satisfy the statement. This requires that they devise repeating patterns, not merely patterns of any kind. Indeed, the Assessment Record Book for the 1991 materials stated specifically that a pupil '. . . *devises a repeating pattern using two colours*'. There was a clear mismatch between the general request made of pupils and the specificity of the performance required. Unless children clearly understand what is called for, then the validity of the assessment is brought into question. In these circumstances the task does not seem to access the required knowledge. When creating their own assessment activities for children, teachers should be reasonably sure that the task is acceptable for the purpose they have in mind.

The apparently reduced demand of this new statement of attainment, which no longer requires that children should be able to copy and continue repeating patterns, might suggest that pupils will now find it easier to attain Ma3/1a. This is not necessarily the case. The ENCA project showed that in a sample of 412 children, over 97% could both copy and continue repeating patterns using coloured circles and using two digits with no repeats. A much lower percentage, 89%, were able to devise their own repeating patterns with circles. The facility for devising repeating patterns with digits was only slightly higher. In effect, *devising* patterns was the only difficult part of the SoA anyway. The results are listed in Table 5.6.

In terms of the time needed to perform the assessment of 'copy, continue and devise', it is sensible to omit those parts which it is established that the vast majority of seven-year-olds find easy.

However, the ENCA project came up with another, rather surprising result about children's ability to devise repeating patterns. Although nearly 90% of the sample were able to devise repeating patterns with circles and with digits, it was not the *same* children who were necessarily succeeding on both tasks. Only 82% of children successfully devised repeating patterns both with circles *and* with digits. This seems to be yet more evidence that the *context* of a task is an influential factor in determining children's responses. There are implications for teacher

| | Percentage of pupils who were able to | | |
	Copy a repeating pattern	Continue a repeating pattern	Devise a repeating pattern
With two colours of circles	98	97	89
With two digits	99	98	89

Table 5.6   Percentage of pupils who could complete the various dimensions of repeating patterns

assessment here. Teachers should not be satisfied with children achieving on tasks which are set in only one context. To ensure that the assessment of pupils is as careful and correct as it can be, a variety of contexts should be used. Children should be expected to achieve *whatever the context*, as long as it is appropriate to their age and maturity.

The *language* which is used in a mathematics assessment task is obviously vitally important. Changes of wording, or the omission of a word in a task or test item, can mean the difference between a child attaining or not attaining a statement. For example, in the ENCA study, a child when asked to devise a repeating pattern using digits responded with '759824'. When questioned further he said that this was his telephone number, which he saw as having pattern, and it was used repeatedly!

In the 1991 Standard Task for the assessment of this statement, teachers were told that they should ask the child to '*devise a pattern*'. The omission of the word 'repeating' casts considerable doubt on the validity of the eventual outcomes, as it is not known whether teachers included the word when questioning a pupil, or indeed whether the pupil knew what was intended if 'repeating' *was* included! Is 1 1 1 1 2 2 2 2 3 3 3 3 a repeating pattern? Does it satisfy the statement of attainment?

Teacher assessment in the everyday classroom situation is often reactive. Teachers observe children responding to questions or performing activities which have been presented orally by the teacher: unplanned assessment often takes place in unforeseen situations. When this occurs, teachers are very often unaware of the words they used in a question or when explaining an activity, so they may not be conscious of how they have helped or hindered a pupil in giving an answer or conducting the task. Such reactive forms of assessment should be recorded as such and the outcomes confirmed in a further, planned assessment experience. Reactive assessment can be used positively, but teachers should recognise its limitations.

The issue of language in the assessment process is, therefore, vital and one that has been stressed throughout this book. It is reinforced here, in the context of assessment in mathematics. Written questions demand high-level reading skill of children, especially at Key Stage 2, when the mathematical vocabulary may be specialised and complex. This is a problem that should not be underestimated in the assessment process. Here, as before, it is not only the language which teachers may use with an individual pupil which is important, but also whether the same language is used consistently from child to child. A further point, with particular significance to mathematics, is the question of children's understanding of what is being said and asked of them. It is natural for a teacher to respond to any uncertainty in a child's response to a task by asking the same questions in a different way. This, it can be claimed, is giving a child the opportunity to demonstrate that they can respond successfully. On the other hand it can be argued that the teacher is invalidating the outcomes, as the responses can no longer be compared: different demands may have been made of different pupils. There is a fine balancing act necessary, on the one hand to guarantee that a child understands the task and the questions which are being asked and, on the other, to ensure consistency of assessment and comparability of outcomes.

In the Graphical Representation strand of Ma3, the statement of attainment at Level 6, Ma3/6c, expects pupils to be able to *'Use and plot Cartesian coordinates to represent mappings'.*

As with the previous statement at Level 1, the content domain from which the assessment items can be chosen is unstated. However, the corresponding Programme of Study casts some light on the possible interpretation of the word *'use'* by suggesting that children should experience activities which involve *'drawing and interpreting simple mappings in context, recognising their general features'.*

So a task which claims to assess children's ability to *'use'* coordinates will require them to plot coordinates and draw the mappings which the coordinates represent. The task may also include a demand that in some way the children interpret the mappings or representations. Only through the Standard Tasks at Key Stages 2, 3 and 4 is the meaning of this likely to become fully apparent.

The 1992 Standard Tasks for fourteen-year-olds at Key Stage 3 included a question which was aimed at this statement. The last part of the question showed the graph of the linear mapping, $a + b = 15$, where a and b were the sides of rectangles which could be made from a piece of string of length 30cm. (Neither the length of the string nor the mapping were explicitly stated.) The pupils were then shown a drawing of a rectangle which had been made with the string, but the length *a* of only one of its sides was given; they had to work out the length *b* of the other side (Figure 5.1). Pupils were required to interpret the graph of the mapping and use it to find the unknown length.

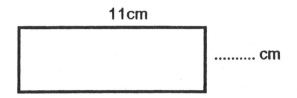

Figure 5.1   The drawing used in the Key Stage 3 Task

A similar question, number 15 in Paper 1, displayed six points which had been plotted, representing the mapping $b = 2k - 1$. Two of the six points had been intentionally plotted incorrectly. Pupils were asked how they could 'see from the shape of the graph that the two points are in the wrong place'. They then had to ring the two points. Here again pupils were being asked to use a representation of a mapping and interpret it, recognising errors in the plotting of points.

Both these questions provide useful insights into the interpretation of statement Ma3/6c. It cannot be overstressed how important it is that teachers consider and analyse all Standard Tasks and so build up a picture of the meanings of the various statements.

However, these two Key Stage 3 questions are of little use in assisting with a definition of the content domain of Ma3/6c. It is not explicit in the statement whether the values of coordinates should be exclusively whole numbers or include decimal and fractional numbers. In the Key Stage 3 tests, question 15, Paper 1, used whole numbers for the coordinates, while Question 14, Paper 3, had one point with coordinates (3.5, 6.5), the remainder involving only whole numbers. The questions may mislead teachers into assuming that only whole numbers will be used for coordinates. However, the early statements of attainment in other Attainment Targets reveal that the plotting of points even at the early levels may involve the use of fractions or decimal numbers. These appear as early as Level 4 in the 'Number' Attainment Target. So familiarity with these types of numbers may be assumed when pupils are assessed on this Level 6 statement.

The two Key Stage 3 questions may also lead teachers to a particular and perhaps misleading interpretation of the statement, since both use only the first quadrant when representing mappings. This is due to the nature of the contexts which give rise to the mappings. When reference is made to the Programme of Study at Level 5 in the 'Algebra' Attainment Target, it is immediately apparent that children should have previously experienced activities involving *'understanding and using coordinates in all four quadrants'*.

Assessment of the Level 6 statement may therefore require the use of all four quadrants of a Cartesian graph. The Programme of Study at Level 6 (and at previous levels) sheds no further light on the *content domain* of this particular statement, however. The corresponding Programme of Study, described above, makes reference to 'simple mappings'. But what may be simple for one teacher could be complex for another.

The four examples adjacent to this statement do provide some help. Three examples are given. Two are linear mappings of the form $x \rightarrow x + 1$ and $x \rightarrow 2 - x$; the third is the simplest possible quadratic, or second degree mapping, $x \rightarrow x^2$. This appears to suggest that the mappings which are appropriate for use in the assessment of this Level 6 statement should be restricted to linear mappings and to only the simplest of the quadratics. However, care must be taken not to jump to conclusions about the restricted nature of the content domain, on the basis of the examples. It must be emphasised that the examples do not define the curriculum, nor determine the type and nature of future assessments. Only over a considerable period of time will future test items in the Key Stage 2 and Key Stage 3 assessments clarify the position. Until precedents have been created over a number of years, it may be advisable for teachers to assess pupils on any mappings chosen from the set of linear mappings $x \rightarrow ax + b$, and second degree mappings of the type $x \rightarrow ax + b$, with a and b taking any values, positive, negative or zero.

A further important issue arises with regard to this statement of attainment, which has implications not only for the assessment of many other statements, but also for teaching the mathematics National Curriculum.

In the 1991 Order, three examples of mappings are presented, in the following way:

$$`x \rightarrow x + 1 \text{ (or } y = x + 1)$$
$$x \rightarrow 2 - x \text{ (or } y = 2 - x)$$
$$x \rightarrow x^2 \text{ (or } y = x^2)'$$

It is apparent that because the curriculum specification fails to state the format, symbolism and notation that should be adopted, teachers are left in a dilemma as to which to use when teaching their children. Of course, this only has serious implications when children are assessed nationally, using the Standard Tasks which present activities using only one kind of notation. A child who has only been taught to use the notation $x \rightarrow ax + b$ is likely to be confused by an alternative form, such as $y = ax + b$, which may appear in a Standard Test item. Teachers should guard against this problem by teaching their pupils all variations of format and notation until an agreed system becomes established.

One of the questions in the 1992 Standard Tests at Key Stage 3, discussed earlier, employs the word *'formula'* for the mapping $b = 2k - 1$. An early statement of attainment at Level 4, Ma3/4b, says that pupils should be able to *'Use simple formulae in words.'*

Thus children will be introduced to the idea and the word *'formula'* well before Level 6. Also, in Ma3/5b, pupils are expected to be able to express simple functions symbolically. This statement is amplified by a Programme of Study element which refers to *'understanding and using simple formulae or equations expressed in symbolic form.'*

As a consequence of a study of Ma3/6c it is apparent that pupils will be expected to understand and use almost interchangeably the words *'mapping'*, *'formula'* and *'function'*. Unless teachers are aware of this demand, their pupils may be at a disadvantage when questions asked in Standard Tests use one or more of these words to express what appears to be the same idea.

In two of the 13 statements of attainment in the first six levels of Ma3, the operational verb *'explore'* is used. This is a very open requirement to satisfy. It is difficult to determine what *behaviour* is demanded that will indicate that children are exploring number patterns in a way which satisfies the statement. This uncertainty is repeated at Level 6 where the statement says that *'pupils should be able to explore number patterns using computer facilities or otherwise'*. Neither statement stipulates that the exploration should result in any findings arising from the *actions* which a child performs on number patterns, nor that if findings are produced, they should be accurate.

The use of such operational verbs is unhelpful to teachers when making their assessments of children. Until clarification of required and acceptable behaviours are produced, either in the Standard Tests or in future SEAC publications, teachers should seek assistance from the moderating teams in their local authorities. At least in this way a consistency of assessment should be possible, if only within authorities.

Shape and Space (Ma4)

This Attainment Target requires that:

> *'Pupils should recognise and use the properties of two-dimensional (2-D) and three-dimensional (3-D) shapes and use measurement,*

location and transformation in the study of space.'

The statements of attainment in this Attainment Target are divided into four distinct yet inter-related strands:

(i)   **Shape** – properties of 2-D and 3-D shapes,
(ii) **Location** – direction and position,
(iii) **Movement** – transformations and symmetries,
(iv) **Measures** – perimeter, area and volume.

There are many opportunities throughout Ma4 for teachers to assess pupils by the *outcome* of an activity rather than by a task devised to consider only one statement of attainment. This is because of the close relationship between the statements at successive levels in the four strands. However, unlike Ma1, there will be occasions when the latter approach is more appropriate and desirable.

In Ma4, the deferring of assessment, referred to on page 79, is particularly evident. Much of the mathematical content in the Programme of Study at a given level is often assessed at higher levels. In the **Shape** strand, for example, the statement of attainment at Level 1 requires only that the children should *'Talk about models they have made.'*

Associated with this statement are three Programme of Study elements which require children to engage in a variety of activities. A decision has to be made which, if any, of these elements is appropriate for assisting with assessment at Level 1. The PoS elements suggest that the activities include the following six kinds of *action*;

- sorting shapes
- classifying shapes
- building shapes
- drawing shapes
- describing shapes
- describing position

As the *actions* sorting, classifying, building and drawing do not relate in an obvious way to *'Talking about models . . .'*, it would seem that the last two on the list, 'describing shapes' and 'describing position', contribute in some way to amplifying the statement. However, consideration of statements of attainment at higher levels in the 'shape' strand indicates that 'description' (and perhaps 'classification') are assessed at Level 2, where the use of mathematical terminology is required. If this behaviour is evidence of attainment at Level 2, it cannot also be a requirement for attainment at Level 1. Can it be that the only part of the

Programme of Study which is appropriate to assessment at Level 1 is 'describing position'? Obviously not.

The answer to this problem lies in the realisation that the activities listed in the Programme of Study can be used to stimulate children's discussion about what they are doing. Sorting, classifying, drawing and description activities which children working at this level might be engaged in, are part of the development of skills which are assessed at higher levels. 'Description' and 'classification' are assessed at Level 2, while 'sorting' is assessed at Level 3 when children are also expected to give reasons for the shape sort which they produce. This latter requirement is important to distinguish the assessment from a similar one at Level 1 in Ma5 (Handling Data). Here pupils should be able to sort a set of objects describing criteria chosen. When the data is specifically 'shapes' and mathematical criteria are used, the demand rises from Level 1 to Level 3.

Building (construction) and drawing 2-D and 3-D shapes is eventually assessed at Level 4. It is the children's use of language while engaged in these activities which is important for assessment at Level 1, and not the outcome of the activities themselves.

Assessment at Level 2 in the 'shape' strand involves describing shapes and objects in mathematical terms. There are two associated elements in the Programme of Study:

SoA: *'Use mathematical terms to describe common 2-D and 3-D objects.'*

PoS: *'recognising squares, rectangles, circles, triangles, hexagons, pentagons, cubes, rectangular boxes (cuboids), cylinders and spheres and describing their properties.'*

   'recognising right-angled corners in 2-D and 3-D shapes.'

The Programme of Study elements refer particularly to the recognition of shapes, as well as the description of properties. *Recognition* and *description* are, clearly, not the same thing, although closely related. Nor is *naming* shapes the same as recognising or describing them, because the name of a shape is not strictly a property of the shape; it is merely a way of identification for communication purposes.

In this instance, the relationship between the statements of attainment and Programme of Study is not very clear, and the examples given in the Statutory Orders do not help much. There are three *actions* in the Programme of Study – 'describing', 'recognising' and, by implication, 'naming' – of which only the first is mentioned in the Statement of Attainment. Most teachers would regard naming a shape as part of the description of a shape, even though its name is not mathematically a property of the shape.

This is the kind of situation where reference to Standard Assessment Task and Standard Test materials is helpful. In 1991 the Standard Assessment Task for Ma4 involved showing children a shape and asking them to say two things about it, one of which could be giving its name. The 1992 SAT included two items relating to this statement: one in which children joined shapes to their names and the other in which the children joined descriptions of properties (for example, '3 corners') with drawings of shapes. On the basis of both these assessment activities, it seems clear that both the naming of shapes, and the description of the properties of shapes are appropriate and necessary for attainment. Standard Assessment Task and Test materials are also likely to be the only source of guidance available to teachers in the matter of *mastery* – in other words 'how many properties' and 'how accurate a description' is required for attainment?

The *content domain* in the '*shape*' strand is essentially the number of different classes of 2-D and 3-D shapes with which the children are expected to be familiar. The word '*shapes*' without qualification is used throughout the curriculum specification, except at Level 2, where the phrase '*common shapes*' is used. The *content domain* is, therefore, open ended, particularly as a given shape might well be commonplace in one child's experience and quite novel for a different child. The Programme of Study at Level 2 refers to ten specific 2-D and 3-D shapes, although many interesting shapes such as trapezia, ellipses, prisms and cones are not mentioned. In the face of these disparities and omissions, a sensible approach might be to give the children experience of a wide variety of shapes in their learning activities, but to restrict assessment tasks to the ten specifically mentioned in the elements.

The ENCA project produced evidence to show that children are much better at finding a shape given the name, than they are at remembering the name when a shape is shown to them. Unsurprisingly, it has been found that children have much more difficulty with the names *pentagon, hexagon* and *rectangle* than with the names *circle, square* and *triangle*, and that in general children have less facility in naming and describing the properties of 3-D shapes than of 2-D shapes.

The ENCA study established a distinct order of difficulty in the naming and describing of the ten shapes mentioned in the Programme of Study at Level 2.

Easiest ←			→	**Most Difficult**
2-D shape: square circle		rectangle	hexagon	pentagon
triangle				
3-D shape:			cylinder	cuboid
		cube		sphere

While this ordering is representative of children in general, it should not be assumed that it necessarily holds true for individual children. There may well be children who can name a cylinder, but not a rectangle, for example. If an assessment activity is to involve only a few of these shapes, some care needs to be taken in choosing *which* shapes to include, because the overall difficulty of the task clearly depends on this choice. For comparable assessment, the same shapes should be used with each child.

The study and assessment of **location** in Ma4 is interwoven with the other strands, particularly at the lower levels. The Statement of Attainment at Level 1 refers to children being able to *'follow and give instructions related to movement and position'*.

This is essentially dynamic, emphasising the **movement** dimension. The examples related to Ma4/1b also focus on movement. However, it seems likely that at least some assessment of children's ability to describe the position of objects, in a static sense, by their relationship to other fixed objects, is also intended. The assessment of this ability should be fairly straightforward, although there is one potential pitfall.

Where children are asked to describe the relative positions of two or more objects, there is the possibility that children may be unsure of the objects, rather than the relative position. For example, a child might say 'the triangle is underneath the rectangle' when in fact the opposite is true, only because of a confusion between *'triangle'* and *'rectangle'* and not because the child does not understand what *'underneath'* means. It is, therefore, essential that any assessment clearly focuses on one issue with the knowledge that pupils have already attained any other mathematical knowledge which is part of the activity.

When assessing **movement**, particularly with younger children, it is important to ensure that it is the ability to *understand* instructions which is being assessed and not the children's ability to *sequence* instructions. With children who find sequencing difficult, it may be more appropriate, and in assessment terms entirely proper, to give instructions one by one rather than two or three at a time. This will obviously take longer than giving three or four instructions together, but is an example of the kind of situation where there is a balance to be struck between fairness to individual children on the one hand, and economy of time on the other.

The assessment of **measurement** in the context of 'Shape and Space' does not appear until Level 4, when perimeters, areas and volumes are considered. From Level 4 onwards, the statements of attainment and Programme of Study relating to the measurement of area and volume proceed in a straightforward way, with the SoAs and PoS at each level corresponding fairly obviously and with an orthodox progression in the content. It is well established that children often have difficulty in conceptualising area and volume, so it is important to introduce these ideas at an early stage, even though formal assessment of the children's ability to quantify and calculate area and volume of shapes is not required until Level 4.

The concept and measurement of *angle* arises in all four strands of this Attainment Target. Angle is introduced as an idea at Level 2 in the 'shape' and 'location' strands, although none of the statements at Level 2 or Level 3 explicitly involve the measurement of angle other than as points of the compass. At Level 4, angle and distance are introduced in the Programme of Study as a means of specifying location, and there is a corresponding statement of attainment. This is the first time that children would need to be formally assessed in their ability to measure angles.

A particular problem arises in the assessment of Ma4, particularly in the 'measures' strand, but also to some extent in 'location'. It concerns the *degree of precision* which is appropriate in different activities and at different levels. Accuracy in drawing and measurement is introduced explicitly at Level 5, but at Levels 1 to 4 it seems to be left to the teacher to decide how 'straight' a straight line ought to be, whether a quadrilateral is as nearly square as makes no difference, or if the location of a point is adequately defined by a coordinate stated to two decimal places when four decimal places would be more precise.

While these decisions are largely a matter of common sense and personal judgement, it is difficult to see how comparability between the assessments of different teachers can be assured. Teachers will need to share examples of children's work, taking account of any guidance offered by Standard assessment materials, and carefully consider the question of appropriate precision before any real degree of comparability between different classes and different schools can be achieved.

Handling Data (Ma5)

The goal of Attainment Target 5 'Handling Data' is:

> *'Pupils should collect process and interpret data and should understand, estimate and use probabilities.'* (DES, 1991)

The three strands listed on the NCC poster correspond with the three old Attainment Targets, ATs 12, 13 and 14:

(i)   **Collecting and processing data,**

(ii) **Representing and interpreting data,**
(iii) **Probability.**

Ma5 is unusual in the proportion of Programme of Study elements which are not explicitly matched by statements of attainment. The first four levels of the 'probability' strand provide a good example of the variety of relationships between the two. This is shown in Table 5.7.

At Levels 1 to 4 of the 'probability' strand, three of the eight elements in the Programme of Study have equivalent statements of attainment at their own levels, three are not directly assessed but are necessary precursors for attainment at later levels, and two elements are never assessed at all.

Although these relationships are particularly evident in Ma5 they do occur in other Attainment Targets in the mathematics curriculum, so it is worth exploring each of these three kinds of Programme of Study element in some detail.

Directly assessed elements

These elements, which have a directly equivalent statement of attainment, are in the majority in the mathematics curriculum as a whole, and although they are in this sense 'normal', understanding the relationships between such elements and their statements of attainment is not always straightforward, as already noted. In the examples given in the Table 5.7, three elements were described as having either directly or broadly equivalent statements of attainment. These occur at Levels 2, 3 and 4.

The Level 2 element is matched with a statement of attainment worded in exactly the same way, but this is not true of the elements at Levels 3 and 4, where there are slight differences in the wording of the elements and their respective statements. In these two cases, the differences are not significant and therefore the PoS and SoAs are broadly equivalent.

Small differences in the wording of PoS elements and SoAs cannot always be ignored, however, as the following example from Level 1 of the 'collecting and processing' strand shows:

PoS: *'selecting criteria for sorting a set of objects and applying them consistently.'*
SoA: *'Sort a set of objects, describing the criteria chosen.'*

Superficially, these seem to cover the same ground. However, careful comparison of the PoS element and the SoA reveals that they are *not* exactly equivalent. The difference lies in the way in which the criterion for sorting arises. In the Programme of Study, children are expected to

Programme of study	Level	Statement of Attainment
	1	
*Recognising possible outcomes of random events.	This element contributes to the understanding required at later levels, but is not directly assessed.	
	2	
*Recognising that there is a degree of uncertainty about the outcomes of some events and that other events are either certain or impossible.	This element has a directly equivalent SoA.	b) Recognise that there is a degree of uncertainty about the outcome of some events but that others are certain or impossible.
	3	
*Placing events in order of 'likelihood' and using appropriate words to identify the chance.	This element has a broadly equivalent SoA.	c) Use appropriate language to justify decisions when placing events in order of 'likelihood'.
*Understanding and using the idea of 'evens' and saying whether events are more or less likely than this.	This element is not assessed.	
*Distinguishing between 'fair' and 'unfair'.	This element is not assessed.	
	4	
*Giving and justifying subjective estimates of probabilities.	This elements has a broadly equivalent SoA.	d) Estimate and justify the probability of an event.
*Understanding and using the probability scale from 0 to 1.	This element describes a skill which is probably appropriate at this level, but is only required for assessment at later levels.	
*Listing all the possible outcomes of an event.	This becomes important at level 6, but is not directly assessed.	

Table 5.7 Programme of Study elements and statements of attainment in the probability strand of Ma5

be selecting criteria whereas in the statement, only describing the criteria is required. The following two examples of activities show why the difference is not trivial.

Activity One (based on the statement of attainment)
- Give the child a set consisting of red objects and blue objects, and ask the child to put the red ones in one tray and the blue in another.
- If the sort is successfully achieved, ask the child *'what is the difference between these* (pointing to one tray) *and these* (pointing to the other)*?'*.
- Note whether the child answers something along the lines of *'these are red and these are blue'*, or *'different colours'*.

Activity Two (based on the Programme of Study and example)
- Give the child a collection of objects of various shapes, sizes and properties. Ask the child to sort the objects in some way.
- When the objects have been sorted, ask the child to explain the basis of the sort.
- Note whether the child's explanation matches the way the objects have been sorted.

The first of these activities, a rather minimalist although still perfectly legitimate interpretation of the statement of attainment, is clearly much less demanding than the second activity.

Indirectly assessed elements

There are Programme of Study elements which describe learning activities which are important for the development of skills and knowledge needed for attainment at higher levels. These elements often form part of a 'chain' over two or more levels in the Programme of Study, even though the 'links' at each level are not necessarily assessed individually. The elements relating to the organised collecting of data are structured in this way;

Level 1 *'recording with objects or drawing and commenting on the results.'*
Level 2 *'designing a data collection sheet, collecting and recording data, leading to a frequency table.'*
Level 3   no element
Level 4 *'collecting, grouping and ordering discrete data using tallying methods and creating a frequency table for grouped data.'*
Level 5 *'designing and using an observation sheet to collect data; collating and analysing results.'*

Although the activities in the Level 4 element do contribute to a rather more general statement of attainment at that level, direct assessment of the skill and understanding which is developed in this chain does not happen until Level 5 with the statement of attainment *'Design and use an observation sheet to collect data.'*

The chain of PoS elements given above is an unusually long one, and was chosen to emphasise the importance of informal monitoring of children's progress even where there is no formal assessment structure. Teachers should remember that although the National Curriculum assessment structure in mathematics is wide-ranging and complex, its purpose is to systematise the reporting of achievement and not to provide a fully comprehensive scheme for monitoring the fine detail of children's development; it records attainment, not progression in learning.

Unassessed elements

Two of the PoS elements in the 'probability' strand shown in Table 5.7 are never formally assessed. Both these elements occur at Level 3:

- *'understanding and using the idea of "evens" and saying whether events are more or less likely than this'*;
- *'distinguishing between "fair" and "unfair".'*

It is a common characteristic of this kind of element that they are independent pieces of knowledge or understanding which are considered important in themselves, but which are not essential precursors to development elsewhere in the curriculum, and are not important enough to warrant inclusion in the formal assessment process. Teachers will have to decide for themselves whether informal monitoring and recording of children's progress in these areas of the curriculum is appropriate.

Many of the statements of attainment in Ma5, in particular those relating to data collection, are much more amenable to teacher assessment than they are to Standard assessment. There are two distinct reasons for this: firstly, there are time constraints; and secondly, there is an element of choice in some of the statements. If data collection and analysis is to be a meaningful and non-trivial exercise, children have to be allowed time to think carefully about the reasons for collecting the data, the best way to go about its collection and appropriate ways to process the data once it has been collected. The actual collection of the data itself may also be a time-consuming process.

The statement of attainment at Level 2 states that *'pupils should be able to interpret relevant data which have been collected.'* The statement is not explicit about where this data should come from. A possible amplification could be that children are asked to interpret data collected by someone else. Both the Programme of Study and the example in the *Non-Statutory Guidance* suggest that this would be an inappropriate strategy, and that children should collect the data themselves.

At Level 6, the statement of attainment *'design and use a question-naire to survey opinion'* is unambiguous in requiring the data collection to be conducted by children themselves. On the question of choice, the statement of attainment at Level 4 is quite explicit: *'conduct a survey on an issue of their choice'*. It is obviously very difficult to arrange an assessment activity which combines an element of choice for the children, *and* standardisation. It is notable that in the 1992 Key Stage 3 Standard Task, no attempt was made to assess the statements of attainment relating to data collection in Ma5.

Clearly, it is a demanding task to become professionally informed about the statements of attainment. It is, however, not only essential in order that assessment of a statement of attainment should be valid, but it is also personally rewarding to move toward total command of the mathematics National Curriculum. The exercise should ideally be a cooperative effort in which the whole staff of a primary school becomes involved. It is essential that those teaching Years 5 and 6 are as conversant with the progression from Level 1 as it is for teachers of the early years to have knowledge and understanding of progression in the different Attainment Targets to at least two or three levels beyond that at which their children are operating. Consistency of assessment is not possible unless there exists agreement between teachers about the interpretations which will be applied to statements of attainment, a message constantly repeated throughout this book. All valid and dependable criterion-referenced assessment relies upon well defined objectives and shared interpretations.

6

Assessing Science

At a time when primary teachers are facing more pressures than ever, science teaching and assessment is making considerable demands on their time and energy. To begin to justify such expenditure of resource, two issues must be addressed: *What are the goals and purposes of assessment of science in primary classrooms?*, and *What makes these purposes valuable and important?*

In a famous quotation, the American psychologist David Ausubel (1968) stated:

> *'The most important factor influencing learning is what the learner already knows. Ascertain this and teach him accordingly.'*

Matching the learner to the task by formatively assessing their understanding and knowledge, then planning appropriate experiences to extend and develop these, was viewed by Ausubel as the teacher's first priority. However, as early as the mid-1970s, concern was being expressed in Britain by HMI about the *lack of match* in primary science:

> *'The work in observational and experimental science was, at all ages and for each ability group, most commonly found to be less well matched to the children's capabilities than work in any other aspect of the curriculum. Children were not sufficiently challenged in over two-thirds of all groups. This lack of challenge occurred more frequently in the most able than the least able groups.'* (HMI, 1978)

Accordingly, the DES undertook a major programme of research and training in primary science. It become prioritised as an area of development under the Educational Support Grant Scheme in the mid-1980s. Growing numbers of teacher advisers worked alongside teachers in classrooms in an attempt to upgrade both the quantity and quality of science done in primary classrooms. There *were* improvements, but a survey carried out in 1987 in seventeen countries placed British primary children close to the bottom of a league table of understanding in basic science. And in a survey carried out by HMI into primary science immediately prior to the introduction of the National Curriculum in 1989, it was reported that:

> *'For the most part existing arrangements for assessing, recording and reporting on children's performance are inadequate and inconsistent. They rarely provide an effective basis for planning*

> *work which takes account of the difference in the teaching group and of the difficulties encountered by the children.'*   (HMI, 1989)

Formative assessment in primary science was rudimentary or non-existent.

It is worth noting that whereas the TGAT Report (DES, 1988) placed emphasis on a national *formative* system of assessment, most of the statutory requirements have in practice focused on *summative* purposes (see Chapter 3). There are indeed important purposes for summative assessment: reporting to parents is a significant function and one which may serve to emphasise the links between school and community. However, further consideration needs to be given to the precise relationship between summative assessment and furthering the quality of learning for individual children.

The enhancement of a child's positive self-image through the effective feedback of his or her achievements has been found to be particularly effective in generating and sustaining intrinsic motivation. A well constructed and well utilised summative record of achievement can form an important element in this process, particularly for young children.

Science in the primary curriculum

Science is a relative newcomer to the primary curriculum, when considered alongside English and mathematics. Studies conducted during the early 1980s (APU, 1988) found only around 5% of time being devoted to teaching primary science. Also a consensus view of the nature of science did not really exist in schools until the advent of the National Curriculum.

To understand the nature of the primary science curriculum is to understand the nature of both science itself and children's developing knowledge and understanding of it. National Curriculum science presents two perspectives on science: the *process* of scientific investigation and the systems of *knowledge* generated by it. Process science is about methodologies for acquiring and refining knowledge, methods that can be used to construct theories which enable the explanation and understanding of phenomena in the physical world. By employing such methodologies, it is possible to construct systems of knowledge, such as the subjects of physics and biology, which incorporate the ideas and theories that have been developed. This is often referred to as scientific *'content'*. Science is concerned with *how* we find out and *what* we find out.

The problem is that the particular ideas that a person holds – their *personal theories* – may not coincide with agreed theories. For example, we all know that when a car breaks down we have to push it to get it to the garage; our own 'theory' of motion tells us that it is not enough just to start a car moving, we have got to keep pushing it to get it there. However, Newton's theory of motion states that '*A body continues in a state of rest or uniform motion unless acted upon by an external force*', which means that once you've got it moving, that should be that. Of course, we may have elaborated our theory to take in the notion of frictional effects or we may quite happily operate two contradictory theories side by side, and utilise each according to the situation. But that is not the point. A child's state of knowledge is not 'wrong' because he or she hasn't integrated ideas about friction into his or her theory: it is just naïve and undifferentiated. 'Knowledge' in this sense is not a 'once and for all' state, and National Curriculum science does not acknowledge this.

On the one hand, National Curriculum science proposes a curriculum that is *investigative*, where children construct their own knowledge and understanding through first-hand investigations; on the other, the curriculum is *pre-specified*, conforming to ideas agreed within the wider (adult) scientific community. It presents knowledge as reflexive, problematic and variable, at the same time as being received and fixed. It is not much fun for the teacher who encourages her children to find out for themselves to be faced with the dilemma of what to do when they discover the 'wrong' facts.

This dilemma has considerable significance for the assessment of children's performance in science. Stenhouse (1975) described a number of processes which take place in education:

- **training**, leading to the learning of skills;
- **instruction**, leading to the retention of information;
- **induction**, leading to thought processes which result in 'the capacity to grasp and make for oneself relationships and judgement'.

Whereas skills and the retention of information are relatively easy to assess, one of the key features of science is that its 'thought system' is speculative rather than fixed, making assessment much more difficult. A fundamental aspect of measuring children's attainments in science is concerned with how understanding has been deepened and explored. As Stenhouse puts it:

   '*Education as induction into knowledge is successful to the extent that it makes the behavioural outcomes of the students unpredictable.'*

This places considerable limitations on the reliability of assessment outcomes in this central area of science. If only simple skills and the retention of information can be assessed, the speculative understandings which are critical to the subject are neglected as not amenable to measurement. For example, in the 1991 Standard Assessment Tasks, many children were debarred from attaining Level 3 on Sc1 because their thinking, despite being valid and supportable, was not what was required. Their ideas became 'unpredictable' and therefore 'unmeasurable'.

This debate in primary science between *process* and *content* has been ongoing since at least the 1960s. For example, *Oxford Primary Science* (Redman *et al*, 1983) concentrated on producing a programme through which children could develop *conceptual* understandings, whereas *Science 5 to 13* (Ennever and Harlen, 1973) concentrated on developing children's *cognitive processing skills*, using a framework derived from Piagetian theory. This 'process science' approach took the view that as long as starting points for investigations were sufficiently widespread, scientific content would take care of itself. Given the pre-eminence at that time of the 'child-centred' approach, as proposed by the Plowden Committee (CACE, 1967), it was not unexpected that 'process science' would find favour among educationists.

A series of surveys and reports in the late 1970s and early 1980s by HMI, APU and researchers such as Harlen and Driver culminated in the DES publishing *Science 5–16: A Statement of Policy* (1985). This set out a more balanced framework emphasising the importance of developing both investigational skills and conceptual understandings.

However, the two perspectives have remained largely unintegrated within the present curriculum: the 1989 National Curriculum Statutory Instrument for Science placed process science and scientific knowledge in separate Profile Components; the 1991 version abandoned Profile Components, placing process science in the first Attainment Target and biology, materials/chemistry and physics in the other three, with a recommendation in the accompanying Circular that process science and scientific knowledge should be equally weighted. What it failed to address is the nature and manner of the relationship between process and content. Such links are possible, however: Harlen and Osbourne (1985) describe a model of teaching and learning where process and content are closely related.

Scientific Investigation (Sc1)

The aim of the curriculum in Scientific Investigation is that:

> '*Pupils should develop the intellectual and practical skills which allow them to explore and investigate the world of science and develop a fuller understanding of scientific phenomena, the nature of the theories explaining these, and the procedures of scientific investigation.*' (Science in the National Curriculum, DES, 1991)

This is divided into three strands:

(i)   **Ask questions, predict and hypothesise**
(ii) **Observe, measure and manipulate variables**
(iii) **Interpret their results and evaluate scientific evidence.**

The statements of attainment as well as the Programmes of Study at Key Stage 1 present science as a set of individual, *atomistic skills*: they do not indicate what the *global process* is meant to be. The only reference to the scientific process was given in the *Non-Statutory Guidance* accompanying the 1989 Orders (NCC, 1989), where a circular model with no apparent beginning or end was proposed. Yet to begin to unravel the assessment issues in scientific investigation, an understanding of what scientific methodology comprises and how this relates to children's theory building is helpful.

Lawson (1989) identifies three elements within *investigative learning cycles*:

- During *exploration* children explore a context with minimal guidance, raise issues, examine the adequacy of their existing conceptions and identify relationships and patterns.
- During *term introduction* new ideas and concepts are introduced.
- During *concept application* children are encouraged to recognise patterns, separate these from specific contexts and apply them to new contexts.

This embodies aspects of learning which are central to the development of children's conceptual understandings as well as their cognitive abilities.

Lawson proposes three forms of this learning cycle which are directly related to scientific methodology: the *descriptive*, the *empirical-inductive* and the *hypothetical-deductive*. This framework allows us to examine how process skills are promoted in National Curriculum science.

■ **Descriptive learning cycle**

Children learn and describe patterns in specific contexts (*exploration*). The teacher then gives this a name (*term introduction*). The pattern is then identified in additional contexts (*concept application*). This common procedure is carried out at most levels of development, particularly as an introductory activity. It enables the introduction of class inclusion terms such as 'mammals' or 'minerals'.

Sc2/2b *Pupils should be able to sort familiar living things into groups, according to easily observable features.*

Sc3/2b *Pupils should be able to group materials according to observable features.*

Here, statements of attainment relevant to scientific investigation, appear to be located in the 'wrong' Attainment Targets (i.e. Sc2 and Sc3, which deal with content not process). The situation is further confused by the Key Stage 1 Programmes of Study for Scientific Investigation (Sc1) indicating that *'these activities'* (scientific investigations) should include *'encouraging the sorting, grouping and describing of objects and events . . . and noting similarities and differences'* (DES, 1991).

■ **Empirical-inductive learning cycle**

This learning cycle forms an important part of young children's theory building. First children discover and describe a pattern within a specific context (*exploration*). A possible cause is suggested, using *reasoning by analogy* to transfer a concept learned in one context to another new one (*term introduction*). The initial exploration is sifted to see if it is consistent with the new concept (*concept application*). For example, the child knows that all birds have mouths (*exploration*). The child knows that mammals such as human beings, dogs, etc., use their mouths for breathing, so they infer (induce) from this that birds breathe in much the same way as human beings (*term introduction*). The child might then re-examine the birds to see if there is anything else that they do which is consistent with breathing in mammals and may note that there is regular body expansion and contraction in birds consistent with breathing (*concept application*). The child has not rigorously examined an hypothesis: he or she has only looked for consistency and induced a more general idea from particular examples. This is a very commonly used method of concept formation in both children and adults.

■ **Hypothetical-deductive learning cycle**

In hypothetical-deductive investigations a question is posed and pupils are asked to suggest hypotheses. Pupils deduce logical consequences from their hypotheses, design experiments to test these predictions and carry them out (*exploration*). They then analyse the results and either reject or modify their hypotheses. Terms are introduced to describe these generalities (*term introduction*). Pupils then discuss their new theory and try out applications in new contexts (*concept application*). For example, a child might be asked to find out why a toy car travels farther from the bottom of some slopes than from others. He or she might hypothesise that this is due to the steepness of the slope down which the car travels and try this out using ramps with differing gradients (*exploration*). Having analysed the results the child might frame a general proposition that the steeper the slope, the farther the distance travelled (*term introduction*). The child might then try this out in other contexts, e.g. skateboards, pram wheel 'trolleys', etc., to find out if it holds true there (*concept application*).

An examination of Sc1 (Scientific Investigation) reveals that Level 1 has an element of all three learning cycles, Level 2 corresponds with the empirical-inductive, and Level 3 and beyond with the hypothetical-deductive. That is, from around the age of seven, children are primarily being required to think *deductively*. But, as indicated above, *inductive* thought is a very important aspect of how both children and adults construct understandings. The development of the first two of Lawson's three learning cycles are at least as important in planning for and assessing progression as the developing emphasis on quantification, the use of more complex variables and the design of 'fair tests' which are overtly identified within the National Curriculum. It is important to take this into account if a valid assessment of young children's developing process skills is to be made.

Assessing scientific investigations

There are three commonly used methods for the assessment of scientific investigation. Firstly, individual skills within the process are identified and assessed separately. The Assessment of Performance Unit (1988), working with eleven-year-olds, identified a series of skills and abilities that form elements within scientific methodology. These are set out in a framework, with similar elements grouped into given categories (see Figure 6.1). Many of their assessments were of individual elements from within this framework using short, specific assessment items.

Secondly, a child's performance of *a complete investigation* can be assessed. APU examined and constructed a model of the overall process (see Figure 6.2). This was an attempt to show how the individual elements might fit together within an investigation. APU then selected a range of contexts through which they assessed a pupil's ability to perform each of the individual elements within a complete investigation, thereby enabling the effect of different contexts on children's attainments to be examined.

Category	Sub-categories	Form of test
1 Use of graphical and symbolic representation	Reading information from graphs, tables and charts Representing information as graphs, tables and charts	Written
2 Use of apparatus and measuring instruments	Using measuring instruments Estimating physical quantities	Individual practical
3 Observation	Making and interpreting observations	Group practical
4 Interpretation and application	(i) Interpreting presented information *Judging the applicability of a given generalisation* *Distinguishing degrees of inference* (ii) Applying science concepts to make sense of new information *Generating alternative hypotheses*	Written
5 Planning of investigations	Planning parts of investigations Planning entire investigations *Identifying or proposing testable statements*	Written
6 Performance of investigations	Performing entire investigations	Individual practical

Figure 6.1   The skills and abilities within scientific methodologies

Thirdly, an *activity* which a child might commonly carry out under the heading of science is selected, and the *individual elements are 'spotted'*. An example of this was the investigation into floating and sinking carried out by children as part of the Key Stage 1 SAT investigation in 1991, where most of the statements of attainment were assessed within a single activity, although not necessarily very well. The investigation did not seem to fit any of Lawson's learning cycles described above.

The ENCA project constructed a model of Scientific Investigation (Sc1) where the elements contained within the statements of attainment were placed within the framework of a total process. The project of course had to work with the 1989 Statutory Orders, but the principles remain very much the same for 1991. Once a general framework had

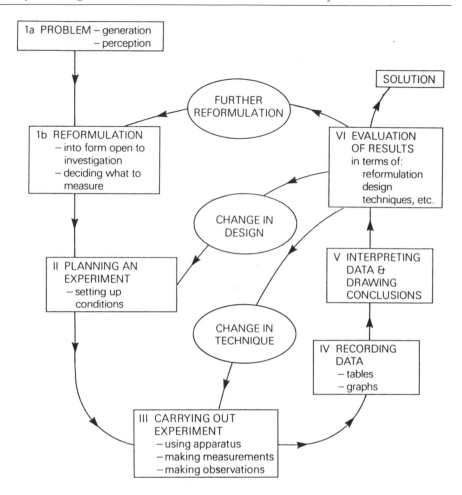

Figure 6.2   The APU model of the scientific investigative process

been constructed, specific elements within the process were identified and the statements of attainment related to these. Essentially the whole process was specified and then statements of attainments were incorporated. Once this had been done, a suitable investigatory activity was selected and related to the model.

When planning assessments of young children's attainments in scientific investigations, the following need to be considered:

Scientific context

- This should be *novel*. If the child has already investigated the topic area (the context), then recall rather than process skills may be being measured.

- It should be *within the child's experience*. If he or she is required to investigate obscure, unfamiliar or inaccessible topic areas and concepts, then investigational skills may not be being assessed.
- It needs to engage the child's *interest*, suggest obvious ways of purposeful, practical exploration, be stimulating and be likely to cause spontaneous discussion.
- It has to be *feasible* within classroom and time resources.
- The child must attain an *outcome* which satisfies his or her *purposes*. At the end of the investigation the child should draw conclusions that he or she regards as appropriate and satisfactory, and events that are being investigated should be consistent and repeatable.
- *Variables* must be easily identifiable, controllable and measurable. Investigations requiring the use of 'control experiments' are not appropriate for young children. Measurements should be made with simple instruments (e.g. rulers – see below).

The assessment context

- This can be *either holistic or atomistic*. Assessments can be carried out holistically as complete investigations or atomistically by assessing individual skills in isolation or at a more central point on this continuum where a group of skills would be assessed. Holistic assessments are likely to give more valid measures, atomistic more dependable measures (see Chapter 2).
- The *context* can be *open or closed*. In a completely 'open' investigation, no constraints would be placed upon the learner about what to investigate and how to go about it. In a 'closed' activity, both the topic and methodology would be pre-specified. 'Open' investigations may yield assessment outcomes that are high in validity. 'Closed' investigations may yield outcomes which are high in dependability if they have performance criteria which are standard and specifiable.
- Open, holistic investigations lend themselves to assessment via *differentiation by outcome* as the child can demonstrate his or her own level of attainment. Closed, atomistic activities require assessment to be carried out via *differentiation by task* as each skill or ability is assessed individually.

Classroom context

- Assessments are likely to be more valid if they take place in the *environment* normally experienced by the child. In most primary classrooms, science lessons take place with children working collaboratively in small groups of between two and four. In this situation, several issues must be considered.

- *Groupings* must be carefully chosen so as not to influence unduly children's attainments.
- Children may *collaborate* under other circumstances, in fact this may be what the teacher wants to encourage! However, for assessment purposes this may cause problems, since the teacher must decide what contribution each child has made.
- Children should be assessed individually, since *imitation of responses* may occur. The opposite process to this is of course possible too. Children may hear what one child says and think they have to say something different.
- The performance of one child should not be assessed through the *performance of a group*. Group outcomes are undependable indicators of the individual performances within them.

Performance criteria

These need to be made explicit. Having determined what statement is to be assessed, and through which activities, it is necessary to determine *what performance would constitute attainment*. Judgements in science are often concerned with the interpretation of terms such as 'measurement', 'hypothesis', 'prediction', 'generalisation' and so on. This can prove to be demanding and problematic. Good assessment is concerned with making interpretations and evidence explicit.

Assessment domains in scientific investigations are often fairly open, i.e. there is an indeterminate number of *possible outcomes*. For example, whereas there are a limited number of addition facts involving numbers up to 10 and one unique correct answer for each, the same is not true for the possible reasons associated with why objects float or sink. The teacher may be faced with making fairly difficult decisions about how much and what parts of the domain are required for mastery to be attained. Information concerning science investigation was available from SEAC in the School Assessment Folder for both the 1991 and 1992 Standard assessments. Although this has been of some value, it has not always been consistent about statements within the Statutory Orders or about the performance criteria and the mastery definitions contained in the different examples.

The nature of the evidence

Any evidence of attainment may be in one of four forms: *verbal, written, behavioural* or *artefactual*. Much of the evidence that is important to the assessment of scientific investigations arises from what a child says or does. During classroom assessment it is important to have *planned* for what evidence is to be gathered, since recording forms with performance criteria explicitly stated and room for comments or verbatims are helpful, even vital.

One further point arises concerning *verbal responses*. A central skill in scientific investigation is a child's ability to generalise. Great care needs to be taken to ensure that children's ability or inability to handle the language involved does not act as a barrier to demonstrating that a general principle has been understood.

'*The stone sank because it was heavy. The wood floated because it was light*' may be individual statements about two different objects or they may be the child's way of making a general statement by relating it to specific events. Only by discussing this with the child is the teacher able to make a judgement.

Changing the *physical resources* available may also affect the demands on the child and the dependability of the assessment. For example, in the 1991 Standard Assessment Task (Sc1) 'Floating and Sinking', children were required to use a top pan, spring compression balance (kitchen scales). The ENCA project investigated the range of balances commonly available to schools. The project found tremendous diversity in terms of the range, method of operation, unit calibration, scale markings and even the linearity of the scale. The balance used could significantly change the demands of the task for the child. The quantity being measured, the nature of the instrument, the graduations and labelling of the scale all have an influence on the outcome of any assessment. The same was true of the objects provided to the children to test for flotation. For example, a small stone and a large block of wood represents a more cognitively demanding situation than a large stone and a small block of wood. For consistent, dependable assessments:

- *Objects and materials* to be investigated should be carefully chosen and controlled.
- *Measuring instruments* should be familiar to the children. They should have scales that are linear and, wherever possible, are graduated in appropriate units.
- Resources need to be *appropriate* to their use and in *good condition*. The ENCA project found many schools with poor, scratched, low quality magnifiers, with a degree of magnification that was too low to be of any benefit.

More specific assessment issues in Scientific Investigation

A number of the findings from the 1991 evaluation of Key Stage 1 assessments are relevant to the new Attainment Targets (DES, 1991).

Strand (i): 'Ask questions, predict and hypothesise'

There are considerable difficulties with interpretation here, similar to those that existed in the 1989 Statutory Orders. At Level 2, children are required to: *'ask questions such as "how?", "why?" and "what will happen if?", suggest ideas and make predictions'*. At Level 3, they are required to *'suggest questions, ideas and predictions based on everyday experience which can be tested'*. It is difficult to discern the difference between these statements other than the words *'which can be tested'*, and almost any question can be tested in some manner. Both statements seem to imply that all three elements – questioning, suggesting ideas and predicting – are necessary for the statement to be attained. The ENCA project found that:

- 98% of seven-year-old children could suggest an idea when given a question;
- 38% of children could suggest a question about the specific topic in hand and suggest an idea.

This might indicate that suggesting ideas and making predictions is a more appropriate demand for Level 2 children and asking questions could be kept until Level 3.

Strand (ii): 'Observe, measure and manipulate variables'

There is no mention in the statements of attainment at the first three levels in this Attainment Target of the term *'variable'*, yet the identification and control of variables is a fundamental aspect of a child's developing ability to investigate scientific phenomena. Given appropriate scientific contexts and easily manipulated variables (see above), young children are quite capable of doing this.

At Level 1 children are required to *'observe familiar materials and events'*. The ENCA project found significantly differing facility levels for *materials* (92%) and *events* (60%), suggesting that these two aspects present different demands for the child. This suggests that they should be at different levels. The project also found that there was considerable diversity in *what* children observed: some described in considerable detail whereas others gave very basic accounts. Observation is not a 'once and for all' state; rather, it is something that becomes increasingly differentiated as the child develops. It would be appropriate to have statements at each level, indicating how a child's performance might be expected to improve. Similarly, one would expect to see some progression in the child's ability to make and record measurements and to deal with more complex and cognitively demanding variables during investigations.

At Level 3 the statement provides an interesting illustration of difficulty of interpretation. It states: '*Pupils should observe closely and quantify by measuring using appropriate instruments.*'

Firstly, there is a syntactic problem here. Are pupils being encouraged to observe closely and measure at the same time or are these two distinct and possibly unrelated activities? If the latter, are pupils being required to (*a*) observe closely and (*b*) quantify by measuring using appropriate instruments? Secondly, what constitutes '*appropriate*'? What degree of accuracy is required? Is the child to state the units? Is the measurement to be recorded? All these aspects will bear on the outcomes of an assessment.

Strand (iii): 'Interpret their results and evaluate scientific evidence'
Some of the vagueness that characterised Sc1 in the 1989 Statutory Orders appears again in the 1991 version. As we have emphasised throughout this book, agreeing how statements of attainment are to be interpreted is fundamental to the dependability of a national system of assessment. For example, the 1991 Level 3 statement from this strand states that '*Pupils should . . . distinguish between a description of what they observed and a simple explanation of how and why it happened.*'

What does this mean? The performance verb here is '*distinguish*', which is given in the dictionary (OED) as 'divide into classes, differentiate, draw distinctions'. So, given a description of what they observed and given a simple explanation of how and why it happened, the child, at most, is required to draw distinctions between them. There is no suggestion in the statement that the child is either to state what he or she observed or give a simple explanation. But the non-statutory exemplification printed alongside indicates that pupils could 'come to a generalised statement'. Nor is it clear how the Level 2 statement differs from the Level 3 statement.

Both the SEAC exemplification material in the School Assessment Folder and the Evidence of Attainment in the 1991 SATs indicated that the critical difference is whether children can make a *particular* statement (Level 2) or a *general* statement (Level 3). This was found to be an important step for children in the ENCA project. Whereas 34% of children could draw a general statement from the results of their investigation, 78% could make either a general or a particular one.

The ability to generalise is very important in describing relationships between variables, constructing hypotheses, making and testing predictions, and drawing and evaluating conclusions.

Teachers, however, had some difficulty in determining what was a general as opposed to a particular statement. One part of the ENCA project presented teachers with an assessment task and asked them how they would judge the evidence. Possible pupil responses were given and teachers were asked to judge where they were suitable to attain the Level 2 statement of attainment (*particular*) or the Level 3 (*general*). For all types of statement, both particular and general, more teachers awarded Level 2 than Level 3, and there were no significant differences between the proportion of teachers awarding both Level 2 and 3 to either particular statements or generalised ones. The only pupil response for which teachers were less inclined to award attainment at either level, was of a general statement that was obviously untrue: they appeared to be judging its *truth value* rather than its generality. There are obvious training needs here in terms of clarifying the issue and agreeing judgements.

The 1991 Attainment Targets appear to give a much more coherent view of how the idea and practice of 'fair testing' might be accomplished. Firstly (Level 3) children should see the need for it and then (Level 4) carry it out in practice. But what *is* a fair test and how many primary teachers could provide an appropriate answer? Fair testing is concerned with identifying the key independent and dependent variables which are to be investigated, and either controlling the independent variables or keeping them the same for different values of the key independent variable. This may sound complex, but it is not. Given simple, easily identifiable variables it is almost commonsense. But this does not provide a teacher with the knowledge needed for assessment. What is needed is 'on the job' training to help teachers to understand this in practice.

Time costs

Time was a major issue in assessing Sc1 on the 1991 Standard Assessment Tasks. No single Attainment Target required more time. One teacher spent 18 hours assessing her class on this AT! Perhaps it is not surprising that 16% of pupils did not complete the Level 3 assessment who should have been assessed at that level. It is not without significance that the AT was not included in the assessments in 1992, nor in the Key Stage 3 assessment pilots.

The influence of Sc1 on science Subject level scores

In 1991, Sc1 was the only science Attainment Target on which *all* the children were assessed by SAT, and of course the score obtained on the SAT outweighed scores given by teacher assessment, except in specially contested cases. There was also a complicated aggregation process to be carried out on the scores. The scores obtained in PC1 (Sc1) were, in the vast majority of cases, higher than those obtained in PC2 (all the other science ATs). The net effect was that the score obtained on 'Floating and

Sinking' in the Standard Assessment Task became the final level awarded to nine out of ten children for the whole subject.

Some conclusions about assessing Scientific Investigations (Sc1) at Levels 1 to 3

When teachers assess scientific investigations in the course of children's normal work, they are not subject to the time and content constraints of the Standard assessments. In practice, both teachers and children find it taxing to assess so many statements at the same time, and it is possible to achieve a saner approach to the whole process. A more sensible strategy would be to target a group of children and assess them on a limited, related group of investigative skills at one time.

As the child's performance is likely to vary according to the scientific context chosen, assessment should be carried out using a variety of different topic contexts to give an overall indication of a child's attainment. Perhaps most important is that suitable activities for scientific investigation are identified using the guidelines above. There is ample scope for identifying contexts with the Programmes of Study for Attainment Targets 2, 3 and 4.

Normal classwork is much more likely to give rise to open, holistic investigations and therefore highly valid assessments. A teacher must then determine whether the requirements of the statement have been met. In exercising these judgements, the teacher needs to be aware of what is taking place in her own decision-making process and continually evaluate how these judgements are being made. If not, they are unlikely to remain consistent and are likely to be marred by bias or the effects of teacher expectation.

Scientific Knowledge (Sc2, Sc3 and Sc4)

The remainder of the Attainment Targets – 2, 3 and 4 – in science are concerned with scientific knowledge: that is, the content aspect of the subject. All three of these Attainment Targets begin with the words *'Pupils should develop knowledge and understanding of . . .'* and are then qualified by information relating to the particular areas of knowledge under consideration, such as life processes and the organisation of living things or electricity and magnetism. Each of these Attainment Targets contain a number of strands: Sc2 (Life and Living Processes) contains four strands, Sc3 (Materials and their Properties) contains four and Sc4 (Physical Processes) five. Most of these strands correspond to the 'old' Attainment Targets from the 1989 Statutory Orders.

A major issue is still that of the performance verbs included within the statements of attainment. The first three levels require (in total) that pupils should *'know that'* (16), *'know about'* (1), *'know'* (1), *'understand'* (5) and *'be able to'* (6). Thus children are being asked for knowledge, understanding and the performance of scientific skills. The issue of where process skills are appropriately placed in these ATs has been discussed above. Aside from the nuances of meaning involved between 'knowing', 'knowing that' and 'knowing about', the use of the term *'understand'* implies a fuller grasp of the meaning and application of concepts. This is certainly borne out by the guidance contained in the science working group's report *Science for Ages 5 to 16* (DES, 1988). It is worth noting that, in the first three levels, four out of five of these 'understand' statements are in Sc4 (Physical Processes) and three are within one strand (Forces and their Effects). From an assessment perspective, one would expect fewer children to attain 'understand' statements compared with 'know that' statements.

Some background on scientific knowledge and children's developing conceptual understanding

Many researchers have sought to describe the development of children's conceptual understanding in science: Piaget, Ausubel, Carey, Driver and many others have studied children's developing ideas about the physical world. This has helped to chart the 'conceptual map' of these developing ideas. But as teachers and educators we need more than just a map. As Rowell (1984) describes: *'. . . the theories of the basic discipline (in our case psychology) differ from those of the applied discipline (in our case education) much as maps differ from itineraries.'*

In this analogy, psychology plots the map and the curriculum provides the destinations which, in this case, are the strands of the Attainment Targets. If effective learning is to take place, itineraries (*Programmes of Study*) are required and to assess a child's progress along these routes, critical points or milestones (*statements of attainment*) need to be provided.

These routes have not proved to be simple and straightforward: children do not always acquire knowledge sequentially within a concept field and therefore children do not necessarily master ideas in the same order. Learning is not invariably linear but can be branched or parallel, often with backward steps along the way. It is important therefore that the *milestones* (statements) do not become *millstones*: if a child appears to regress, important new knowledge may be in the process of being constructed and understood.

Just as there is no clear evidence to support *within concept* sequences, there is also questionable support for *between concept* sequences. Two concept statements may appear at the same level within the National Curriculum, but this should not indicate that they are in any way related developmentally. In practice, the ENCA project found that this was often not the case. For example, children's knowledge of sounds being heard when they reached the ear (95%) was much greater than their ability to explain how sounds were made in musical instruments (61%), despite these being both Level 2 statements.

A common element in all the current perspectives on children's learning in science is that they emphasise *constructivism*: that is, they subscribe to the view that knowledge is constantly and socially constructed. One of the most important implications for science education is that children are not blank slates but bring their own understandings and concepts to the learning process before any teaching takes place. These ideas are frequently resistant to change and persist even into adult thinking. They are relatively context-specific and children will often hold a number of conflicting ideas at the same time.

This has important implications for children's learning. Driver (1989) suggests that children need to be active participants in revising and reconstructing their ideas and concepts. Interestingly, the ENCA study found that less than 10% of the children in the sample had been involved (by their teachers) in setting targets or planning future work. Teachers ought to be able to provide appropriate experiences for bringing about changes in children's thinking rather than just supplying information, however practically this is done. As stated earlier, it is fundamental to the provision of appropriate experiences to the learner that an assessment is made of what a child knows, so that learning programmes match the needs of each child. If this planning process is to be accomplished, if the next step is to be identified, then accurate concept maps are required.

How good is the map provided by the Statutory Orders, and how well does it relate to what we know of children's developing conceptual understandings in these areas? As an example, let us examine Sc2 strand (i), 'Life Processes and the Organisation of Living Things'. Considerable research has been carried out on young children's ideas about living things, most notably by Carey (1985, 1987). Young children's thinking (from around the age of 4) is best characterised from a *psychological* rather than a *biological* subject perspective. One of the underlying principles in a *young child's* psychological theory of living things is *intentionality*, e.g. 'I eat because I am hungry'. Carey describes how young children see human beings and animals as alive because they exercise intentionality, and plants as not alive because they don't. *Older children* start developing a biological theory which is concerned with life processes and adaptation.

As described earlier, inductive inference is a basic mechanism for learning. Young children attribute animal properties from human beings to other living things according to the similarity between the species. For example, children attribute breathing and feeding in other living things according to their perception of similarity with themselves: young children do not seem to explain such things from a biological perspective, as they lack a biological theory which would allow it. At four, children are largely ignorant of their bodily organs and processes, and even at about age 10, when children have acquired a more differentiated picture of their bodily organs, these are seen as containers or conductors rather than processors. Ten-year-olds seem to have little understanding of what is involved in bodily processes.

A child's knowledge of bodily organs commonly precedes an understanding of the processes going on within them. National Curriculum science, on the other hand, indicates that children should know the basic life processes first (Level 3) and then name and locate the major organs (Level 4) later. At Level 5 children should be able to outline the functions of the major organs. This appears to be a rather simplistic view of how children construct their understandings in this area. The development of all these concepts – the processes, the organs and the functions of the organs – are interrelated; as children get older, for example, Carey found that their ideas about bodily organs become increasingly more differentiated. Here again, 'knowledge' is not of a 'once and for all' nature. Similarly, a Level 1 statement from Sc2 refers to 'living things' without any reference to the problematic nature of this term for young children.

The Programmes of Study appear to be better. At Key Stage 1, it is stated that children should have first-hand experience of a wide range of living things: they should develop their understanding of themselves in terms of how they grow, feed, move and use their senses. In Key Stage 2 they should identify living things using observable features. They should be introduced to the functions of the major organ systems, and investigate feeding, support, movement and the bodily functions of breathing, circulation, growth and reproduction. But there is no indication to teachers of how and what children might learn from these experiences, nor do the demands of statements of attainment always match with the Programmes of Study. For example, Level 2 demands that children *'know that plants and animals need certain conditions to sustain life'* and therefore most Key Stage 1 children would be expected to attain this. But this does not appear in the Programmes of Study until Key Stage 2. Routes are all very well, but you have to know where you are going and you have to make sure that your route will take you there.

Assessing scientific knowledge

The introduction of an assessment system alongside the curriculum provided the first experience for many primary teachers of assessing children in science. Whereas the assessment and monitoring of reading and mathematics were relatively commonplace, few teachers had experience of how to go about assessing children's knowledge and understanding of scientific concepts. Nor, with the exception of a very limited amount of commercially available material, were any assessment items available to teachers. How then might teachers go about assessing scientific knowledge?

As before, a key issue is *purpose*. If the purpose is formative, so that work can be planned to match the learners' needs, assessment needs to prefigure and be integral to the learning programme. If, however, the purpose is summative – for example, to evaluate what a pupil has gained from a learning programme – then this clearly needs to take place afterwards.

Some specific issues concerning the assessment of Scientific Knowledge

There is a series of methods that can be used to make an assessment of a child's scientific knowledge. Most of these come from educational research, but they are entirely appropriate and practical within classrooms:

- **Interviews.** Wherever possible, 'open' questions should be used to enable children to demonstrate the range of their knowledge.
- **Interviews about instances.** This technique involves showing the child an actual event, or a drawing or photograph of it. Children are then questioned about their understanding of what is happening. The teacher should use the child's own language rather than any technical or scientific terms. The use of a tape recorder allows the re-examination of evidence after the interview.
- **Annotated drawings.** Children watch an event (such as rolling a car down a slope) and are asked to draw a picture of what they have seen. They are then told to describe by annotating the drawing what is going on in it and why it is happening. The child might look at the event again and then refine the annotated drawing.
- **Free writing or drawing using 'log books'.** This is particularly useful for recording and assessing long-term changes (such as germination). Children are told to write or draw anything that changes and record their explanation of what is happening.

- **Structured writing or drawing**. Here children respond to specific questions such as '*What is energy?*' or '*How does sound travel?*'
- **Sentence completion**. Part of a sentence is provided and the child is required to supply the rest. This can be administered in either written or oral form.
- **Picture completion**. This is similar to sentence completion, but the relevant points are added to a picture. This allows children to use pictorial representations without requiring facility in drawing.
- **Matching and sorting activities**. Actual objects or living things, or photographic or other representations are provided and sorted or matched, to assess whether a concept can be applied. It is particularly useful for assessing conceptual knowledge involving the understanding of concept categories such as 'living things', 'things that melt when heated', 'transparent things', etc.

Resources

Changing the resources used may change the cognitive demands of an assessment. Wherever possible, assessment needs to be integral to the learning process going on in the classroom, both from the point of view of obtaining valid measures and also of contextualising the knowledge for the learner. However, this may not always be realisable within the classroom context, especially in the case of living things. The aim should be, then, to utilise the best possible representations. However, this can be fraught with danger. In the work carried out by the ENCA project, a picture of a toadstool was chosen, showing the underside. When children were asked to classify it as living or non-living, several classified it as 'dead' or non-living since it was no longer growing.

Assessment domains

Assessment domains in science, as outlined in the statements of attainment, are often difficult to define, open to different interpretations, or infinite. For example, '*know that some materials occur naturally while many are made from raw materials*' has an unspecifiable number of elements. What proportion of this domain (i.e. how many materials) do children have to know about before they can attain the statement? Other domains are entirely open to interpretation. For example, the assessment of '*be able to name the main external parts of the human body and a flowering plant*' relies on determining what is meant by '*main*'. There are over fifty commonly described external parts of the human body. The ENCA project found that whereas 100% of seven-year-olds could name a 'finger' and 85% could name 'wrist', only 22% could name 'forearm'. But the latter would seem much the most likely to qualify as a 'main part'. From both the teacher assessment scores and the SAT scores, it appeared that teachers had only required children to name the more commonly described parts of the body. In criterion-referenced assessment, all parts of the possible knowledge domain should be carefully considered when the assessment is being planned.

Timing of assessments

Since the aim of the assessment process is to obtain a valid and dependable picture of what a child knows and understands, the issue of how learning affects attainment must be considered. If assessment, as it is generally recommended, is integral to the learning process, then we should expect that the state of knowledge would change during learning. At what point then should the child be assessed? Clearly, telling the child the answer and getting the child to repeat it is not enough. For example, to tell a child that light travels faster than sound, and then to ask him or her which travels faster, does not indicate very much about the understandings being constructed.

The SPACE project (Harlen and Russell, 1989) found that important changes in children's understanding frequently occurred in the weeks following a learning experience. This seems to be the time when children revise and reconstruct their ideas. It suggests that 'tests' separated in time from the learning experience may be useful as part of summatively assessing children's conceptual knowledge. There is also no reason to suppose that once a child has attained a particular state of understanding, he or she will not regress. Indeed, regression can be a prerequisite to constructing further understanding. The measurement of attainment of conceptual understanding must be expected to vary with time: at best, all that can be indicated is the child's state of knowledge at one point in time.

Enabling children's performance

In assessing a child's state of knowledge, they must be given sufficient scope to demonstrate what is known or understood. For example, in the 1989 Statutory Orders, children were required to *'be able to describe the main stages of the human life cycle'*. The ENCA assessment involved the children in making a 'comic strip' of the different stages from when someone begins to grow, to the end of their life. During trialling, one teacher expressed surprise at what some 'low ability' children could achieve, given sufficient time and scope. She was surprised at the degree of detail within their responses. The 1991 SAT required only four stages of the life cycle to be described by the child for the statement to be attained. In fact, in the instructions to be presented by the teacher, four stages – the infant, the child, and the adult and old age – were actually *given* to the child! Children need to be provided with suitably open opportunities to allow them to demonstrate the full extent of their knowledge and understanding.

Some conclusions about assessing Scientific Knowledge

As with the assessment of scientific investigation, planning for assessment is of vital importance, including the choice of an appropriate *context*. Once assessments have been made, then these will need to be recorded in some way so as to build up an overall picture of the child's attainments. With the statutory demand that these be reported to parents at the end of each Key Stage, these records are a most important resource. It must not be forgotten, however, that learning occurs outside the classroom too, so checks need to be made that these records are up to date.

In criterion-referenced assessment, all elements within the assessment domain should, in principle, contribute equally to the award of attainment. Where the domain of the statement of attainment is large, or there are an unspecifiable number of elements, items covering the whole range of difficulty in the domain could be sampled. Choosing items that either all children find easy or all find difficult, effectively changes the domain and thereby changes the assessment criterion. For example, if most children at age 7 are expected to attain Level 2, then there is a temptation to choose items from the domain that ensure that this happens. The justification may well be that 'you can't expect a seven-year-old to know that', but such justifications *may* change the assessment from a criterion-referenced one to one that is norm-referenced. Norms may be used to calibrate the criteria, provided that the calibration does not change with the attainment of the cohort. The use of such norms may, in fact, make sense under certain circumstances. They may be useful in distinguishing levels of performance.

7

Special Educational Needs

One of the central messages of this book has been that the issues and questions surrounding the process of assessment apply, irrespective of the characteristics of any child or group of children. It is a message that was implicit in the chapters on the three core curriculum areas, since the discussion there covered many levels of attainment. This is not to say, however, that there are no issues and circumstances that warrant separate consideration, as this chapter and the subsequent one show. Whilst always stressing continuity and broad application of the ideas, nevertheless there are two groups of children who raise particular questions for assessment, particularly national assessments. Children with special educational needs (SEN) are one such group and are the focus of this chapter.

Such children are not a homogeneous group, but display a continuum of need which is varied and wide ranging. Current definitions of need are *relative* in nature and relate to *context*. The lack of a standard set of criteria which indicate SEN is problematic and it is interesting to consider whether a national system of assessment may begin to produce more defined criteria for the purpose of identification. As well as examining the purposes of assessment, consideration is given to current policy and legislation and the evidence which is so far available on the outcomes of National Curriculum assessment for children with SEN.

What is a special educational need?

The 1944 Education Act had established eleven categories of children with 'handicapping conditions'. Local education authorities were obliged to make specific provision for the special educational 'treatment' of these groups. Official guidance in 1946 gave estimates for each category, which constituted between 14% and 17% of the school population. Clearly not all 'treatment' was provided in special schools and the greater proportion of these identified children remained in ordinary schools. Until April 1971 a whole category of children, at that time referred to as 'mentally handicapped', were not the responsibility of the LEA and therefore were not entitled to educational provision. It was as a result of the Education (Handicapped Children) Act 1970 that a further sub-category, Educationally Sub-normal (Severe) or ESN(S) was created and this group then became entitled to special educational provision.

The Warnock Committee (1978) adopted a concept of special educational need (SEN) which related to the child's abilities, disabilities and all the factors which had a bearing upon educational progress. In attempting to assess the extent of SEN, wide variance was found between LEAs in the numbers of children 'ascertained' as having handicaps. Special schools and special classes were taken into account, as well as the temporary nature of the disability for some children. The Warnock Committee drew upon four studies which suggested that: '*at any one time about one child in six is likely to require some form of special educational provision*' (para 3.16) and that '*up to one child in five is likely to require special educational provision at some point during his school career*' (para 3.17).

The Warnock '20%' has become almost enshrined in educational folklore. Interestingly, it is not far removed from the upper figure given in official guidance in 1946.

Provision for this group of children with SEN was likely to take the form of:

- special means of access to the curriculum;
- a special or modified curriculum;
- a particular social structure and emotional climate in the education environment.

A new system was suggested to replace categorisation of children. Terms which described the child's difficulties instead of labelling the child were felt to be more useful.

- 'Children with learning difficulties, *mild*, *moderate* or *severe*', replaced the educationally sub-normal categories and described those children in receipt of remedial education.
- The term *specific learning difficulties* was used to describe those children with difficulties related to what is sometimes called dyslexia.
- The term *maladjusted* remained 'serviceable'. This group of children today are most usually referred to as having emotional and behavioural difficulties, or as exhibiting challenging behaviours.

A meaningful distinction, it was felt, could not be made between remedial and special education. As well as establishing the concept of SEN as a *continuum* rather than as discrete categories, the Committee also linked to this the concept of a continuum of provision:

> '*This framework is intended to establish once and for all the idea of special educational provision, wherever it is made, as*

additional or supplementary rather than, as in the past, separate or alternative provision.'   (Warnock, 1978, para 3.45)

Undoubtedly the Warnock Report was a watershed, which established a different way of conceptualising need and provision which has significantly shaped current thinking in this field.

The legislation which followed the 1981 Education Act took up the concepts of need and provision, and hence they became enshrined in law. However, the definitions provided by the Act, with a rather more vague notion of a continuum, are fraught with difficulties when identifying and assessing children with SEN.

The 1981 Act defines that: *'a child has "special educational needs" if he has a learning difficulty which calls for special educational provision to be made for him'*   (Section 1 (1)).

The definition under the Act of special educational provision is that: *'in relation to a child who has attained the age of two years, educational provision which is additional to, or otherwise different from, the educational provision made generally for children of his age in schools maintained by the local education authority concerned'*   (Section 1 (3) (a)).

The Warnock Report (1978) had also given emphasis to the notion of the integration of children with SEN into ordinary schools. Such integration could be:

- **locational** – that is, sharing a site with an ordinary school but having little other contact;
- **social** – having social contact with pupils from mainstream but not sharing the classroom or curriculum;
- **functional** – which would be the optimal level of integration.

The changes in thinking which have taken place since 1978 are widely recognised among educators as positive. Children's needs are described in terms which are helpful to those engaged in their education. Those needs are not regarded as static but can change, increase or diminish over time, and the idea of a continuum of provision has allowed greater flexibility and creativity in responding to children's needs.

The SEN assessment process

As well as providing a new framework for thinking about needs and provision, the Warnock Report also suggested a framework for assessing children with SEN. Five stages of assessment were to replace the idea of 'ascertaining' children with SEN. Assessment over time was felt to be good practice, with the early stages of identification and assessment taking place within the school setting, and with parents as partners at each stage. Stages four and five of the assessment process would take the form of a multi-professional assessment and the provision of a statutory assessment under the 1981 Education Act which may result in a 'statement' of SEN.

But this change of emphasis is not without its problems. The earlier process had fairly clearly defined, normative criteria, unlike the system that has replaced it. The boundaries have become somewhat blurred, and the criteria less distinct. Dessent (1987) points out that need relates to context and therefore the assessment procedure becomes more individualistic. It cannot be a standardised procedure and therefore the line between those children who are 'formally' assessed under the 1981 Education Act and those who are not becomes arbitrary.

It is interesting to consider therefore what effects a national assessment process may have on this debate. Certainly a more standard – though not standardised – set of data will be available at the end of each Key Stage of a child's education. At Key Stage 1, for example, the average range of attainment is likely to be between Levels 1 and 3 in each subject. It may be possible therefore to draw up certain patterns of attainment which may suggest a child has a SEN, whether it be 'minor or temporary' or 'major and lasting' (Warnock, 1978).

For example, it may be possible to identify pupils working within Level 1 in the core subjects of mathematics, English and science at the end of Key Stage 1 as having SEN. However, in the context of a mainstream school where the *majority* of children at this age are attaining within Level 1, then these children would not be perceived as having a learning difficulty 'which calls for special educational provision to be made'. Such a school may be meeting the needs of its children from within its ordinary resources. In a different context, a child who attains Level 1 in only one Attainment Target in one core subject, and attains Level 2 or 3 in all others, *could* equally be perceived as having a SEN – as do highly gifted children. Mostly, children have been identified as having a SEN if they have a difficulty relating to literacy or numeracy, but often with a greater emphasis on reading skills. It will be interesting to note whether a more equal weighting given to the three core subjects means that children may be identified in future as having a SEN because they have difficulty in understanding scientific concepts.

Policy and legislation

The introduction of a National Curriculum has clearly challenged educational practice, especially in primary schools. There seem to be

tensions between the kinds of cross-curricular approaches widely practised and the separateness suggested by defining skills and knowledge in
a subject-based way in the National Curriculum. From having a great
deal of autonomy about what and how to teach, teachers across the age
range – and across the range of provision – are expected to follow much
more clearly defined programmes of study at each Key Stage. This
particularly challenges the notion of a 'special or modified curriculum'
and puts heavy emphasis on 'special means of access to the curriculum'.

The DES (1989) document *National Curriculum: From Policy to
Practice* clearly stated that '*All pupils share the same statutory entitlement to a broad and balanced curriculum, including access to the
National Curriculum.*' This document, however, goes on to discuss
ways of adapting the curriculum by exempting groups of pupils or
modifying their curriculum, by using the statement of SEN to modify
or disapply National Curriculum requirements, or by enabling the
headteacher to disapply or modify the National Curriculum in circumstances set out in the regulations. It further suggests that, if necessary,
assessment requirements can be disapplied or modified whilst still
applying the Attainment Targets and Programmes of Study.

Although the principle of entitlement applies to all children with
SEN, the majority of these would have difficulties of a mild, moderate
or temporary nature. However, concerns have been and continue to be
expressed about the applicability of a National Curriculum for children
with severe or profound and multiple learning difficulties. It is not an
easy debate to resolve, but the present position would seem to be
helpful, starting from a position of *inclusion* rather than exclusion.
However, the skills and resources of special educators need to be
brought to bear in suggesting adaptations and modifications for these
particular groups of children.

The NCC (1989) Circular No. 5 suggested that only a few children
should require 'exceptional arrangements' to be made and emphasises
profiles of achievement which encourage self-assessment and which
record all that the pupil has achieved and experienced both in the
National Curriculum and more widely.

As regards assessment, it emphasises that '*careful assessment is a
hallmark of good practice*', and that the essential formative purpose is to
monitor achievement against each Attainment Target. It is suggested
that when administering the Standard Assessment Tasks, special measures may be needed, but only for a very small number of children
would the assessment procedure need to be modified or disapplied. The
use of *small steps* in assessment, common practice in many special
schools, is advocated for children with SEN. Most importantly, it was
felt that teachers' continuous assessment would play a central part in

National Curriculum assessment for pupils with special needs.

The DES Circular 15/89 covers regulations made under Section 19 of the 1988 Act which allow headteachers to make *temporary* exceptions from the National Curriculum. However, the circular *'does not constitute an authoritative legal interpretation of the Act or Regulations'*, which is a matter for the Courts. The guidance given in this Circular is about the use of temporary exceptions which can modify or disapply any or all of the provisions of the National Curriculum, which of course would include the assessment arrangements. It is stressed that such arrangements should be used 'sparingly' and 'only in rare cases'.

There are two kinds of temporary exception which can be used at the discretion of the headteacher:

- A **general direction** can be made in rare circumstances, for a period initially of six months. The three cases given are for pupils arriving from a different educational system; pupils who have had spells in hospital, home tuition or have been excluded; and pupils who temporarily have severe emotional problems. In each case the temporary nature of the difficulty would be stressed.
- A **special direction**, which initially can last only for six months, would be given if a pupil has a longer-term need for exceptions or modifications *'which can only be made through a statement of SEN, and temporary exception is necessary while the process of assessment or reassessment takes place'* (DES, 1989).

A special direction can only be given when a headteacher can present a clear-cut case. However, it remains for the LEA to determine whether there are sufficient grounds for assessment. It is also the case that:

- before giving a direction, the headteacher must discuss the arrangement with parents and the child's teachers, and consult an educational psychologist, medical officer or other specialist staff;
- before giving a special direction, the headteacher is required to consult the LEA.

General directions can be renewed twice for a period of three months only each time. In the case of a special direction it will automatically end when the statement of SEN is made, amended or denied. At this point it will be superseded by the special educational provision specified in the statement. It should be noted also that parents may ask for either kind of direction to be 'given, varied, revoked or renewed'.

The emphasis in this Circular is on the temporary nature of the exception and the anticipated rarity of usage. Although a direction is given at the discretion of the headteacher, she or he must consult a variety of significant others, including parents, governors, the LEA, educational psychologists, medical officers and other specialists. These safeguards mean that a headteacher cannot make a unilateral decision about excepting a child from the National Curriculum arrangements.

The later Circular 22/89 replaced DES Circular 1/83 and suggests three main ways of taking account of SEN under the new arrangements resulting from the 1988 Education Reform Act:

- In the first case the Secretary of State can modify or disapply parts of the National Curriculum and related assessment arrangements 'in specified general cases or circumstances'. This applies to pupils with or without statements.
- In the second case, for pupils with a statement of SEN, Section 18 of the 1988 Act provides that such a statement may modify or disapply any or all of the requirements of the National Curriculum if they are inappropriate for the individual pupil concerned.
- The third case given in Circular 22/89 repeats the general and special directions previously outlined.

Although an outline is given in these two Circulars about the special arrangements, LEAs will need to develop their own guidelines for headteachers, parents and other interested professionals. Some LEAs have already developed such guidance, or at least advice to schools, whilst others are adopting a 'wait and see' stance.

National Curriculum assessment arrangements did not apply to pupils with statements of SEN in 1991, although such pupils could be assessed at the discretion of the school. The 1992 assessments, however, included all non-excepted pupils with statements, whether in mainstream schools or in special provision.

The LEA should have a role in monitoring the circumstances and frequency of usage of these regulations. It would seem to be important to monitor the effects of arrangements for giving special directions on the numbers of requests for statutory assessment under the 1981 Education Act. It would be a retrograde step if special directions were used to request assessments for children whose educational needs could be met from within the school's resources. It could be argued that with increasing delegation of budgets to schools, it might be envisaged that the majority of pupils in mainstream schools could have their needs met without recourse to a statement of SEN. It would not be desirable to have an increase in 'mainstream statementing' prompted by a desire to modify or disapply National Curriculum arrangements. Special directions may lead to an increase in statutory assessment and in this case would also lead to a reduction of the usage of the stages of assessment recommended by Warnock (1978) and widely regarded as good practice.

A more positive approach to the assessment of children with SEN is to consider what adaptations may be made when administering Standard Assessment Tasks. Of course, when carrying out their own assessments, teachers will also need to be adaptable and creative in their approach. Teachers in special schools or units may already have a heightened awareness in the area of assessment. For example, they may be less likely to present some of their groups of pupils with either written instructions or written recording tasks. In such instances assessment would reflect classroom practice. For teachers in mainstream classrooms, where pupils with SEN are not the majority, special consideration will need to be given to presentation, operation and recording when designing assessments for pupils with SEN. As already stated, these children do not present as a homogeneous group and therefore such consideration would need to be given on an individual basis.

The 1991 Standard Assessments

In the 1991 Standard Assessment Tasks at Key Stage 1, advice was given in the *Handbook of Guidance for the SAT*. This stated that the SATs were written to accommodate the needs of a 'wide range' of children and that they allowed for teacher choice in how the tasks would be communicated and in how the child could respond. It was emphasised that adaptations could be made without invalidating the assessment. However, teachers were to consult about arrangements for children with statements.

In 1991 the emphasis was upon careful planning for children with SEN, with careful use of entry and exit points. The tasks were not time-limited, so individuals could theoretically work at their own pace. Apart from very few tasks which required group work, a child could also be allowed to work individually throughout. Further, it was recommended that support staff working with the child should be involved at the earliest stage in planning and carrying out assessments. The teacher was urged to use her or his judgement in discontinuing the assessment and finishing it at another time.

Children with a specific learning difficulty could be given help with sequencing before either oral or written reporting took place. Letter or number reversals could be accepted as long as the child's intention was clear to the teacher. Reversals were not acceptable when assessing En5 (Handwriting), and spelling errors could be accepted at Level 2 in En4 (Spelling) but not at Level 3. Children with physical or sensory impairments could use technology or aids which were usually available to them. Those with language disorders or hearing impairments could communicate 'in their usual way' and teachers were urged to ensure that these children understood what was being asked of them. Presumably for children with visual impairments, pupil sheets could be enlarged or tactile representations made if this was normal practice.

Throughout the teacher's book, specific adaptations were noted where they applied to particular Attainment Targets. No specific adaptations were suggested for English, but five were given for mathematics, in Ma1, Ma8 and Ma10: five were also given for science, in Sc1, Sc3 and Sc5. None of these particular ATs reappeared again in 1992. Specific adaptations in these cases referred to working individually rather than as part of a group, dictating findings to a helper, giving an oral report instead of a written report, 'indicating in their customary way' understanding of specific conceptual terms, or using a doll to name parts of the body for those with either physical disabilities or cultural objections, if necessary. The other specific note was a caution, rather than advice, about not affecting the assessment if a task (Ma8) was to be broken down into smaller steps.

The 1992 Standard Assessments

The general advice given in the Teachers' Handbook for the 1992 Standard Assessments was no doubt designed to complement the 1991 advice. In 1992 'exceptional cases' could be assessed in small groups or individually. The teacher or helper could explain the activity rather than have the child rely on written instructions. The term 'convey' was used to signify any responses which indicate attainment:

> '*Children may convey what they know or understand by any means appropriate to them: talk (in languages other than English for mathematics and science), writing, gesture, pictures, models or any combination of these, or other normal means of communication.*'

Such flexibility in the mode of response no doubt benefited many children assessed in 1992, especially those with significant language difficulties, severe learning difficulties or profound and multiple learning difficulties.

The National Curriculum Council (1989) had suggested extending the time that was normally allowed for an assessment activity or adapting the mode of presentation, operation or recording. The Council further recommended providing a series of intermediate goals when structuring schemes of work. It would therefore follow that the assessment of the schemes of work should also be broken down into smaller steps.

Whilst *general* guidance is given by the NCC, the DES and the SAT developers, the individual circumstances of each pupil are best known to the teachers, support staff and parents. Teachers have been advised about adaptations, but in reality this extends considerably the planning and preparation time involved in administering the assessments. Further, it is up to the LEAs to provide adequate training, both for teachers and support staff in special provision and for those in mainstream schools who are educating children with SEN in their classrooms.

Purposes and uses of assessment

According to SEAC (1991), the main purpose of assessment is '*to discover a child's level of knowledge, skills and understanding so that you can plan the next steps for that child.*' This gives emphasis to the formative use of assessment, which for most teachers is the daily reality. However, the purposes and uses of assessment are many. Some of these were discussed in Chapter 2. Gipps *et al* (1983) identify three main purposes: political, organisational and professional:

- The *formative* assessment process, as defined above, is clearly a **professional** purpose.
- Part of the national assessment process is also monitoring and accountability, a **political** purpose.
- Assessing for transfer (between Key Stages, classes, schools) and screening, are **organisational** purposes.
- The outcomes of assessment can be used for the allocation of resources and are therefore a **managerial**, organisational tool. In a climate of formula funding, this kind of information becomes particularly significant.

A major purpose of assessment is to help with the process of *decision-making*. Therefore screening and the identification of children with SEN should inform decision-making about the allocation of resources. In some LEAs children with statements already have an individual 'budget' attached to them. The effective grouping of identified children could, of course, make the implementation of resources more efficient. The identification process could also inform as to where in the school resources may best be directed, whether in a particular class or year group, or in a particular curricular area.

Assessment will also be used to plan the curriculum, evaluate learning, evaluate teaching, monitor standards, compare schools and inform the community. There are, however, many dangers in the notion of using assessment outcomes as effectiveness measures or performance indicators, and the notion of 'value-added' will be touched upon later. Comparison of raw results between schools, and indeed between LEAs, is potentially simplistic and dangerous, without any reference to context.

Galloway and Edwards (1991) view assessment as essential in the planning of future learning experiences. *Diagnostic* assessment will give a greater understanding of the child's mastery of identified skills and concepts. *Formative* assessment will inform teacher decision-making about what to teach next. *Evaluative* assessment will help teachers to review their practice, schools to review their policy, and will allow for evaluation of the curriculum. Gipps (1990) identifies the uses of assessment results for screening, diagnosis, record-keeping, feedback on performance, certification and selection.

In the case of children with SEN, early identification is important in order that an appropriate intervention, or response, can be planned. A child may be identified as having a SEN for the first time as a result of end-of-Key Stage assessment. The assessment at age 7 could therefore take on a *screening* function, as envisaged in the TGAT Report. However, the school would need to be cautious in the interpretation of assessment outcomes and to discuss what various profiles of attainment might mean. A child with a specific learning difficulty would have a very different assessment profile from the child with moderate or severe learning difficulties.

Screening of course is only useful if it is followed up in some way. At this point, once a child is identified as having a SEN, then further diagnosis would be needed. For example, a child may be initially identified because he or she attains Level 1 in reading at seven years old. In a criterion-referenced system such as the National Curriculum provides, the teacher should also know *which* of the Level 2 statements of attainment the child had reached. Perhaps the child has only failed to attain EN2/2f: *'read a range of material with some independence, fluency, accuracy and understanding'*.

This statement clearly has several attributes, which would require further investigation. A new teacher would not necessarily know whether the child was reading with accuracy, but not fluency, or with independence but not understanding. Therefore the teacher would need to carry out further diagnostic assessments to identify the area of need and set appropriate learning objectives.

The *transfer of records* containing summative assessment information provides a baseline for learning at each Key Stage. In establishing a *baseline of skills* for young children entering school for the first time,

Lewis (1991) points out the importance of classroom observation and information gathering from care givers. For some children, identification of a difficulty or need at age 7 can be rather late in the day. With baseline assessment on entry to school, the assessment at the end of Key Stage 1 would indicate progression as well as serving a screening purpose. A measurement would be made of the *'value-added'* by the school:

> *'It is said that assessments of value-added would distinguish between a school which has initially high-attaining pupils who nevertheless make relatively little further progress over the next few years in school and a school which receives a relatively low attaining intake but makes great progress with the children.'* (Lewis, 1991)

The idea of 'value-added', borrowed from the world of marketing, may serve to make schools less reluctant to admit children with SEN in the first place, or to continue to meet their needs within mainstream education. This may begin to counteract the idea that, if assessment outcomes are to be published and used as performance indicators, then children with SEN may be less accepted in mainstream schools.

There are many questions which arise from the idea of *baseline assessment on entry*. Which skills and concepts would be used in order to create a baseline? Would we, for example, use Level 1 assessments from the National Curriculum Orders, which do not formally apply until Year 1, or would we need to identify a level of skills prior to these? Would some children be labelled from their first day at school as being low attainers? At what age is the identification of, or screening for, SEN appropriate?

Labelling is a significant issue in any assessment system. Although educators generally have welcomed the move away from normative assessment (see Chapter 2), which previously had been used to categorise children as educationally sub-normal and the like, perhaps the new system of assessment will herald the advent of *'the Level 1 child'* or worse *'the working towards Level 1 child'*. Despite Warnock's (1978) emphasis upon describing the child's needs, one can still witness the descriptions being used as labels.

Whilst statements of attainment will indicate *learning objectives* for children, for some these will be long-term rather than short-term objectives. For a child with SEN, the statement quoted earlier (En2/2f), which requires independence, fluency, accuracy and understanding in reading, may be either very long term or unattainable throughout the child's school career. The skills of the teacher will be vital in order to set much shorter-term objectives, depending upon the needs of the child.

Such short-term objectives as defined by the teacher must also be assessed against, in order that progress can be monitored, feedback can be given to the child and parents, and feedforward to the teacher when planning the next steps in teaching and learning.

Reason (1989) points out the need for a finer gradation of steps for children with SEN, as progression between levels will be slow for some and non-existent for others. Pearson (1990), in discussing what had been learned from pilot SATs, asserts that:

> 'Assessment is part of a positive process whether this is teaching, designing more detailed instructional plans for individual pupils, identifying and solving problems or helping. To be valid, reliable and fair, assessment needs to be designed for each child, each class, each school, each purpose'.

This is a highly individualised model of assessment which sits much more comfortably with teacher assessment than with Standard assessment. It could be argued, however, that the setting up of a standard set of assessment tasks has led to very useful discussion, debate and training which will help to fine-tune teacher assessment, making it more valid and reliable in its own right.

Finally, perhaps, in this discussion of the purposes and uses of assessment for children with SEN, some mention should be given to *ipsative* assessment. This means that a child is measured against previous *personal* performance rather than against a group. This model of assessment shifts the emphasis towards notions of achievement for the individual.

Approaches to Teacher Assessment for children with SEN

Teacher assessment, according to SEAC (1991), is *'the continuing process of judging individual children's work. It can have both formative and summative purposes'*.

There are several approaches to teacher assessment, some of which have been introduced in Chapter 2. These include *general* classroom observations and *systematic observation*. Systematic observation implies that the teacher has planned to observe something specific, perhaps using a checklist of some kind. The assessment situation may be purposefully set up to see if a child, or group of children, can achieve a particular assessment task. Evidence from observation is more difficult to record than, say, evidence of writing or drawing. Video cameras, tape recorders and photographs can usefully provide evidence of attainment, but the teacher needs to be aware that such aids, unless used regularly in the classroom, may influence assessment outcomes.

Child-adult conferences are rarely found in primary schools, but could provide a forum for finding out the strategies a child uses to reach an outcome. Given a child who has completed a few addition sums, the teacher would not know *how* the answer had been reached without discussing the process with the child. A discussion could illuminate, for example, whether the child 'knew' number bonds to 10, used concrete aids, including less obvious ones such as fingers, was able to 'count on', and so on. There is a stronger tradition of child-adult conferences in the SEN context for diagnostic purposes. Lewis (1991) gives the example of using miscue analysis when listening to children read, but stresses that this technique can be extended to spelling, handwriting and mathematics.

When using curriculum-based assessment, it is suggested that a bank of *differentiated tasks* should be available for some areas of assessment. However, some tasks, such as writing, lend themselves much more readily to *differentiation by outcome*. In reading, the teacher would clearly try to match the text to be read to the reader, therefore differentiating by task. In writing, the teacher may ask the whole group or class to write a description or story, and to assess the outcome of this task separately for each child against a set of criteria. When differentiating by task the teacher plans to assess by certain criteria, whereas when differentiating by outcome the teacher decides after the activity which criteria best describe the child's response.

Assessment can be organised perhaps more easily with this kind of task, where the teacher can take the evidence away from the classroom and spend time considering the work against the criteria set. Much more difficult to manage are assessments of a child's speaking and listening skills, where instant judgements are to be made and where the criteria need almost to be internalised by the teacher. Attempts to tape or video children's speaking and listening may, as pointed out earlier, influence their performance. More complex still is the task of trying to assess a child's performance within a group. Here the teacher has to decide whether to focus upon one child's performance at a time or to try to assess all of the members of the group at the same time. Clearly En1 (Speaking and Listening) is felt to be problematic in terms of assessment, as it is not included in the formal Standard Assessment Tasks.

SEAC (1989) outline three principles for teacher assessment:

- the assessment activity should arise from current classroom practice;
- a task should build on a pupil's previous experience;

- a task should be clearly introduced to the pupils – who need to know what is expected.

Unlike traditional tests, the teacher assessment task should reflect closely the child's experience in the classroom and should not be unusual to the child. This suggests that assessment should be contextualised and should match the practices of the school, whether mainstream or special, where the assessment takes place.

For some children the units of learning need to be smaller and therefore the units of assessment need to be finer also, possibly occurring more frequently. Precision teaching, for example, involves teaching to specific targets on a regular, perhaps daily, basis. These targets may be a few words to be read by sight or some identified number bonds, e.g. number bonds to five. The ultimate learning objective would be broken down into smaller steps to reach this target. There would be frequent checks on learning against a set criterion. For example, the child might have to read three out of four words correctly on two successive days before 'mastery' could be said to be achieved. Only then could the learner move on to the next step.

In many special schools an objectives-based curriculum has been used for a number of years. Although this has been criticised as a somewhat sterile approach to curriculum planning, the use of fine objectives in assessment terms has merit. Objectives, of course, need to be drawn up with due regard to National Curriculum Programmes of Study and Attainment Targets.

For the first time in 1992 all pupils with statements of SEN, unless disapplied, were assessed at Key Stage 1. It is, of course, possible for children to access Programmes of Study and to undergo teacher assessment, but to be disapplied from the SATs. This may be an appropriate option for children with profound and multiple learning difficulties. The work of Aherne *et al* (1990) has given a useful lead in this area for teachers of children with severe and profound and multiple learning difficulties.

The 1992 *School Assessment Folder* gave more guidance on SEN than the 1991 version because of the wider inclusion in the second year of the full national assessments. The advice was intended for the administration of the SATs, but it has merit for teacher assessments also. During assessment activities, prompt cards can be used for complicated sequential tasks which incorporate symbols or simple words. Forms of communication other than language can be used, as can technological aids. Print can be enlarged or text translated into braille. Indeed, all the adaptations allowed in the SATs are also allowable in teacher assessment.

Teachers are well advised to draw upon the specialists from within the LEA for support and advice. Educational psychologists have assessment as an important part of their work and many services have now moved over to curriculum-based assessment and away from the traditional normative model of assessment. Many LEAs have teams of specialist teachers and advisory teachers, also well versed in issues relating to SEN and assessment. As well as drawing upon the support services available within the LEA, schools should also draw upon each other for support. More integration between special and mainstream schools in terms of teaching and non-teaching staff would benefit and inform practice in both.

The outcomes of National Curriculum assessments for children with special educational needs

The evidence currently available comes primarily from two sources, the reports on the Pilot work for the development of the Standard assessments and from the ENCA project which evaluated the first national assessments in 1991. These studies involved relatively small samples of pupils with SEN, but the information is nevertheless useful in shaping questions which need to be asked as the basis for future research and evaluation.

The SAT Pilots

Three development agencies piloted Standard Assessment Tasks at Key Stage 1 in 1990, as well as considering teacher assessment. These agencies were the Consortium for Assessment and Testing in Schools (CATS); the National Foundation for Educational Research and Bishop Grosseteste College consortium (NFER/BGC); and the Standard Tests and Assessment Implementation Research body (STAIR).

The **CATS** approach reflected the Warnock philosophy that children with SEN do not constitute a separate group of children to be treated differently. They advocated a flexible route through the SAT structure and gave guidance for teachers on adaptations and allowable prompts. Their sample was drawn from a group of children either identified by teachers as having a SEN or who had statements of SEN. There were no children with severe learning difficulties in the sample, but the materials were given to some special educators for comment. Their findings can be summarised as follows:

- Some of the provisions on children's statements were not being met during the SAT period (e.g. speech and physiotherapy).
- Children were generally motivated and not stressed, as perhaps anticipated.
- A 'pre-Level 1' set of materials was felt to be required, but there are no criteria before Level 1, making this problematic.
- For some pupils, more finely graded steps were required in the assessment tasks.
- The language of instruction was difficult for some groups.
- The SATs were particularly appropriate for children with visual and hearing impairments.
- Children with physical disabilities were easily included when adaptations were made.
- Children with emotional and behavioural difficulties sometimes had difficulty working in pairs or groups.
- Carrying out assessments on an individual basis made greater demands on teacher time.

The approach of the **NFER/BGC** consortium was also to present the same range of tasks to all children. Adaptations could be made to presentation or response mode, or to the time required for an assessment. There was felt to be some tension between the integrity of the assessment system as a whole and designing assessments which would do justice to children with SEN. The main findings were as follows:

- Children with physical disabilities were readily included in the tasks.
- Teachers in EBD (emotional and behavioural difficulties) provision found it almost impossible to deliver the tasks.
- It was more difficult to administer the tasks where there were large, as opposed to small, groups of low attaining pupils in a class.
- The majority of children with statements who were assessed, attained Level 1 or below.
- There was some tendency for teachers to underestimate the achievement of children with SEN.

The **STAIR** consortium adopted a differentiated approach to assessment tasks and recommended that thought be given to defining the content of a 'working towards Level 1' assessment. Children with SEN, it was felt, could best demonstrate achievement if differentiation was by task rather than by outcome. The main findings were as follows:

- Children with SEN in mainstream schools were given less support and prompting than usual.
- Ancillary staff needed some training.

- Children with emotional and behavioural difficulties fared worst because of difficulty working in groups.
- Children with moderate learning difficulties were able to succeed with a 'good proportion' of Level 1 tasks.
- Children with physical, sensory or language disabilities could achieve beyond Level 1 with appropriate support.
- There were prerequisite social achievements assumed in the assessment process (cooperative play, reasonable attention span, self-help and manipulative skills).

Further investigation into presentation, operation and response modes was recommended for all groups of children with SEN, as it was felt that minor adaptations were not always adequate. There were concerns about classroom management during the SAT period, as well as the issues of reporting to parents and judging schools on their results.

It must of course be emphasised that the pilot tasks were quite different in scope from the current versions, which are considerably pruned down. However, the pilot studies highlighted some important issues which bear further consideration. The SATs appear to be most accessible to children with physical and sensory disabilities where suitable adaptations can be made. Children with emotional and behavioural difficulties are potentially able to attain, but there are organisational difficulties where children find it difficult to work cooperatively. Although this is a real difficulty for teachers working with such children, the often very favourable staffing ratios in this kind of special provision should go some way to easing such organisational problems. For children with statements of SEN in mainstream schools who have emotional and behavioural difficulties, it is likely that their statements would make provision for some additional support where necessary. Adaptations to presentation or recording would also in many cases make the assessment tasks accessible to those children with moderate learning difficulties. Again, if these are children with statements of SEN, whether working within special provision or in a mainstream classroom, it is likely that they may benefit from a more favourable staffing ratio than is usually the case.

The groups for whom there is little information to date are those children with severe learning difficulties or profound and multiple learning difficulties. For these groups of children the pre-Level 1 criteria, which are non-existent at present, are a real issue. How do we record the achievements of children with such significant learning difficulties within the current framework? Access to the Programmes of Study at Key Stage 1 is a separate, but of course closely related issue to the question of standardised assessment. The STAIR consortium also raised the important issue of assumed prerequisite skills. No doubt these important areas will be the subject of further investigation.

The 1991 ENCA project findings

The ENCA project at Leeds University did not include any special provision in its sample but did include a group of children with SEN, either with a statement (8%) or as identified by teachers (92%). The total number of children with SEN included in the data was 233. The majority of these pupils were described as having learning difficulties. However, the sample also included children with language difficulties, behavioural and emotional difficulties, hearing and visual impairments and physical disabilities. Overall, the results indicated that:

- The attainment of children with SEN was significantly lower than the attainment of children without such needs.
- Those who did attain at Level 3 were those with physical disabilities or sensory impairments.
- Most children in the SEN sample attained at Level 1 in English and mathematics, but at Level 2 in science.
- More of this sample attained Level 3 in science than in the other core areas.
- More children were awarded 'W' (working towards Level 1) in mathematics than in English and science.

The size and diversity of the sample makes it difficult to draw any detailed conclusions from this data. However, comments were also elicited from headteachers of mainstream schools about the effects of SATs on their school. Many of these headteachers expressed concern that support was being focussed on Year 2 classrooms, with resulting detrimental effects on other children who should have been receiving support. Not only was teacher support redeployed to Year 2 classes, but so were parent helpers, ancillary staff and E2L teachers. The headteachers in the sample negatively rated the influence of the assessments on the wider aspects of school life – for example, the general behaviour of children and the provision for children with learning and behaviour difficulties. All these are significant points, to be taken seriously, since the year-on-year effects could be considerable.

Conclusions

The principle of entitlement to a broad and balanced curriculum is now established, under the 1988 Education Reform Act, for *all* children regardless of ability. It follows that, if children are to follow a curriculum, then progress within this curriculum must be assessed. In mainstream schools, various profiles of attainment may inform the teacher as to the nature of the child's SEN if this has not previously been identified. The assessment process will also help to define specific teaching objectives and provide a wealth of diagnostic information about an individual. More rigorous screening and identification may also inform the way in which resources are distributed within schools. There are, however, dangers in publishing raw results, which are open to misinterpretation. The notion of value-added would therefore seem worthy of further exploration in the educational context.

In special schools and units it is more likely that children's SEN have already been formally identified under the 1981 Education Act. The focus of assessment would therefore be formative and ipsative. Teachers may need to finely grade assessment tasks in order that progression can be monitored. This would serve to emphasise the notion of achievement rather than attainment, especially for those pupils who will spend most of their school career working within Level 1. A standardised set of assessment criteria which work towards Level 1 attainments may be helpful to teachers and to parents in sharing a common understanding of what their children can do and what the next steps in learning are likely to be. Earlier assessments could be considered, in conjunction with baseline information gathered on entry to the mainstream primary school. This would be important if the value-added by a school was to be measured.

In both mainstream schools and in special provision, there are many non-teaching staff who work alongside children in the classroom, and who support the role of the teacher. It is of real importance that teaching *and* non-teaching staff are trained together for assessment training, so that they share a common understanding of the assessment process. When so much assessment is based on observation, then it is important that all those involved in the classroom are able to interpret their observations, to inform both assessment and planning.

Although the Standard Assessment Tasks at Key Stage 1 can potentially be made accessible through adaptation to the majority of pupils, it seems likely that as the child moves through the Key Stages, the Standard assessments may become less appropriate. The practical nature of the assessment will almost certainly diminish and the demands on literacy skills and cognitive skills will no doubt increase. For some children, the SAT will therefore become an insurmountable obstacle. By judicious use of differentiation, programmes of study should remain accessible to most pupils even if their attainments remain within the Key Stage 1 range. A written SAT will be totally inaccessible for children with severe, and profound and multiple, learning difficulties. The focus should therefore be upon refining Teacher Assessment so that it is of the very highest standard whilst being readily tailored to meet individual needs.

8

Assessing Bilingual Children

The second group of children whose qualities and skills pose particular challenges in terms of accurate assessment are children for whom English is not a first or home language. These children may be or may become bilingual, trilingual or even multi-lingual, frequently displaying enormous facility in two or more languages. However, many arrive in school with little initial experience of English and must rapidly learn in order to benefit from what the school has to offer. Learning to function in another language, however, takes time and experience, experience which many seven-year-olds have not really had the opportunity to exploit. Yet they must mostly be involved in the end-of-Key Stage assessments, posing particular challenges for their teachers and for the system.

This chapter looks at the needs of bilingual children in the context of the National Curriculum assessment system. In doing so, attention is given to basic questions of the nature of bilingualism and the issue of language proficiency. Central questions about assessment, covered in Chapter 2, are picked up again here. Direct reference is made to the available research evidence. It is important to recognise the distinction between a *special need* which relates to linguistic proficiency and a *Special Educational Need*, as defined by the 1981 Education Act. In this context, the situation for some children in Wales must be borne in mind.

Defining terms

What is problematic about the term *bilingualism* is that it gives no indication of the degree of proficiency in the languages spoken, nor does it always indicate the full range of languages in use.

A group of so-called bilingual seven-year-olds might display a continuum of language skills. Some would have parents who were educated in Britain and for whom English is the preferred language for daily communication at home, to others whose parents have little or no use of English, so that English is rarely used in the home. Where there are several school-age siblings in a family, a situation sometimes exists where the children use mostly English among themselves, but not with their parents.

Some definitions of bilingualism demand complete fluency in two languages, without accent, in all language skills, including reading and writing. However, less rigorous definitions involve being able to use and understand some words in a second language. Those included in the first kind of definition would be referred to as *balanced bilinguals* or *dual bilinguals*, but the majority of two-language speakers would not fulfil such criteria. Speakers who have only surface aspects of a second language would be referred to as *incipient bilinguals*.

When considering the degree of bilingualism which a person has achieved, such factors as the timing and origin of learning a second language, the context in which the languages were learned, the degree of proficiency in each language, the current frequency of usage of both languages and the ability smoothly to alternate, or *'code switch'*, between languages should be considered. These factors give greater understanding of the nature and level of a person's bilingualism and, for a child, such factors are crucial to assessment in all areas of the curriculum.

The term *bilingual* can also be an understatement of the number of languages to which a child is exposed. A recent example is given by an educational psychologist seeing a primary school-aged child, with his father, as part of an assessment of possible special educational need. At home the child only used Punjabi with both parents, but a mixture of Punjabi and English with his siblings. For five evenings a week the boy spent two hours learning to read the Koran in Arabic. At weekends he attended two three-hour classes in reading and writing Urdu. This situation would not be uncommon in many communities.

Although some adult bilinguals (Grosjean, 1982) have reported that their two languages sometimes get mixed, affecting their ability to convey precise meaning, bilingualism is mainly perceived as positive and contributing towards increased cultural understanding. As the project team for Language in the National Curriculum (LINC, 1992) suggests:

> *'Discussions of multilingualism have in the past often been afflicted by the misunderstanding that for a school to increase its knowledge of and support for languages other than English implies a devaluation of responsibility to give pupils a confident control of English. This is not so; multilingual language learning is not subtractive . . . but mutually additive, whereby the growth of competence in one language enhances that in another through constant comparison of the ways that the two languages achieve – or sometimes fail to achieve – identical or similar meanings.'*

This view is consistent with Cummins' (1984) 'dual iceberg' representation of language proficiency, as shown in Figure 8.1.

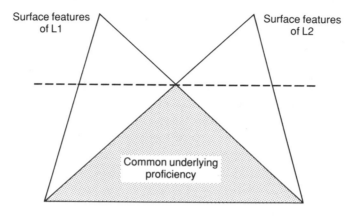

Figure 8.1   *Cummins' (1984) 'dual iceberg' representation of language proficiency*

In this model he affirms that experience with either language can promote 'common underlying proficiency'. This underlying proficiency makes the transfer of cognitive skills possible across languages. Further, he suggests that *'For minority students academically at risk there is evidence that strong promotion of L1 proficiency represents an effective way of developing a conceptual and academic foundation for acquiring English Literacy.'*

The theory of 'threshold levels' is discussed by Skutnabb-Kangas (1981) and is represented in Figure 8.2.

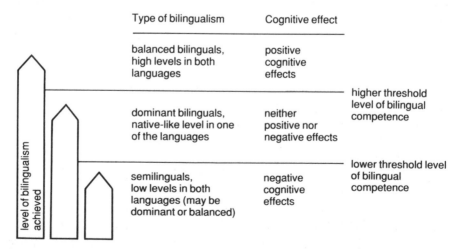

Figure 8.2   *Threshold levels of language proficiency*

The positive effects of bilingualism are clearer, as illustrated here, for balanced bilinguals. It is argued that bilingual children show greater flexibility in thinking and a greater awareness of language as an abstract system than their monolingual peers. There is also a tendency to be more sensitive to the social aspects of language, because of their more diverse cultural and linguistic experiences.

The question remains then that if we regard multilingualism as additive rather than subtractive, why are home languages not more widely promoted within the education system? Apart from the Welsh language, there is no evidence to suggest that the National Curriculum and its related system of assessment recognises or promotes the concept of multilingualism as additive and culturally enriching.

The status of language

Although this chapter focuses on the issues related to the assessment of bilingual children, it is important to underline the broader importance of language in gaining status and success both within and beyond the educational context.

In our society, language is a marker of status and power. High status is given to standard English, especially if spoken with Received Pronunciation (RP). However, Edwards (1983) argues that all languages and dialects are equally adequate for purpose, well-formed and rule-governed. So closely linked are language and identity, that to give up one's dialect or language is to give up a sense of group identity associated with solidarity, integrity, social attractiveness and persuasive quality. Also, any attack on the way we speak is likely to be perceived as an attack on our personal worth. Speech style may have a significant effect on teacher assessment and bias may be shown in favour of middle-class pupils. Certain speech cues may also trigger social stereotypes. It is important to recognise that such comment *'applies not only to bilingual children, but to speakers of non-standard dialects of English which have originated both in Britain and overseas'* (Edwards, 1983).

Black British children whose parents have a Caribbean background cannot be excluded from consideration when looking at issues to do with bilingualism and assessment. These children have not traditionally been perceived as bilingual, and the use of creoles may not even be recognised by teachers as distinct from English. It is more likely to be seen as an inferior form of English. It can be argued also that for many 'poor white' children, class and economic conditions are such that their needs should be seen as those of 'black' pupils.

We need therefore to avoid generalisation and understatement when we speak of bilingual children and to try to understand the uniqueness of each individual. To understand the complexity of assessment in this context is to recognise that it will always be incomplete and often inaccurate. We need to be conscious of the potential ethnocentrism of those involved in assessment and the prevalent perspective on 'mother tongues' as, at best, aids to acquiring English and, at worst, a hindrance and problem.

Edwards (1983) suggests that the educational establishment is slow to respond to the needs of bilingual pupils. A change in population should constitute a challenge to accepted values and practices in our mono-lingual, monocultural institutions. Above all, linguistic diversity should be seen as a classroom resource so that children feel more valued and therefore are better motivated:

> *'The failure by educators and academics to critically examine the implicit acceptance of middle-class dominant-group values in the assessment and pedagogical process has served to perpetuate the educational (and societal) status quo in which cultural and socio-economic differences are frequently transformed into academic deficits.'*   (Cummins, 1984)

Certainly, the message that is conveyed by English, rather than Language, being one of the core areas of the National Curriculum, is that it is English in our culture which is one of the most important areas of learning in our schools. A similar point can be made about Welsh, also represented as a core subject of the National Curriculum in Wales.

In the context of the situation in England, however, if a child is not a 'balanced' bilingual, then she or he will clearly be disadvantaged when being assessed against English Attainment Targets. Unlike in science and mathematics, the use of the child's preferred or most proficient language is not allowable. Assessment purely in English also fails to recognise the degree of linguistic achievement which a child may have acquired in the home language. Language is central to learning in school and therefore bilingual children, as well as being denied their full entitlement to the curriculum, may also be exposed to bias in assessment. The clear message to these children and their families is that their languages are not valued, either in our schools or in our society.

Cultural and linguistic bias in assessment

Gipps (1990) puts forward the proposition that although tests were originally introduced in Britain to promote equal opportunities, as opposed to patronage, testing is now felt to deny opportunities to certain groups. Further, teachers' assessment of certain groups of children can be influenced by behavioural rather than cognitive criteria, and can lead to low expectations of their group's performance.

The Race Relations Act 1976 defines two kinds of racial discrimination, one of which – indirect discrimination – is described as follows:

> *'Indirect racial discrimination consists of treatment which may be described as equal in a formal sense as between different racial groups but discriminatory in its effect on one particular racial group.'*

It is now widely recognised that it is impossible to achieve 'culture-*free*' assessment, although every effort can be made to make assessment 'culture-*fair*'. In examining cultural bias in assessment, the following factors need to be considered:

- the testing/assessment situation,
- item content bias,
- statistical norm bias,
- statistical item bias,
- the language of assessment.

The testing/assessment situation. However 'natural' assessment situations are made, for some children the unfamiliarity of being tested, particularly by a white adult, can create disadvantage. When questions or tasks are presented to a child and little or no response obtained, the most that can be said is that under those assessment conditions it has not been possible to establish what the child does and does not know, or can and cannot do.

Some assessment activities, for example reading and screening tests, are unfamiliar to certain groups of children. The assessment items are not contextualised and the very strangeness of the task may cause some children to panic and give up. Clearly, a fair measure of the child's attainments in reading could not be gained under such circumstances, but the results might be accepted as valid and reliable. This kind of flawed interpretation of test outcomes can be extremely misleading in any debate about 'standards', as well as providing misleading information about the individual on which to base further teaching.

Item content bias. As already stated, tests or assessment items or activities cannot by their nature be culture-free. The selection of items cannot fairly represent the previous learning experiences of children from diverse cultural and linguistic groups. The ethnocentrism of some standardised reading and language measures can easily be seen by looking at the illustrations and vocabulary content – for example, the use of farm animals and tea sets in test kits, or pictures of white children and their parents. Test items can be as prone to gender bias as to racial stereotypes and therefore can potentially disadvantage several groups.

Assessment tasks based on the classroom curriculum should be as culturally fair as the curriculum content itself. The content of assessment tasks needs to be firmly based on the children's life experiences.

Statistical norm bias. Norm-referenced assessment hinges on a child's performance being compared with a 'representative' wider sample of children of the same age, including children from a similar background. Given the unique and diverse language backgrounds of bilingual children, it is difficult to see how a truly representative sample could be obtained.

Statistical item bias or differential item functioning. This is where certain test or assessment items favour one group disproportionately. Again, this can apply to gender or cultural groups. Assessment items about certain food or social customs would clearly advantage and therefore disadvantage certain groups.

The language of assessment. The whole issue of the language of assessment cannot be separated from the much broader issue of the language of instruction, as earlier chapters emphasised. Even where there is acknowledgement and use of first language or mother tongue or dialect in the classroom, these tend to be seen from an assimilationist perspective, as aids to the acquisition of English rather than as vehicles of learning to be developed in their own right. If the child has been taught in English, then it may not be advantageous to assess the child in a first language, as terms and concepts learnt in English may not be easily translatable and may only be known to the child in English.

Good practice in the assessment of bilingual children should be incorporated within good practice in the assessment of all children, rather than developing policy and practice which is marginal to 'mainstream issues'. It is by improving assessment practice for all pupils, by seeing it as an ongoing formative process, by focusing on the assessment context, by questioning the validity of normative data, by taking account of the child's previous experiences and by raising teacher expectations, that most benefit will occur for the majority.

Whilst developing good practice for all, there are clearly components of the general approach to assessment where additional care should be exercised when assessing bilingual children. The areas outlined in this section ought to be emphasised and caution exercised. There would seem to be most risk in the use of standardised, norm-referenced forms of assessment. Although it has already been stated that no assessment can be culture-free, it can be argued that the most culture-fair form of assessment is Curriculum Related Assessment, with the proviso that the curriculum which is to be assessed is also culture-fair.

Curriculum Related Assessment (CRA)

A general trend away from standardised or psychometric assessment is actually upheld by the National Curriculum assessment arrangements which give emphasis to teacher assessment as well as to Standard (rather than standardised) assessment tasks. This shift in assessment practice also heralds a move away from psycho-educational explanations of difficulty or need to context-related explanations. Therefore Curriculum Related Assessment is viewed by many as a less discriminatory form of assessment than either standardised assessment or that which is based solely upon teacher opinion.

The importance of context

A model of CRA is put forward by Frederickson and Cline (1990) in materials produced by University College London, with particular reference to bilingual pupils . This model is based upon the work of Cummins (1984) and his ideas of language proficiency as context-embedded or context-reduced communication. In turn, Cummins drew upon the work of Donaldson (1978), who wrote about disembedded thinking, that is, abstract thinking not operating within supportive contexts. Donaldson drew attention to the 'apartheid' of disembedded thinkers (so-called intellectuals) and embedded thinkers. She pointed out that IQ tests offered only disembedded tasks, reflecting the value system of our society, which admires and rewards abstract thought:

> *'The attempt to become skilled in the disembedded modes of intellectual activity is for most of us defeating or repugnant . . . If this were not so, we should not have a small, smug intellectual elite, convinced that this one attainment is enough to justify their whole existence and establish outright their superiority.'*   (Donaldson, 1978)

In order then to support the learning of all children, but especially bilingual learners, tasks should be embedded as far as possible in context. Cummins (1984) points out that many classroom activities are context-reduced, whilst 'real life' is context-embedded. This would seem to be especially pertinent as a child passes through the Key Stages of the curriculum. The learning style of the classroom is likely to become less 'experiential' as the child increases in age. Cummins argues that the more 'embedded' the task, then the higher the levels of cognitive performance which will result.

Cummins and Swain (1986) put forward a model for thinking about language proficiency. This model has two axes, one horizontal with context-embedded at one end and context-reduced at the other, the other vertical with cognitively demanding at one end and cognitively undemanding at the other (see Figure 8.3)

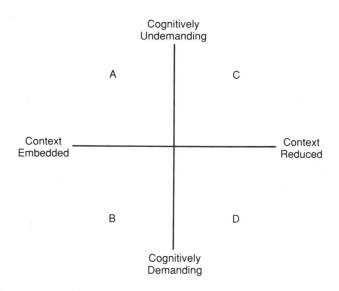

Figure 8.3   Language proficiency in different contexts and tasks

This draws on the work of both Donaldson (1978) and Cummins (1979), and makes the distinction between 'basic interpersonal communication skills' (BICS) and 'cognitive/academic language proficiency' (CALP). Frederickson and Cline (1990) suggest that:

> 'bilingual pupils are likely to benefit more from the learning experience if their classroom tasks, when difficult, are moved across the context-embedded continuum rather than down the cognitive dimension'.

It is proposed that the more cognitively demanding the task, then the more context-embedded it should be. It is not appropriate to reduce the cognitive demands of the task because of a child's limited language proficiency. In practice the teacher is urged to consider:

'a) *What the task requires of the child; an analysis of the task and its cognitive demands.*
 b) *What the child brings to the task in terms of his/her experience and current skills.*
 c) *How the task is presented to the child: to what extent it is context embedded or context reduced.*
 d) *What is to be acceptable as evidence of learning.*
 e) *How to assess the quality of different types of evidence of learning.'*

(Frederickson and Cline, 1990 , p.26)

Straightforward simplification of tasks is not appropriate for children who are bilingual and have no additional learning difficulty. This will lead to an inappropriately low conceptual level of work. The over-simplification of a task can also lead to the omission of important cues which support the child in 'making intelligent guesses', as demonstrated for example in the reading process. This 'guessing' at purpose and meaning is a valid and legitimate part of the learning process, if we view learning as a dynamic rather than transmissional process (see Chapter 1).

A helpful example is provided, drawn directly from the UCL materials, which illustrates the Cummins' model in practice. This example relates to Attainment Target 1 in mathematics (Using and Applying Mathematics) Level 1 (*'pupils should use materials provided for a task e.g. compare objects to find which is the longest, tallest etc'*.) The example uses several dimensions which can be altered to increase the context embeddedness of tasks. Within each dimension, context is reduced by moving from (a) (most embedded) through (b), (c), etc. (least embedded), under each of the relevant headings:

- **Materials**   Here, the emphasis is on activities based on using actual size, real-life objects (the most embedded), through using scaled-down objects and finally, pictures and more abstract representations (the least embedded).
- **Setting**   The most embedded settings are real-life situations, where the children may, for instance, arrange toys in size order as they tidy

them away. The least embedded activites may involve the use of apparatus on a desk top.

- **Proximity of adult support/feedback** The continuum here is from tasks where an adult is present, through the intermittent presence of the adult, and on to independent work
- **Language of instruction used, oral/written** The most embedded situations under this heading would involve the flexible use of everyday vocabulary, in the oral mode, through to using formalised, written instructions, for instance on a work-card.
- **Response expected of the child** Responses could vary from direct physical responses (pointing, for instance) which are the most embedded, through group and individual verbal responses and finally, written responses.
- **Task demand/cognitive complexity** This could vary from straightforwardly comparing numbers of objects, through comparing the number of dimensions of comparison, and finally increasing the total complexity of the problem presented.
- **Child factors**
  (a) *Motivation*. Using items that the child has an interest in, e.g. animals or cars. The child is likely to have a larger vocabulary in 'interest' areas and find working in such areas more motivating.
  (b) *Background/Experience*. A task which has a familiar content is likely to be more motivating and less cognitively demanding (the child can concentrate on the task processes rather than the unfamilar content).

In these ways, the child can gradually be progressed through context-embedded activities, towards more abstract, disembedded approaches, along these varying dimensions and according to the particular needs of each child. This kind of analysis potentially allows for a more differentiated and appropriate provision for children.

Language proficiency

Another crucial issue to be considered when undertaking an assessment of any kind is the child's language proficiency. There is often a failure on the part of teachers to distinguish between conversational or surface fluency in a language and cognitive/academic aspects of language proficiency (BICS and CALPS). Because of this, there can be a tendency to extrapolate from face-to-face conversational fluency, supported by many visual and auditory cues, to overall proficiency in English. Cummins (1984) gives an example of a six-year-old and a fourteen-year-old English monolingual child. Both can express themselves in conversation without obvious errors. However, the older child's English proficiency would be much greater overall.

If a teacher then assumes that a child is more proficient in the second language than is actually the case, this may influence how the teacher interprets the outcome of an assessment. As a result of this assumed proficiency in the assessment situation, a lack of attainment may be attributed to lack of ability, whereas it is really a question of linguistic proficiency. It is pointed out that 'immigrant students' (*sic*) require on average five to seven years to approach 'grade norms' in second language academic skills, yet show quite high-level conversational skills within about two years of arrival in the country, or indeed school if this is their first real experience of the English language. The danger of course is the underestimation of children's academic potential and the possibility that they will be identified as having a special educational need as opposed to a special need in language learning. It is also important to note that there may be a 'silent period' before the child achieves surface fluency in a language and that this can be regarded as a normal stage in the developmental process.

In the light of these issues it is crucial that the teacher becomes as informed as possible about each child's linguistic background and about his or her proficiency in mother tongue. As well as finding out about the child's language proficiency, it is important that the mother-tongue skills of the child are valued and are seen as enhancing and supporting the child's learning. One of the richest sources of information about any child are the parents, who will have lots of information to share about their child's language and culture. Frederickson and Cline (1990) highlight the importance of having detailed knowledge about what the child brings to the learning situation and what the child is like at home and in the community. It is of course good practice for teachers to have this information about all children, but it is particularly significant when attempting to make assessment judgements about a child whose language is not shared by the teacher.

National Curriculum assessment and bilingual pupils

The 1991 *School Assessment Folder* made clear that the child's first language could be used to assess all Attainment Targets other than English and Welsh. Bilingual assistance could be used, if this was normally available in the classroom. Therefore it was permissible for the children to be assessed in their first language in mathematics and science, although it was pointed out that the child may not have certain subject-specific words in her or his first language vocabulary, if those words had only been learnt in English. Teachers were cautioned not to equate a lack of English, or Welsh, with a lack of knowledge, skills or under-standing. They were encouraged to use mime or gesture to elaborate instructions and to accept a wide range of responses from the child. What was not acceptable was for parents to help their own child in the classroom during assessment periods.

The 1992 Folder added that non-standard English, including creoles and regional dialects, is acceptable in response to assessment tasks. Other acceptable responses included drawing or demonstration to support oral description. It was advised that children who share a language may benefit from being grouped together, which would allow for 'code switching' during assessment activities. The document cautioned against grouping children with limited English proficiency with children of lesser attainments. The bilingual child, it was felt, would benefit from being with children of similar capabilities, whether or not there was a mismatch in term of linguistic proficiency.

The *Guide to Teacher Assessment, Pack C* (SEAC, 1989) had this to say about second-language learners:

> *'The actions that promote the learning of a child who is not very proficient in the normal language of the classroom are the same as those which promote effective assessment.'*

This underlines the idea that teaching and assessment are inextricably linked where assessment is formative, and each informs and supports the other. It is also highlighted in this document that bilingual children may initially choose an observer's role if they share little of the language of the school. This is consistent with the 'silent period' referred to earlier. The use of home-tongue materials and support were recom-mended to ensure continuing language development. The use of other bilingual children or adults is recommended in both presentation of tasks and in eliciting responses. It is advised that a familiarity with the child's language and culture is needed in the interpretation of responses, as well as an awareness as to whether the kind of task presented is familiar or unfamiliar to the child.

The *Handbook of Guidance for the SAT* (SEAC, 1991) picks up some of these issues in the section on 'Fluency'. However, it clearly states that children should not be used as translators during assessments, and that support teachers need to be as familiar with the assessment requirements as the class teacher. Clearly, there are implications here for the LEA training of support staff of all designations alongside class teachers. Of course, the same issue will apply at the end of each Key Stage. So with these points in mind, what actually happened at the end of Key Stage 1 in 1991?

The findings of the ENCA evaluation project

The ENCA project looked at a national sample of 2,471 seven-year-olds in summer 1991. Within this group were 309 children whose first language was not English. Of these 309 children, 72% had as their first language either Urdu, Punjabi or Gujerati. Other languages represented in this sample were Bengali, Chinese, Malay, Arabic, 'other' European, and 'other' non-European. It is also interesting to note that a further 11% of this sample had another first language, but the teacher who completed the pupil information did not know what the child's first language was.

At Subject, Profile Component and Attainment Target levels in both teacher assessments and in the SAT, the performance of children whose first language was not English was significantly lower than that of their monolingual peers. Children from different ethnic backgrounds showed different patterns of attainment. In many Attainment Targets, children from Pakistani homes attained at lower levels than children from Black Caribbean, Indian or White homes.

The largest body of data was obviously available in the compulsory Attainment Targets. In these, there was good agreement between teacher assessment and SAT outcomes in reading (En2) only. In other compulsory Attainment Targets (En3, 4, and 5, Ma1 and 3, and Sc1), children generally did better in the Standard assessments than in teacher assessments.

It would be possible to draw from these results all kinds of conclusions about teacher expectation. However, it must be pointed out that this trend for children to perform better on the SAT was general and applied to the whole sample, as well as to the sub-sample of bilingual pupils. This may indicate that teachers had set more stringent criteria for all children than did the SAT.

During the SAT period there was only a small amount of redeployment of E2L staff to Year 2 classes. This applied in 9% of the schools in the survey. Although there was an increase in support in Year 2 classrooms, the converse is that it was withdrawn from other areas of the school in order to make that provision. No school in the sample had full-time E2L support.

The implications of these results (which did not apply in the case of fluent Welsh-speakers) are that certain bilingual children attain at lower levels in the national assessment system . There are two probable factors at work here. Firstly, this group of children could be being denied their full entitlement to the curriculum, with the assessment outcomes actually reflecting underachievement. Secondly, the assessment process itself could be putting these children at a disadvantage for one or more of the reasons outlined earlier above. Again, it must be emphasised that the bilingual child's language proficiency in his or her home language is not assessed or recorded, but that as second-language learners they are being compared in English with children who have English as their first, and probably only, language.

Underachievement

Cummins (1984) lists a set of variables related to underachievement in bilingual children: bilingualism, lack of exposure to the school language, linguistic mismatch between home and school, cultural mismatch between home and school, inferior quality of education provided to minority students, factors associated with socio-economic status, disrupted patterns of inter-generational cultural transmission as a result of majority-minority status relations.

These are all possible explanations for underachievement. However, he goes on to emphasise the last of these:

> 'Children's cognitive and academic development is a direct function of their interaction with adults both in the home and school and whatever can be done to validate and strengthen this process of cultural transmission is likely to contribute to children's overall personal and intellectual growth.'

This brings us back to the points made at the beginning of this chapter. The status given to English in relation to other languages within the education system sends a clear message about the value of the child's home language and hence culture and identity.

There was further cause for concern when the raw results of National Curriculum assessment were published in national newspapers (*The Guardian*, 20.12.91), showing certain LEAs as top of the assessment league tables and others, of course, at the bottom. It surprised few that those LEAs with a high proportion of bilingual children in their schools were identified as 'bottom of the league'. Along with these published results was an article which affirmed them:

> 'Ministers immediately seized on the proportion of pupils at level one as an indicator of a local authority's efficiency in delivering education standards, and discounted other factors

> *which might have a bearing on results such as levels of social
> deprivation or the proportion of children from homes where
> English is not the first language.'*   (*The Guardian*, 20.12.91)

There is therefore clearly a need for those with influence to understand
some of the explanatory hypotheses for underachievement rather than
simply to interpret raw data in an uninformed way.

9

Conclusions, Issues and Prospects

In the Introduction, the basic principles guiding this book are set out. It is argued there that assessing children in a classroom context, in a curriculum-based way, demands that certain issues be addressed. These are that we need to:

- understand more about learning and development in young children;
- understand more about teacher judgements and classroom characteristics/interactions;
- understand more about the nature of assessment and its role in the teaching-learning process;
- understand more about the subject-matter of the curriculum that provides the basis for the assessments.

The following chapters then seek to provide this information. Chapter 1 emphasises several important messages about children, teaching and classrooms. Our view of children, their learning and development has changed over the past decade or so, away from the Piagetian framework. Children are indeed active learners and constructors of knowledge, but that is not to say that the adult, as parent or teacher, does not have a significant role. Productive intervention can take place, and learning can be structured and enhanced through sensitive guidance and careful matching of new information or skills to the needs and present capacities of the child. Some understanding of how we take in information, process it and make it our own is important here. Attention and perception are very selective processes and this is crucial information for teachers.

As adults, too, we deal with information, learn and develop in a similar way – a fact that has particular significance in classrooms. Our perceptions of children, their responses, behaviour, work and attitudes are likely to be selective and partial, and it is important to recognise this.

Classrooms are places where complex social processes and interactions occur, which no doubt influence the learning process and our assessment of that learning. Social interactions constantly take place, behaviours are defined, judged and responded to, and relationships constantly negotiated. In such a context, expectancies are formed by all the participants – teachers and children – which serve to sustain, develop or change ongoing relationships and interactions. The expectations that teachers form about children and that children form about themselves and each other may be a significant factor both in the delivery of the curriculum and in the assessment process.

Chapter 2 outlines some general points about assessment, discussing different kinds of tests, different approaches to assessment and the important question of reliability. Since all assessment judgements will always contain a degree of error, it is important to understand how this can be minimised, leading to better quality assessment and more valid and objective judgements. An important message conveyed there concerned the central role assessment (of all kinds) plays in effective teaching and learning.

The approach to assessment embodied in the National Curriculum is discussed in Chapter 3. The characteristics and issues outlined there seem to represent, in principle, a positive approach to assessment and one that might enhance the quality of teaching and learning in primary classrooms. However, this will only happen if the emphasis is on formative assessment, seen in appropriate relationship to summative assessment, especially the limited kinds of summative assessment of the Standard Assessment Tasks at the ends of Key Stages.

Such assessment, whether carried out in an ongoing way during the Key Stages or at the end, should be informed by the kinds of issues discussed here. The strategies are, in general terms, the same. They involve the systematic noting of children's responses, careful analysis of their work, retaining some items as reference points and, from time to time, constructing special assessment activities for specific purposes (particular skills or knowledge). It is still very much early days in coming to terms with this new dimension of teaching and learning. More emphasis will need to be placed on teachers' developing skills of observation and on the skills of analysing children's work – written products or products of other kinds – with very focused questions in mind.

All of this has major implications for record-keeping. It is unlikely that any single approach or method of recording children's performance and progress would be suitable for all schools and all teachers. An imposed and uniform system would probably meet with little approval or success. Experience would seem to indicate that it is the *process* of arriving at an agreed and workable system in any school, group of schools or LEA that leads to the most productive outcomes. Discussion among teachers, with its attendant professional development, seems to be the key.

However, there is no point in creating elaborate systems of recording if they are not used, and used effectively. Records of children's performance need to be shared actively with relevant colleagues within school, and where appropriate across schools, as children progress. It is especially important at the ends of Key Stages which may coincide with changes of school.

The National Curriculum itself embodies progression for this very reason, but the standards implied at each level in this progression have yet to be established throughout the system. Again, this could prove a significant vehicle for professional discussion, leading to shared judgements across the 5–16 age range. If this happens, it is more likely that the full attainments of each child will be acknowledged, and learning not constrained or inhibited at any stage.

However, some aspects of the curriculum specifications, in the core subjects as well as the wider foundation subjects, may be unfamiliar to some teachers. Since effective assessment relies upon teachers themselves possessing the knowledge to be able to judge when children are demonstrating complex and high-level insights and understanding, this represents a challenge. Without appropriate knowledge on the part of the teacher, the quality of performance of some children may go unrecognised. Clearly, in-service courses have a role to play here, as have the subject specialists within a school or group of schools. This could be a particular issue at the end of Key Stage 2, one that urgently needs to be addressed. The introduction of non-mandatory assessments in a wider range of subjects only serves to increase the problem.

The three chapters that focus on the core-subject curriculum areas, begin to draw attention to these matters, and specific points will not be repeated here. However, certain general messages arise in relation to the three subjects:

- The curriculum specifications in the core subjects, the listings of the statements of attainment at each level, may or may not be appropriate. Some modification has already taken place in mathematics and science, and further evidence is needed on these. However, information so far suggests that some of the statements are not **correctly located** at their present level.
- This review and revision process will also need to address the issue of **comparability across subjects**. It is not at present clear that the attainment requirements at the same level in different subjects are equivalent.
- There has been much discussion over the years about the role of **context** in assessment. The essence of the argument is that the theme or topic area in which assessment items and activities are set, may have an important influence on scoring outcomes. Some children, for instance, may demonstrate higher or lower levels of performance if they are asked to carry out number operations in the abstract, using counters or counting pencils or sweets. Evidence from the evaluation

study has raised questions that still need to be addressed. It is certainly an important matter for teachers to consider when they are carrying out their own assessments of children.

■ When Standard tasks and tests are used for summative Key Stage assessments, it is vital that they are as **standard** as possible if they are to deliver dependable judgements. Administration procedures, instructions and materials must be equivalent for all children. This may give rise to a certain amount of professional controversy, especially among teachers of younger children. There may be sound arguments for allowing some flexibility, but the more leeway that is allowed, the less dependable and comparable are the results. Ideally, any variation in procedure, questioning or materials must be known and in some way allowed for or controlled in the scoring outcomes.

The chapters on children with **special educational needs** and on children for whom English is not a **first language** raise many specific assessment issues. However, this is to focus on only two of the many **background variables** which seem to have important effects on assessment outcomes. Children with special educational needs and children for whom English is a second language show particular patterns of scoring in terms of the levels of the National Curriculum. This is also the case for boys and girls, for children of different ages within the same year-group, for children from different social backgrounds and for children with and without nursery experience. The evaluation study analysed the results in the light of each of these variables and has reported the findings (ENCA 1 Report, Shorrocks *et al.*, 1992). Only some of the most significant findings will be discussed here.

The effects of certain background variables on scoring outcomes

Three of these variables were very pervasive in their effects. These were birth date, social background and first language. When scores were analysed at all the possible levels of aggregation in the assessments (Subject, Profile Component and individual Attainment Target) then **younger children consistently scored lower than older children** in the year-group. These differences were statistically significant throughout and applied both to the teachers' own assessments and to the scores on the SATs. The age-range within the total sample was between 6 years 9 months and 7 years 8 months. This birth-date effect was not confounded with the number of terms a child had spent in school. Given that this outcome is in line with other findings both in the present system and in analyses of other kinds of assessment outcomes (eleven-plus scores, for instance), then there is every reason to suppose that similar outcomes will occur at the later Key Stages too.

For **social background**, similar results were found. It is not easy to arrive at a straightforward measure of children's family background: really detailed and accurate judgements would imply quite heavy intrusion into families and very personal information being requested. A measure such as entitlement to free school meals is not reliable, since definitions of entitlement may vary from area to area and entitlements may not always be taken up by parents. For this reason, the child's address and postcode were used to give a general measure of social background through neighbourhood status. This is also not a perfect measure, but it is one that is becoming widely accepted in its validity and use. For children in the ENCA sample, neighbourhoods were divided into four groupings: high status, intermediate status (high and low) and low status. When scores were analysed on this basis, at Subject, Profile Component and individual Attainment Target levels, there were significant differences in scoring. Children from high-status neighbourhoods scored higher than those lower down the social scale. There was a clearly declining pattern of attainment with declining neighbourhood status.

The third variable, **English as a first or second language**, has already been commented on in Chapter 8, but is worth pointing out again in this wider context. Once again, the analysis showed that at all scoring levels (Subject, Profile Component and individual Attainment Target), statistically significant differences were found in the scores. However, Wales proved to be a special case here, since *Welsh-speakers* performed better than their non-Welsh speaking counterparts.

Some of the variables were less pervasive in their effects than these three, namely **gender** and **nursery education**. Here the effects were more variable. With regard to **gender**, some differences were evident in the scores of boys and girls for English but few in mathematics or science. Girls outperformed boys in all the English Attainment Targets and in the mathematical areas of number concepts and number patterns and relationships. In science, there was a slight indication that girls did better than boys in the area of 'Human Influences on the Earth' but few other statistically significant differences emerged.

Schools in the ENCA sample were also asked if the children had **nursery experience** of any kind, and roughly half the children (over 1000) fell into this category. Precise details of the type of nursery experience were not sought, so the results were of a rather general nature, but interesting. At Subject and at Profile Component level, in English and mathematics, children with nursery experience performed better than those without. This finding was not repeated for science because the outcomes were heavily dominated by the results in Sc1 (Exploration of Science), where no differences were found between children with and without nursery experience. At the level of the individual attainment targets, children with nursery experience performed better than those without on En2 (Reading), En3 (Writing), both in the SATs and in teacher assessments. For En1 (Speaking and Listening), this was also the case, but based on teacher assessments only. In mathematics, there were *no* significant differences in the number Attainment Targets (Ma2, Ma3 and Ma5) or in Ma11 (Shape). *All* other Attainment Targets, in teacher assessment scores, showed significant differences in favour of children with some nursery experience. For scores in the SATs, significant differences were found in Ma10 (Shape, conceptual aspects) and in Ma13 (Handling Data). In science, notwithstanding the earlier comment about Sc1, teacher assessment scores showed significant differences in all the other Attainment Targets, in favour of nursery experience. The scores in the SATs revealed a significant difference in Sc3 (Processes of Life).

However, this issue of the effects of nursery education is a complex one. Earlier findings from the pilot studies have not always been clearcut in their interpretation. For instance, the NFER (1991) found no such relationship in their analysis. In fact, in their sample, children who had received nursery education performed *less* well than those who had not. They did, however, explain that nursery education was being confounded with social background factors: their sample contained many children with nursery experience from deprived, inner-city areas. Nevertheless, the data from the ENCA project did show the effect and the finding is robust when social background factors are taken into account.

It is important to consider the wider implications of all these significant differences in scoring outcomes. The National Curriculum is an entitlement curriculum: it is the right of each child. Yet the results of assessing how well children have responded to and learned that curriculum show that there are systematic patterns of scoring differences. It is not just a case of individual children performing differently: this is to be expected and is one of the important dimensions the assessments are designed to reveal. Instead, it seems to be a case of *particular groups* being advantaged or disadvantaged in the outcomes.

In one sense, they are not new insights: analyses of scoring outcomes of many kinds have revealed such patterns, with younger children and children from more deprived social backgrounds performing less well than their older or more advantaged counterparts. The reasons are no doubt complex. It certainly has to be established that the *assessment materials themselves* are not producing the bias, whether produced by a national agency in the form of Standard Assessment Tasks or by teachers themselves in their own classrooms. It may be comparatively easy to monitor obvious sources of potential bias (gender-related, cultural, etc.), but less easy to recognise the more subtle ways in which bias may enter into assessment materials, through implied attitudes and values, pictorial representations and even particular kinds of language use over and above the obvious gender and culturally-related ones. It is unlikely that all such bias could ever be eliminated entirely, but very considerable care must be exercised.

Another explanation could lie in the *attitudes and expectations of the teachers* administering the assessments and making the judgements. Chapter 2 raised the issue and it is clear that it is a most significant matter to address. No one would suggest that such bias is consciously or deliberately exhibited by teachers. However, there exists by now sufficient evidence that teacher expectations may play a role, and that the best way of countering it is first to recognise it and then to devise strategies for attempting to reach more objective judgements, such as enlisting the help of colleagues from other classes and other schools. Even when such matters have been addressed, it seems unlikely that all these group differences in performance would disappear, since they are no doubt related to wider societal influences and processes.

In the present system, it could of course be argued that such differences in scoring patterns are irrelevant. What we have is a criterion-referenced approach, not founded on the idea of comparing individuals, but rather focusing on the attainments of children in terms of the specified curriculum. With time and appropriate learning experiences, all children will attain higher levels. In fact, the nature of the National Curriculum should provide a means of facilitating this. Such arguments have a great deal of face validity, until it is acknowledged that summative assessments are made and that the results may be used as a means of judging teachers and schools. In this situation, unless the comparisons are made in a careful way, based on properly interpreted scoring outcomes, then schools with disproportionate numbers of younger children, second-language children or socially deprived children will be misjudged and disadvantaged. Again, this needs urgent consideration.

Further issues

The original proposals for the assessment system, produced by the Task Group on Assessment and Testing, represented an innovative approach, grounded in up-to-date theories of assessment and testing. In theory they should have been workable, but in practice, given the kinds of curriculum specifications produced by the working groups in the different subjects, problems have emerged. At Key Stage 1 and at Key Stage 3, the points where we now have experience of implementing both the curriculum and the assessment system, it has not proved easy to produce appropriate Standard test materials, that effectively assess the relevant levels of the curriculum in the core subjects in ways that are both dependable and acceptable in the classroom. Also, it has not proved easy to generate dependable teacher assessments, largely due to the complexity and ambiguity of some of the curriculum specification in the statements of attainment. This has particularly been the case at Key Stage 1 and will doubtless prove to be the case at Key Stage 2.

Above all, adequate training and agreed interpretations of the meaning and standards implied at the various levels, is needed. In 1991, the ENCA project found that teachers were very confused about the meaning of certain terms – *'know'*, *'sight vocabulary'* or *'fluent'*, for instance. They were also not clear about the mastery levels they should use (*how many* correct sums out of a set of 10? *how many* 'signs, labels and notices'?) or whether they should consider each child's *average* work or only their *best*. The performance criteria used in the SATs were helpful, as were the exemplification materials produced by SEAC. With time, better agreement will no doubt be reached, which should help to improve the dependability of the scores. Validity will only be enhanced if these agreed interpretations of the statements and standards reflect adequately the curriculum intentions and richness.

Teacher responses to the assessments

The SATs for Key Stage 1, as deployed in 1991 and 1992, evoked a variety of responses from teachers and other educationists. Teacher responses to the manageability and usefulness of the assessments have been mostly negative, although the assessment materials themselves were often judged quite positively: many teachers indicated they might use them again, at other times and for checking their own judgements. Such strong rejection of assessment of this kind on the part of teachers requires explanation, explanation that does not oversimplify causes and motives. Evaluations of the 1990 pilot work showed that teachers often felt threatened and overwhelmed by the demands being placed upon them, giving them a sense of becoming deskilled. Such feelings do not seem designed to encourage professional development and change in classroom practice. Criticising the assessments and suggesting that nothing new had been learned about the children are effective ways of defending against this threat.

However, it has to be pointed out that such comments are difficult to reconcile with other kinds of responses from teachers. The fact that in some cases teacher assessment scores and SAT scores were different, might be expected to raise important questions about the performance of the children or the assessment process itself. This is surely a significant kind of teacher 'learning' and the potential basis for further professional development. It is also the case that in-service work with teachers on assessment often reveals that important aspects of children's responses are not picked up or acknowledged, once again highlighting the new insights and skills that can and should be developed through the process of engaging in a systematic way with assessment. More training and more experience may reduce these responses, engendering more productive outcomes and better assessment.

The evaluation of the 1991 experience showed that the *children* themselves were quite positive in their comments about the assessment activities they experienced. The vast majority enjoyed them, when talked to immediately afterwards, and few seemed to connect them with any national assessment purpose. Very few were upset by the experience, and many seemed to come away with a sense of success, perhaps a tribute to their teacher's skill or to the correct 'match' of the activities to their capabilities. As already reported, many parents were also in favour of the ideas of national assessments, both by the teachers and through Standard Tasks.

Aggregating scores

The fact remains, however, that the detailed assessments carried out by teachers for ongoing recording purposes or for the SATs need to be aggregated. Discussion of some of the major theoretical issues in aggregation was presented in Chapter 3, but the realities of the 1991 experience have not yet been addressed. Aggregation of scores happens at several levels within the National Curriculum assessments:

- aggregating the smaller elements, the attributes or aspects, within each statement of attainment;
- aggregating the scores for the statements at each level, to arrive at a Level score for each Attainment Target;
- aggregating the scores for each Attainment Target to reach a score for the Profile Component, where appropriate;
- aggregating the scores for the Profile Components to reach a score for each Subject.

Most of these aggregations are done according to rules set out in the documentation, except for the first. It is still not clear how the individual attributes or aspects within any statement are to be treated. It is also the case that some of the scores for the individual Attainment Targets are weighted differently in the overall calculations. The reason for this is the perceived importance of that dimension of the curriculum in relation to the rest. In mathematics and science, in some of the Profile Components (under the old curriculum specifications) many Attainment Targets were being combined, often from quite disparate areas of the curriculum.

In 1991, some significant issues arose with regard to the aggregation of scores. The first of these was the highlighting of the (perhaps obvious) fact that it was more difficult for children to attain some levels in some Attainment Targets, because of the number of statements at the level. This is a finding that continues to have relevance for the new specifications for mathematics and science, where the number of Attainment Targets has been reduced but the number of statements at the levels has been increased. It is also clear that the ease or difficulty of attaining the levels will be directly related to the ease or relative difficulty of the statements at the level. These sometimes vary widely in their difficulty level, as measured by **facility** calculations. Missing out a statement in the assessments and scoring is therefore fraught with problems, since the effects of doing so will depend on both the number of statements at the level and the difficulty of the omitted one.

Teacher assessment and SAT assessment

Early in the development of the Key Stage 1 assessment approach, it seemed to be considered feasible to administer Standard Assessment Tasks in *all* the Attainment Targets in the core subjects. Experience rapidly demonstrated that this could not be the case, at least with the number of Attainment Targets then existing. Reducing these in number has made this strategy more viable, always bearing in mind that any selection of Attainment Targets for the Standard assessments carries important messages to the classroom about their relative importance.

If all Attainment Targets are to be assessed summatively at the end of each Key Stage, yet not all can be addressed through the Standard Tasks, then the question of the relationship between the two kinds of assessment is brought to the fore. In principle, the two kinds of assessment should produce similar results: after all, the same children are being assessed against the same Statements by the same person. In fact, this can be seen as a measure of the dependability of the scores, the fact that two assessments agree. The two kinds of assessment may be different in terms of the nature and breadth of the evidence available, so the question is, how far should or will this fact create differences in the assessment outcomes?

In 1991, the two kinds of assessment took place at different times (teacher assessment preceding the Standard assessments), a factor that in itself might have been expected to create some differences in scoring, if only because the children may have made progress in the intervening time, or even have regressed. The assessments were also taking place in a situation where most teachers were unfamiliar with the performance criteria implied in the statements or the appropriate mastery levels. Both these factors could account for the disparity of scoring that emerged in the first year (see the ENCA Report, 1992). In some ways it is not surprising therefore that the outcomes were judged rather undependable.

In 1992, some of these problems were either addressed or were reduced as the result of experience. The two kinds of assessment were arranged to occur simultaneously in time, during the second and third terms of the school year. Also, the performance criteria for judging the statements had been to some extent clarified by the Standard Assessment Tasks of the previous year and via additional exemplification material produced by SEAC. Both these factors would no doubt serve to produce scores for teacher assessment and Standard assessment that bore a closer resemblance to each other. The matter perhaps not fully addressed, was the truly 'standard' nature of the supposedly 'Standard' Tasks.

By this kind of argument, teacher assessment and the Standard assessments can be expected to come closer together over time and with more experience on the part of teachers. What is still not clear, however, is whether or not they are so fundamentally different in character to suggest that it is not appropriate to combine them across Attainment Targets, where some are assessed through teacher assessment alone and others by Standard assessments, which in these circumstances outweigh teacher assessments in the same Attainment Target.

Essentially it boils down to the difference between formative and summative assessment. Teacher assessments will no doubt be based on broad coverage of the curriculum, Programmes of Study and the statements at each level, all carried out over a prolonged period of time. The Standard assessments represent a limited set of assessments carried out at one point in time and covering only limited dimensions of the curriculum. Insofar as it is ever possible to summarise detailed, ongoing assessments into an overall, summarised value, then the two may be comparable and even combinable. This leaves aside the theoretical argument about the nature of the content that is being combined in each case.

What all this highlights is the very basic matter of being clear about the precise **purposes** of the assessments and the role of the Standard Tasks within the system. Assessment can serve many purposes, and different purposes may demand different assessment approaches. Perhaps *too many* purposes are being confused at the present time. If the main purpose is to provide **summative** information for national monitoring and obtaining year-on-year data in order to monitor long-term trends, then detailed assessment of every child is not necessary. A carefully selected national *sample* of children would need to be assessed each year for this purpose to be met.

However, if the purpose is to collect summative information in order to allocate resources or to judge the performance of schools and teachers (never an easy matter), then information on *all* children is required. Meeting these purposes, of course, raises the vital question of the kinds of evidence that will constitute valid and dependable measures, appropriately interpreted.

If the main purpose of the assessments is to **raise standards**, then the central question is that of clarifying the ways in which the imposition of an assessment system might achieve this. There seems to exist an almost intuitive belief that requiring teachers to assess the children they teach in a summative way and making public the results, will of itself improve the quality of teaching and learning in primary classrooms. This may be so, but little direct evidence exists at the moment. Perhaps, in this case, time will indeed tell.

With these possible purposes in mind, what is the role of the external Standard Tasks? In a situation of national monitoring through a limited *sampling* procedure, external assessment would no doubt play a central role. A carefully established framework would need to be agreed and tasks produced that were of proven validity and dependability in order to generate comparable statistics from year to year. The actual assessments administered could be quite detailed, since they would not be administered in all schools by all relevant teachers. Different assessments could even be given to different samples to generate even more information.

As we have seen, if summative information on *all* children in an age-group is required, it is unlikely that the Standard Tasks could cover all the curriculum. In this context, the external, Standard assessments are best seen as *calibrating* devices, gradually improving the shared interpretations of the curriculum specifications and the validity and dependability of the assessments as a whole. The professional development of teachers may also be enhanced in this way.

Perhaps a final comment should focus on the kinds of decisions that still need to be made in relation to these purposes. There is clearly a balance to be struck, both at Key Stage 1 and to some extent at Key Stage 2, between fairly tightly controlled, dependable and valid assessment and one which might prove less reliable but more directly in line with good classroom practice for these age groups, not to say acceptability to teachers. Any decisions which move the assessment tasks towards more streamlined, pencil-and-paper forms are less likely to serve the goals of the development of teachers' skills and the improvement of teaching and learning in primary classrooms. Such assessments act in a purely 'monitoring' way, providing no guidance on better teaching strategies and classroom practice. Queries have already been raised about whether such an approach would of itself raise standards. If the quality of teaching and learning is to be improved, it seems more plausible to argue that teachers should be offered the means of effecting change. Waving the stick of published results may or may not be the best catalyst for change and improvement.

References

Adey, P. (Ed) (1989) *Adolescent Development and School Science*, Lewes: Falmer Press.

Aherne, P., Thornber, A., Fagg, S. and Skelton, S. (1990) *Communication for All: A Cross-Curricular Skills Involving Interactions between 'Speaker' and 'Listener'*, London: Fulton.

Alston, J. and Taylor, J. (1981) *Handwriting Checklist*, Wisbech: LDA.

APU (1985) *Practical Testing at Ages 11, 13 and 15*, London: HMSO.

APU (1988) *Science at Age 11*, London: HMSO.

APU (1991) *Assessment Matters No. 5: Profiles and Progression in Science Exploration*, London: HMSO.

Arnold, H. (1982) *Listening to Children Reading*, London: Hodder and Stoughton.

Arnold, H. (1992) *Diagnostic Reading Record*, London: Hodder and Stoughton.

Ashdown, R., Carpenter, B., Bovair, K. (1991) *The Curriculum Challenge: Access to the National Curriculum for Pupils with Learning Difficulties*, Lewes: Falmer Press.

Ausubel, D. (1968) *Educational Psychology: A Cognitive View*, New York: Holt, Rinehart and Winston.

Barrow, R. (1984) *Giving Teaching back to Teachers*, Sussex: Wheatsheaf Books.

Bates, R. V. (1984) Educational versus Managerial Evaluation in Schools, in Broadfoot, M. P. (Ed) *Selection, Certification and Control: Social Issues in Educational Assessment*, Lewes: Falmer Press.

Bennett, N., Desforges, C. et al. (1984) *The Quality of Pupil Learning Experiences*, London: Erlbaum.

Bereiter, C. and Scardamalia, M. (1982) From Conversation to Composition: the role of instruction in a developmental process, in Glaser, R., *Advances in Instructional Psychology*, New Jersey: Erlbaum.

Bereiter, C. and Scardamalia, M. (1985) Children's Difficulties in Learning to Compose, in Wells, G. and Nicholls, J., *Language and Learning: an interactional perspective*, Lewes: Falmer Press.

Bereiter, C. and Scardamalia, M. (1987) *The Psychology of Written Composition*, New Jersey: Erlbaum.

Bloom, B. S., Engelhart, M. D. et al. (1956) *Taxonomy of Educational Objectives: the classification of educational goals*, New York: David McKay Co..

Bruner, J. S. and Haste, H. (1987) *Making Sense: the child's construction of the world*, London: Methuen.

Bullock, A. (1975) *A Language for Life* (The Bullock Report), London: HMSO.

Carey, S. (1985) *Conceptual Change in Childhood*, Cambridge, Mass.: M.I.T. Press.

Carey, S. (1987) Theory Change in Childhood, in Inhelder B. et al. (Eds) *Piaget Today*, London: Erlbaum.

Central Advisory Council for Education (England) (1967) *Children and Their Primary Schools* (The Plowden Report), London: HMSO.

Chi, M. T. H. (1978) Knowledge Structures and Memory Development, in Siegler, R. S., *Children's Thinking: What develops?*, New Jersey: Erlbaum.

Chi, M. T. H. and Koekske, R. D. (1983) Network representation of a child's dinosaur knowledge, *Developmental Psychology, 19,* 29–39.

Cinamon, D. and Gravelle, M. (1985) Bilingualism is not a learning difficulty, in *Gnosis 12,* 19–23, Concordia University, Montreal, Canada.

Commission for Racial Equality (1989) *Code of Practice for the Elimination of Racial Discrimination in Education,* Commission for Racial Equality.

Consortium for Assessment and Testing in Schools (1990) *The Development of Standard Assessment Tasks at Key Stage 1: A Report to SEAC,* London: SEAC.

Cox, B. et al. (1989) *English for Ages 5 to 11* (The Cox Report), London: HMSO.

Cummins, J. (1979) Cognitive/academic language proficiency, linguistic interdependence, the optimum age question and some other matters, *Working Papers on Bilingualism No.19,* 121–29.

Cummins, J. (1984) *Bilingualism in Education,* Longman.

DES (1984) *Curriculum Matters 1: English from 5 to 16,* London: HMSO.

DES (1985) *Science 5–16: A Statement of Policy,* London: HMSO.

DES (1986) *English from 5 to 16: The Response to Curriculum Matters 1,* London: HMSO.

DES (1988) *Language Performance in Schools: Review of APU Language Monitoring 1979–1983,* London: HMSO.

DES (1988) *National Curriculum Task Group on Assessment and Testing: A Report* (The TGAT Report), London: HMSO.

DES (1988) *Science for Ages 5 to 16,* London: HMSO.

DES (1989) *Assessments and Statements of Special Educational Needs: Procedures within the Education, Health and Social Services. Circular 22/89,* London: HMSO.

DES (1989) *Education Reform Act 1988: Temporary Exceptions from the National Curriculum. Circular 15/89,* London: HMSO.

DES (1989) *English in the National Curriculum,* London: HMSO.

DES (1989) *Mathematics in the National Curriculum,* London: HMSO.

DES (1989) *National Curriculum: From Policy to Practice,* London: HMSO.

DES (1989) *Science in the National Curriculum,* London: HMSO.

DES (1991) *A Handbook of Guidance for the SAT – Key Stage 1,* London: HMSO.

DES (1991) *Mathematics in the National Curriculum,* London: HMSO.

DES (1991) *Science in the National Curriculum,* London: HMSO.

DES (1992) *Standard Assessment Tasks Teachers' Handbook – Key Stage 1,* London: HMSO.

Dessent, T, (1987) *Making the Ordinary School Special,* Lewes: Falmer Press.

Donaldson, M. (1978) *Children's Minds,* Glasgow: Fontana.

Driver, R. (1989) Changing Conceptions, in Adey, P. (Ed) *Adolescent Development and School Science,* Lewes: Falmer Press.

Edwards, D. and Mercer, N. (1987) *Common Knowledge,* London: Methuen.

Edwards, V. (1983) *Language in Multicultural Classrooms,* Batsford Academic and Educational Ltd.

Ennever, L. and Harlen, W. (1973) *With Objectives in Mind: Guide to Science 5–13,* London: Macdonald Educational.

Frederickson, N. and Cline, T. (1990) *Curriculum Related Assessment with*

Bilingual Children: A Set of Working Papers, London: University College, London.

Galloway, D. and Edwards, A. (1991) *Primary School Teaching and Educational Psychology*, London: Longman.

Gipps, C. (1990) *Assessment: A Teachers' Guide to the Issues*, London: Hodder and Stoughton.

Gipps, C., Steadman, S. and Blackstone, T. (1983) *Testing Children: standardised testing in schools and LEAs*, London: Heinemann.

Glaser, R. (1963) Instructional Technology and the Measuring of Learning Outcomes, *American Psychologist, 18*, 519–21.

Greene, E. (1986) *Language Understanding: A Cognitive Approach*, Milton Keynes: Open University Press.

Grosjean, F. (1982) *Life with Two Languages: an Introduction to Bilingualism*, Harvard University Press.

Hall, N. (1989) *Writing with Reason*, London: Hodder and Stoughton.

Halliday, M. A. K. (1989) *Spoken and Written Language*, Oxford: Oxford University Press.

Harlen, W. and Osbourne, R. (1985) A Model for Learning and Teaching Applied to Primary Science, *Journal of Curriculum Studies, 17*, 2, 133–46.

Hayes, J. R. and Flower, L. S. (1980) Identifying the organisation of writing processes, in Gregg, L. W. and Steinberg, E. R., *Cognitive Processes in Writing*, New Jersey: Erlbaum.

Hayes, S. (1991) Too Eagerly Awaited Assessment, *British Journal of Special Education 18(2)*, 48–51.

Hegarty, S., Pocklington, K., and Lucas, D. (1981) *Educating Pupils with Special Needs in the Ordinary School*, NFER-Nelson.

Home Office (1977) *Racial Discrimination: A Guide to the Race Relations Act 1976*, London: HMSO.

HMI (1978) *Primary Education in England: a Survey by HM Inspectors of Schools*, London: HMSO.

HMI (1989) *Aspects of Primary Education: The Teaching and Learning of Science*, London: HMSO.

HMI (1990) *The Teaching and Learning of Reading in Primary Schools*, London: HMSO.

Jackson, P. W. (1968) *Life in Classrooms*, New York: Holt, Rinehart and Winston.

Kellogg, R. (1969) *Analyzing Children's Art*, California: Mayfield Publishing.

Kingman, J. (1988) *Report of the Committee of Inquiry into the Teaching of English*, London: DES.

Lawson, A. (1989) Research on Advanced Reasoning, Concept Acquisition and a Theory of Science Instruction, in Adey P. (Ed) *Adolescent Development and School Science*, London: Falmer Press.

Levine, J. (1981) Developing Pedagogies for Multilingual Classes, *English in Education, 15*, 3, 25–33.

Lewis, A. (1991) *Primary Special Needs and the National Curriculum*, London: Routledge.

LINC Project (1992) *Language in the National Curriculum, Materials for Professional Development*, Leeds: LINC Publishing.

Lunzer, E. and Gardner, K. (1984) *Learning from the Written Word*, Edinburgh: Oliver and Boyd.

McTear, M. (1985) *Children's Conversation*, Oxford: Blackwell.

Merttens, R. and Vass, J. (1991) Assessing the nation: blue prints without tools, *Primary Teaching Studies*, 5, 3, 222–39.

Mojet, J. (1991) Characteristics of developing handwriting skill in elementary education, in Wann J., Wing, A. M and Souik, N., *Development of Graphic Skills*, London: Academic Press.

NCC (1989) *Curriculum Guidance 2: A Curriculum for All. Special Needs in the National Curriculum*, York: NCC.

NCC (1989) *Circular Number 5: Implementing the National Curriculum: Participation by Pupils with Special Educational Needs*, York: NCC.

NCC (1989) *Science: Non-Statutory Guidance*, York: NCC.

NCC (1991) *Mathematics: Non-Statutory Guidance*, York: NCC.

NFER/BGC Consortium (1990) *The Pilot Study of Standard Assessment Tasks for Key Stage 1: A Report*, London: SEAC.

NFER/BGC (1991) *Evaluation of the Pilot Study of Key Stage 1 Assessment*, London: SEAC.

NFER/BGC (1991) *Standard Assessment Task, Key Stage 1*, London: HMSO.

NFER (1992) *An Enquiry into LEA Evidence on Standards of reading of seven year old children.*

Nitko, A. J. (1983) *Educational Tests and Measurement*, New York: Harcourt Brace, Jovanovitch Inc..

O'Rourke, E. P. (1990) Spoken and Written English, in Harris, J. and Wilkinson, J., *A Guide to English Language in the National Curriculum*, Stanley Thornes.

Pearson, L. (1990) What have the pilot SATs taught us?, *British Journal of Special Education 17(4)*, 130–32.

Randall, M. (1991) Can Section 19 be used positively?, *British Journal of Special Education 18(2)*, 44–47.

Read, C. (1986) *Children's Creative Spelling*, London: Routledge and Kegan Paul.

Reason, R. (1989) Evidence of Progress, *British Journal of Special Education 16(4)*, 149–52.

Redman, S. et al. (1983) Young Children and Science: The Oxford Primary Science Project, in Richards, C. and Holford, D., *The Teaching of Primary Science: Policy and Practice*, London: Routledge and Kegan Paul.

Richards, C. and Holford, D. (1983) *The Teaching of Primary Science: Policy and Practice*, London: Routledge and Kegan Paul.

Richardson, K. (1991) *Understanding Intelligence*, Milton Keynes: Open University Press.

Robinson, E. J. and Robinson, W. P. (1977) Development in the understanding of causes of success and failure in communication, *Cognition*, 5, 363–78.

Robinson, E. J. and Whittaker, S. J. (1986) Learning about verbal referential communication, in Durkin, K. *Language Development in the School Years*, Kent: Croom Helm.

Rogers, C. (1982) *A Social Psychology of Schooling*, London: Routledge and Kegan Paul.

Rosenthal, R. and Jacobsen, L. (1968) *Pygmalion in the Classroom*, New York: Holt, Rinehart and Winston.

Rowell, J. (1984) Many paths to knowledge: Piaget and science education, *Studies in Science Education*, *11*, 1–25.

Rowntree, D. (1977) *Assessing Students: How shall we Know Them?*, Harper and Row.

Rubin, N. and Henderson, S. C. (1982) Two sides of the same coin: variation in teaching methods and failure to learn to write, *British Journal of Special Education*, *9*, 4.

Russell, T, Harlen, W., and Watt, D. (1989) Children's ideas about evaporation, *International Journal of Science Education*, *2*, 56–76.

Russell, T and Harlen, W. (1990) *Practical Tasks in the Primary Classroom*, Paul Chapman.

Salvia, J. and Hughes, C. (1990) *Curriculum-based Assessment: Testing what is taught*, New York: Macmillan.

Savva, H. (1990) The Multilingual Classroom, in Harris J. and Wilkinson J. (Eds) *A Guide to English Language in the National Curriculum*, Stanley Thornes.

SEAC (1989) *A Guide to Teacher Assessment: Pack C. A Source Book for Teacher Assessment*, SEAC/Heinemann Educational.

SEAC (1990) *School Assessment Folder*, London: HMSO.

SEAC (1991) *School Assessment Folder*, London: SEAC.

SEAC (1991) *A Handbook of Guidance for the SAT (1991)*, London: HMSO.

SEAC (1992) *School Assessment Folder*, London: SEAC.

SEAC (1992) *Standard Assessment Task Assessment Record Booklet (1992)*, London: HMSO.

Shorrocks, D., Daniels, S. et al. (1992) *The Evaluation of National Curriculum Assessment at Key Stage 1: Final Report* (The ENCA 1 Report), London: SEAC.

Skutnabb-Kangas, T. (1981) *Bilingualism or Not. The Education of Minorities*, Avon: Multilingual Matters.

STAIR Consortium (1990) *Evaluation Report of the Standard Assessment Task: Pilot Study*.

Stenhouse, L. (1975) *An Introduction to Curriculum Research and Development*, London: Heinemann.

Stott, D. H., Moyes, F. A. and Henderson, S. E. (1985) *Diagnosis and Remediation of Handwriting Problems*, Ontario: Brook Educational.

Swann, W. (1991) Marching backwards to selection (BACKLASH), *British Journal of Special Education 18(3)*, 96.

Tizard, B. and Hughes, M. (1984) *Young Children Learning: talking and thinking at home and at school*, London: Fontana.

Tizard, B. Blatchford P., et al. (1988) *Young Children at School in the Inner City*, Hove, Sussex: Erlbaum.

Todd, J. (1982) *Learning to Spell*, Oxford: Blackwell.

Vygotsky, L. S. (1978) *Mind in Society: The Development of Higher Psychological Processes*, Cambridge, Mass.: Harvard University Press.

Warnock, M. (1978) *Special Educational Needs. Report of the Committee of Enquiry into the Education of Handicapped Children and Young People*, London: HMSO.

Wastenedge, E. R. (1983) Nuffield Junior Science: The End of a Beginning, in

Richards, C. and Holford, D. *The Teaching of Primary Science: Policy and Practice*, London: Routledge and Kegan Paul.

Wells, C. G. (1987) *The Meaning Makers*, London: Hodder and Stoughton.

Wood, D. (1989) *How Children Think and Learn*, Oxford: Blackwell.

Wood, R. (1986) The Agenda for Educational Measurement, in Nuttall, D. L., *Assessing Educational Achievement*, Lewes: Falmer Press.

Index

ability 23–5, 26
accountability 49
accuracy 44, 64, 103, 108
achievement 26–7
age 84, 99, 177
aggregation 43, 46, 128, 182–3
agreement trials 45, 80
Algebra 95–103
alphabetic knowledge 64
assessment 18–19
  accuracy 44
  bilingualism and 158–73
  domains 32, 39, 134
  goals and purposes 43, 114–15,
    133, 146–9, 185
  process 33
  using first language in 169–70
Assessment of Performance
  Unit (APU) 74, 115, 120,
  122
Attainment Targets 36–7
  Algebra 95–103
  Handling Data 108–13, 179
  Handwriting 73–5, 77
  Life and Living Processes
    129–36, 179
  Materials and their Properties
    129–36
  Number 86–95, 108–13
  Physical Processes 129–36
  Reading 56–65, 76–7
  Scientific Investigation, 118–29,
    179
  Shape and Space 103–8, 179
  Speaking and Listening 50–5,
    76, 150
  Spelling 70–3, 77
  Using and Applying
    Mathematics 81–6
  Writing 65–70, 77
  see also strands
attitude 10–11

baseline assessment 147–8
bias 21, 129, 161–5, 172, 180
  types of 163–4

bilingualism 158–73, 178
  definition of, 158–9

capital letters 68–9
children's development 2–7, 24,
  31, 77, 132
chronological writing 67, 69
classrooms 14–15, 19, 125, 174–5
comparability 41, 42, 45, 60–1, 108
  across subjects 176
  see also statements of attainment
conceptual development 2–5
  see also children's development
conservation of number 4
consistency 80, 93–4, 100
content domain 32, 80, 89–97,
  106, 122–4
context, in assessment 33, 80,
  85–6, 98–9, 123, 165–8, 176–7
conversation, children's 15–17, 19,
  51–2, 54–5
criterion-referencing 25, 27, 30,
  38–41
criterion levels 92–3, 109
curriculum 14, 31–2
curriculum related assessment
  (CRA) 165–9

dependability of assessment 30, 47
diagnosis 9
diagnostic assessment 29, 147
dialects 54, 161
differentiation 10, 43, 150
disadvantage 52, 162
disapplication 141–4, 151
disembedded thinking 66
Donaldson, Margaret 4, 66

eleven plus 47
English 50–78
  status of 161
error, in assessment 30
evidence 20, 34, 84–5, 124–5

fair test, in science 128
familiarity 106

fluency 64
formative assessment 29, 41, 54,
    115, 147, 184–5
full stops 68–9

gender 178, *see also* bias
Gipps, Caroline 31, 146, 147,
    162–3
grammar 56–7

halo effects 11
Handling Data 108–13, 179
Handwriting 73–5, 77

inference 62
informal assessment 26, 28–9
information processing 5
'intelligence' 23–4, 25, 47
interpretation of criteria 39–40, *see
    also* statements of attainment
intervention 84

knowledge 5–7

labelling 15, 43, 148
language
    in mathematics 84, 99–100
    nature of 5
    see also bilingualism,
        conversation, English, reading
league tables 172–3
learning 2–3, 8–9, 48, 52, 118–20,
    135
levels of attainment 36–7, 44, *see
    also* progression
Life and Living Processes 129–36,
    179
literate language 66
LEAs 47, 49, 80, 137–8, 142–3, 152

manageability 47, 82, 123–4, 128,
    181
mastery 27, 40–1, 46, 69, 93–4,
    106
match 10
mathematics 79–113, 179
Materials and their Properties
    129–36
meaning 51, 57
memory 5
miscue analysis 61, 150

moderation 36, 44–5
motivation 1, 10

National Curriculum 36, 45
National Curriculum assessment,
    nature of 36–8
NFER 59, 60, 179
non-chronological writing 67, 69,
    70
norm-referencing 25, 27–8, 40, 60
Number 86–95, 108–13
nursery education 178–9

observation 17–18, 21–2, 149–50
    in science 126–7

parents 48, 169, 182
pattern 95–9
perception 5
performance criteria 93, 124, 181,
    see also mastery
Physical Processes 129–36
Piaget, Jean 2–5, 6, 7, 130, 174
probability 112
process
    in maths 81–6
    in science 115, 117, 118–29
professional development 41, 45,
    84, 113, 181–2, 185
profile components 36, 65, 117, *see
    also* aggregation
programmes of study, 38, 80–1,
    109–12
progression 29, 37, 44, 82, 132, 176
psychometric approach 25

questioning 53

reading
    approaches to teaching 59
    assessment of 49, 59–60, 76–7
    Attainment Target 56–65, 76–7
    cues 64
    model of 58
    process 56
recall 91–2
record-keeping 20, 48, 175–6
Records of Achievement 31
redrafting 67, 69–70
reliability 30, 125, 186
response, mode of 33–4, 125

self-fulfilling prophecy 11–12
sentences 68
science 114–36
  process and content 115–17
  Scientific Investigation 118–29
  scientific knowledge 129–34
Shape and Space 103–8, 179
Speaking and Listening 50–5, 76,
  150
social factors 52, 54, 178
special educational needs (SEN)
  137–57
  assessment of 139–40
  definition 137–9
  directions 142
  disapplication 141–4, 151
  standard assessments and 144–6,
  151, 152–5
Spelling 70–3, 77
standards 185, 186
Standard Assessment Tasks (SATs)
  x, 37–8, 41–3, 89, 144–6,
  179–80, 183
  development agencies 60,
  152–5
  maths 93–4, 98, 106
  pilot studies (KS1) 46–7, 152,
  154, 179
  reading 60, 76–7
  scores 43
  'standard' 42, 177
standardised tests 22–3, 26, 28, 32,
  49, 59–60, 165
statements of attainment (SoAs)
  33, 37–41, 109, 130, 176, 183
  interpretation of 39–40, 79–80,
  87, 89–91, 101, 103, 111, *see
  also* mastery, performance
  criteria
stereotypes 10–11, 12, 161
story structure 69

strands
  in mathematics 80–1, 82, 89,
  95–6, 104, 108–9
  in science 118, 126–7, 129
summative assessment 29, 36–7,
  115, 180, 184–5

Task Group on Assessment and
  Testing (TGAT) 36, 38, 41–3,
  45, 53, 115, 180
teacher assessment (TA) 16, 37,
  42–3, 112, 149–52, 171, 183–4
teaching 8–10, 48
teacher expectations 11–13, 43, 54,
  129, 180
tests
  ability 23–5
  achievement 26
  LEA testing 49
  reading 59
time 128
timing 135

underachievement 172–3
understanding 79–81
Using and Applying Mathematics
  81–6

validity 30, 98–9, 123, 186
'value added' 148
value judgements 18, 21
video recording 21, 55, 149–50

Warnock Report 137–40
Welsh 161, 162, 169–70, 171, 178
Writing 65–70, 77
  chronological 67, 69
  process and purposes 66

zone of proximal development
  7–8, 9

Pupils wall Assessed
at KS1 maths 89

A Guide to T assessment p55

maths
82
83

87